When We Become Men

When We Become Men

The Effeminizing and Devolution of the Black Male and Culture in America

KHALIL BAAQI

ISBN: 1507740654
ISBN 13: 9781507740651

Table of Contents

Preface

Sometime during the summer month of July 2011, I was harangued and then promptly, as was once a common phrase on the streets, "dissed and dismissed" on the C.O.W.S. radio program. The C.O.W.S., which is an acronym for Context of White Supremacy, and the show's host Gus T. Renegade, along with several of his cadre of regulars, very thoroughly made me aware that there was no room for outsiders who demonstrated a lack of knowledge or inability to speak in their codified style of language. Or, no tolerance for any failure to accentuate the methods of replacing a cruel and unjust system of racism and white supremacy with one of justice and equality as only Mr. Renegade and his cohorts could fully understand or consider. Humiliated and ostracized, I could not at that time understand how people who routinely identify themselves as victims of racism could show such hostility toward another victim of racism who, similar to their endeavor, was merely searching for solutions and offering possibilities as to how to overcome such a societal and cultural dilemma.

Yet in hindsight, I can appreciate the intolerance for the ignorance that I displayed. Besides, in disavowing my feelings from the actions of the messenger(s) and instead centering my focus on the message, I was from that day forward inspired to offer my own analysis and perspective of the conditions that adversely affect the lives, psyche, outlook, and trajectory of former slaves and contemporary victims of institutional racism/white supremacy. And as a result of my own thorough analysis, it is my claim that the black male in American society is not a *Man* by standard definition, nor can he consider himself a man after succumbing to centuries of systematic bondage, servitude, oppression, and relegated citizenship status, brought forward and largely determined by way of his former enslavers and present-day Christian masters; a condition that to this day the black male has not fully been able to recover and/or overcome.

It is also my conclusion that the indoctrination of the Euro-minded black male and black female is as much a result of the conditioning process of institutional racism and the ubiquitous white supremacists mindset that envelopes both people, same as they are the result of the continual plight and imminent destruction of the urban poor in America; particularly the black male—whether he be urban, rural, foreign, or otherwise. And lastly, I have determined that the socioeconomic and corporate acceptance and burgeoning union with the black female, and the provisional inclusion of the effeminized, passive, and "nonthreatening" black male is nothing more than a simultaneous act of hegemonic *tricknology*, designed to conceal the ultimate goal of keeping the black male and black female disjointed and at odds with each other in terms of mutually preserving the black family and maintaining communal accord and cultural solidarity.

The title of this book, *When we become Men: the effeminizing and devolution of the Black Male and Culture in America,* implies that because of the system of institutional racism/white supremacy, the black male, along with the culture of which he is ascribed, is gradually either becoming extinct or has become so insignificant that both he and it are no longer relevant or purposeful in American society as both once may have been. It is because of this perspective that my use of the word *effeminizing* is in reference to the external conditions (i.e., racism, socioeconomic disenfranchisement) that are superimposed on black males, and that subsequently have caused a startling transmutation of characteristics that result in partaking in actions and behaviors that are anything but manly, masculine, or culturally empowering.

Ordinarily, the term *feminized* is more commonly accepted or is more literal in traditional usage. Obviously, I am not using it here. Nor do I find its usage relevant to the point and claim that I am making in this book. The reason being is that contrary to the above reasoning for the use of the term effeminizing, feminizing implies a factor or reasoning that is not externally related. For instance, black males can be feminized or act more effeminate than masculine because of strong ties or anomalous connections with their mothers or other strong black females in their respective families or social circles. For this reason, the use of the word feminizing fundamentally implies that these are characteristics that are taken on by choice rather than by circumstances, and are not the direct result of external forces that are designed to emasculate black males in a highly racist society.

The purpose of this book is to offer a theoretical explanation as to why the effeminizing of the black male in America is taking place, as well as offer insight as to how the black male can potentially circumvent this endeavor and overcome the barriers of persistent institutional racism/white supremacy. So, for instance, when I as the writer of this book observe the rapid increases in interracial courtships between black females and white men, while at the same time finding it difficult not to notice an exceedingly increasing number of black males who are outwardly homosexual, transgendered, on the "down low," are either in skinny jeans or are wearing pants that are sagging to their knees (an effeminized calling card for those who may not be aware), I can only assess these permutations and manifestations as being not only the result of an increasing and disturbing trend of self-hatred, family dysfunctions, and bad manners and absent morals, but also the result of the institutional system of racism/white supremacy that continues to pound the heads of black people, particularly black males, like a sledgehammer.

And certainly the fact that western society is directly exposed to a celebrity culture in which high-profile black male entertainers are increasingly clad and/or draping themselves in women's clothing on television and in film has to have some merit, in addition to making credible the claim that black culture, which was once unique and stead-fastly admired, is now being swathed in a maelstrom of both exploitation and stratification for purposes of monopolizing and bifurcating the tal-ent and contributions of black people as a whole in the entertainment industry— a plausible assessment that can only lead to one plausible conclusion. So, in addition to the ever-present national (and global) crisis of institutional racism/white supremacy, it is the result of actions of certain blacks as just described, as well as the unknowing victims of institutional racism/white supremacy—male and female—who have suc-ceeded in negotiating their victim status for temporal wealth and recog-nition that I was compelled to write this book.

It is the actions of those who although are permanently ascribed to skin blackness, treat their God-given culture and hue as conditional to the precepts of institutional racism/white supremacy—perceiving the condition of being black or of having color as amenable to the whims and endeavors of those who represent the dominant culture—rather than as an apotheosis of hue, ethnicity, and culture that has been bequeathed from the creator and well worth fighting for and TRULY being proud to possess. It is because of this point of view that I was inspired by those few black males and black females who, despite its political incorrectness in a society fraught with delusions of grandeur and denunciation of facts, dare/d to speak the truth and call to the attention of those concerned; conditions and social inadequacies that portend a trajectory of immi-nent doom rather than one of peace, prosperity, and prominence.

It is because of the undaunted wills and spirits and indefatigable efforts of those who served as sources of inspiration that I would like to thank the likes of Dr. Francis Cress-Welsing, Michael Eric Dyson, Michelle Alexander, Neely Fuller Jr., Haki R. Madhubuti, Pierre Orelus, Thomas J. Sugrue, Joy Degruy, Cisco Streetlove, and the works and tireless day-to-day efforts of a slew of others who have and continue to engage in the fight for TRUE freedom, justice, and liberation. Moreover, I would like to thank my family, Sheila McClelland, James McClelland, Jala McClelland, and Ericka Brown, my daughters Devin Michelle and Jordyn Marie, as well as Omar Montgomery, and other friends and confidants for closely mentoring me throughout the course of starting and completing this mentally debilitating yet rewarding project. Last and, of course, far from least, I would like to pay homage to all of the civil rights activists and freedom-fighters—both past and present—who because of their in-depth insight and understanding to do what is right, despite the cost, provided for me the latitude, logistics, structure, and the moxie to want to pursue this project irrespective of the rewards or risks.

Introduction

How one defines being a *Man* varies, as does the literal definition of the word. Therefore, questions and/or presumptions in regards to what a man is; what a man does or does not do; how a man acts; how being a man differs from being anything else, particularly from being a woman; and how a man defines or perceives his relationship to global society are important in terms of acquiring an understanding of its literal definition. In Webster's dictionary, the basic definition of *Manhood* is defined as the condition of being an adult male as distinguished from a child or female. This definition, however, may be left to interpretation, particularly depending on how certain individuals go about their day to day dealings and view the world around them. Additionally, *Manliness*, also according to Webster's dictionary, is defined as well as perceived as exhibiting qualities that are associated with the highest characteristics and displays of masculinity—qualities such as strength, virility, and self-sufficiency.

Noticeably, manhood is merely defined as maleness based on biological endowments. Manliness, on the other hand, is defined as possessing certain characteristics that in a patriarchal society, imbues biological maleness with both indelible and incomparable features that are obviously devoid in women and children. Despite the differences—whether feasible or illogical—in a patriarchal and hegemonic purview, both definitions connote a biological ascription and cultural conditioning that speak exclusively to social and cultural preeminence, and are associated with characteristics and attributes that men have always been revered and respected for possessing. Additionally, and once again from a patriarchal perspective, men of particular high standing and status have often been credited for possessing such qualities, as both manhood and manliness are traits and characteristics that represent the pinnacle of human existence. Moreover, both attributes have always been perceived as the epitome of what human beings have the potential to accomplish and can contribute to in their respective geographic locale (i.e., state, country, community).

In a system of institutional racism, however, and a system that is driven by a white supremacists mindset, what it means to be a man and the definitions of manhood and manliness are arguably interchangeable concepts. And despite the biological distinction that men are ascribed and what separates manhood from womanhood, a more plausible definition of manhood or perceived manliness is the ability to control one's situation, success, happiness, livelihood, well-being, and ultimate destiny. For this reason, I would argue that being a Man—which encompasses both manhood and manliness—and as it applies from a humanistic point of view, is the ultimate freedom. Furthermore, it is the ability to live with only the concessions and limitations that one places on self, and not the constraints that are superimposed as they are in a system of racism, vis-à-vis' white supremacy.

From a rational, and not a societal, cultural, or national point of view, when musing and ruminating over what it means to be a man, particularly in a racist society, a feasible conclusion is that one cannot truly call himself a man if his fate, livelihood, and destiny are both shaped and determined by others, particularly if the man in question still languishes under the penumbra of those who once (and still continue to) sought to minimize his humanness, global significance, and national standing.

One cannot truly call himself a man if his ability to acquire the barest of necessities to that of achieving and procuring the highest rungs of success and upward mobility is at all compromised and left in the hands of someone else, especially if that someone else is the former slave master and owner of, again, the man in question. This is especially true and hard to dispute in a present day system of institutional racism/white supremacy, regardless of if that someone else so happens to be a descendant of slave masters and slave owners and, unsurprising yet incredulously, denounces any form or method of racial bigotry and intolerance. One cannot truly call himself a Man if the principles from which his very existence and being are based is systematically torn down and reconstructed to fit a certain mold that is not only fashionable, marketable, or trendy, but is also the basis for his survival and perseverance.

During the era of the struggle for civil rights—a seminal period of substantial upheaval, turbulence, and racial unrest—the black male, and black people as a whole, who were victims of institutional racism/white supremacy were directly and/or indirectly forced to delude themselves into thinking that second-class citizenship was sufficient for survival, despite its obvious limitations and civil restrictions. That ultimately, the offspring of former slaves were still in a state of bondage if they were not entitled to the same freedoms and civil liberties that are guaranteed to other ethnic groups who call the shores of North America their homeland, and do so under the banner and precepts of a constitution that stipulates that these inalienable rights are guaranteed and non-negotiable. Furthermore, I would argue that since equal entitlements to civil liberties and the proverbial "pursuit of happiness" remain elusive to the once slaves and burden bearers of America, second-class citizenship or, in some cases, complete expropriation of humanity and dignity was not only all that seemed was left but was the only non-negotiable alternative that was, more or less, superimposed.

As generally defined, being biologically ascribed to manhood or possessing the characteristics of manliness that I have suggested is arguably what encapsulates being a true man, the black male in America has never truly had the pleasure of enjoying either. Immediately following the transatlantic slave trade, an endeavor that caused hundreds of millions of Africans on the west banks of Africa to be herded and shipped to North America for the sole purpose of chattel slavery, black males were called "boy" and referred to as anything other than a man for the purpose of being stripped of their dignity, humanity, manhood, and manliness. Certainly, the proprietors and financiers of slaves and the slave trade possessed a profound understanding of manhood and manliness and other attributable characteristics—hence, being, acting, and conducting oneself as a man—and the ineffaceable harm and ramifications of being stripped of this earthly right as ascribed by the creator. In other words, taking away from one these God-given rights—the ability to be as well as to live—has caused irreparable damage. Furthermore, it has obfuscated what it means to be a man for the black male in a racist society, as certainly manhood and manliness in black America are on a collision course towards either doom or uncertainty.

For instance, a logical question that could be posed is whether or not one can be a black male in America and make less than his spouse and still be considered as a man? Or, can one have unrestricted means and freedom for the ability to produce offspring, yet fail to raise and financially support these offspring and still be considered as a man? Or, can one spend the majority of one's life as a ward of the state or county that one resides and still be considered as a man? Subsequently, it is with the information, statistics, and analyses offered in this book that I will attempt to address such questions, as well as underscore the claim of how it is first and foremost institutional racism/white supremacy that has emasculated, has effeminized, and has caused dependence on other(s) rather than reliance on self for the black male and black people as a whole in America; a crisis that began with chattel slavery hundreds of years ago and remains a crisis for the black male and black people to this day.

As I write this, Barack Obama, the first black president, is nearing the end of his second term as president of the United States. And although clearly the demography of the North American hemisphere is gradually changing, the significance of this feat is that many black folk can remember a time when it was widely believed that they would never see a black male in the oval office as leader of the free world in their respective lifetime. Arguably, this can in hindsight be looked upon as a stark concession to the reality of institutional racism/white supremacy that has always been a chasm in the consciousness of black people as a whole in this society, as well as the absolute powerlessness that ensued as a result of the conditions of racial discrimination that continues to lay dormant in the mental psyche of those who still either directly and/or indirectly acknowledge the reality of racism and sordid race relations in this country. More telling is that this is still the reality of black people, particularly the black male, as well as the hundreds and hundreds of years of a systematic conditioning process that has been the determining factor in regards to black folk's purpose and usefulness in this society and exactly what it is that both male and female and black children are able to accomplish amid unblemished and undeterred racism and oppression, regardless of who is sitting at the helm of the oval office.

I can recall as a child, an adult black male whom my mother was intimately involved with at the time, witnessing my play with toy action figures on the living room floor and then replying, "that boy is going to be a coach someday!" In looking back, what I find the most interesting aspect of that particular statement is that given what he could've perceived as precocious organizational skills during my play with these toys, or imaginative as well as ingenious creativity, or grandiloquent verbosity and animation, he would instead surmise these qualities as being more commensurate to that of a coach (presumably a football coach, being that it is what I was simulating at the time) as opposed to a trial lawyer, motivational speaker, or fortune 500 CEO. While it is indeed a possibility that Obama's accomplishment as first black president of these United State has changed the scope of such a mundane and trite yet relatable trajectory of young black males, and females, his historical ascent to the presidency, however, should still raise important questions that clearly require equally important answers. Questions such as how far as a society has America really come in terms of race relations? Additionally, how has the polarizing and debilitating scourge of institutional racism/white supremacy gradually taken its toll on the black male and black people— who as America's former slaves and burden-bearers remain the country's premiere victims of its machinations?

The paradox that some might argue is that Barack Obama is indeed the country's first black president in a society that I am claiming is persistently laying down the framework for either the complete destruction of the black male or effeminizing the black male to a point where he is no longer in consideration for being tossed in the competition pool for recognition of manhood and manliness. This is especially true, or at least hard to dispute, in a society that is still as overwhelmingly patriarchal as it is racist, as well as a society that reveres such attributes and characteristics in its leaders, celebrities, and other high-profile figures. Therefore, in addressing the aforementioned hypothetical, another key question is whether or not Barack Obama has plainly and honestly addressed the issues of the poor and downtrodden in this society, many of whom remain disproportionately people of color? With that question being posed, along with some of the previous questions asked as well, what is the real truth of race-relations in America? What is the real agenda in terms of settling the race problem even though America elected its first black president? Have things honestly changed in terms of race-relations since the days of chattel slavery, reconstruction, Jim Crow, and the civil rights era? How much have conditions really improved? How much more stable are black families and black communities? How much more power has the black male and black people as whole truly acquired in the socioeconomic, political process?

Has the black male in America gotten closer to acquiring true manliness, or is he gradually regressing and/or devolving in this endeavor? How much closer has he gotten to being both perceived and treated as a key figure in his respective household, or does this effort also remain elusive? Has the black male in America succeeded in being an unmitigated and undeterred breadwinner in his home, or has he been a total failure? Has he achieved being perceived as a key participant in creating and honing the potential destinies for his children, as well as being viewed and respected as the pillar, strength, and backbone of his community? And, finally, is he at this present stage of his earthly existence able to lay claim to the right to declare himself as a Man?

One

HORSES, SLAVES, AND DRESSES:

How Racism/white supremacy obstructs black manhood and masculinity

History was written by those who hanged the heroes

Neely Fuller Jr., considered to be one of the fathers of counter-racist theory and social activism that is geared towards eradicating racism and racist practices, claims that institutional racism and white supremacy and the stripping of manhood as a result of these practices is premised on the idea that in a purely patriarchal society there can be only one dominant male figure. Congruent with this claim, the progenitors and practitioners of institutional racism/white supremacy set out to extract the manhood and manliness from African *men,* who were subsequently relegated to the powerless and subordinate classification of slaves by way of a system that was contrived for the purpose of keeping them socially, politically, and economically weak and vulnerable. Accordingly, the developing conditions of slavery were exhorted by what were considered the Willie Lynch Slave Doctrines, which were premised on the idea of "man-breaking and slave-making." This would be accomplished by way of a systematic process created for the purposes of stripping the seized of independence and, conversely, creating a state of total dependence.

Over the years, social and political scholars have debated over the authenticity of the Willie Lynch doctrine. Nonetheless, what we have come to know of the slave manifesto is that the basis of the process which, historically is analogous to breeding horses, would be to strip the male subject of the conquered group into complete worthlessness as a means to secure the kind of economic gains that the provisos of chattel slavery dictated. As theorized by Neely Fuller, the idea behind the separation of power of a superior racial group from an inferior and subordinate caste is to make certain that there can be only one Man that exists in society. Therefore, in order to function or assure any semblances of survival, males of the subordinate group can either assume the position of an infant, woman, or boy but certainly can never attempt to act as a man or conduct oneself in a manly fashion.

Making Boys out of Men: A theoretical perspective

"You can't be a black 'man' in Corporate America!"[1]
—LOREN MOYE, THE COLOR OF FEAR

According to Mr. Fuller, in a system that is driven by racism/white supremacy, the black male can never make a claim of ownership of true manhood or possess the qualities of manliness. Therefore, maleness is the only title that is appropriate because it is commensurate with the biological ascription that the black male was brought into existence. This is especially true and hard to dispute while in existence under a system of oppression and subjugation. Regardless of whether one agrees with Neely Fuller's theory or not, what is also difficult to dispute is that the black male in America has lived in complete subjugation due to racism and discriminatory policies and practices. Therefore, if one is to view objectively the gaping disparities that continue to exist between black people as a whole and white people, then, clearly, there must be some merit to any claim of these factors being the result of institutional racism or some method of systemic race-related propaganda.

The Willie Lynch doctrine, purportedly, was a set of guidelines that were designed to preserve the control of slaves and the institution of chattel slavery for a period of three hundred years. Furthermore, the foundation of this method of control was to instill fear in the slave of his or her owner or master, inculcate a distrust of other slaves, and instill envy in regards to the power that slave owners and masters possessed for the purposes of maintaining control. Consequently, the invariable practices of institutional racism/white supremacy have taking their toll in the most insidious and destructive ways (and, yes, there is indeed an institutional system of racism/white supremacy and, yes, white people in American society do still practice it). As stated earlier, it is my claim that functioning as a man in any given society renders one capable of taking care of himself, his family, and having control of his choices, life course, and decisions made that help shape and mold his future. Certainly, when the systematically oppressed are denied jobs to acquire, at minimum, the basics that provide and ensure subsistence; and as a result of such denial, generations and generations of crime, decadence, and operating on the fringe of social decorum and morality are impro-vised as compensation to being denied such basics, how is it then at all possible that those whom have fallen victim to this process can honestly call themselves Men? The answer is that they cannot!

It has been said that sometimes the best place to hide something is in plain sight. Accordingly, America is a nation that is rife with social injus-tices such as racism, classism, sexism, homophobia, and xenophobia, all of which, although can be directly linked to the patriarchal fraternity of racist white male hegemony, instead seems to be obfuscated in a conun-drum of random acts of civil disobedience. Therefore, when speaking on the issue of crime that is perpetrated by black males in almost exclusively black communities, because these are criminal and immoral deeds that have involved males of color and have been seemingly ethnically neutral, the omission of conspiracies and the assertion of there is no one else to blame other than the rogue(s) who perpetrate such misdeeds becomes that much more credible. Furthermore, it is important to note that the idea of classism, which has been argued is a condition that is gradually supplanting racism, is perceived as rendering men who are not of color, vulnerable to being deprived of the same privileges or entitlements that promotes true manhood and manliness.

Regardless, the differences that I would argue are that the status of white men and their unmitigated claim to manhood in American society are not at all being circumscribed or diminished due to conditions such as institutional racism/white supremacy. On the contrary, the status of white men might be compromised because of the escalating dearth of resources due to the gradually expanding global society. Not to mention a society that has been projected as becoming more and more of a gradually expanding non-white population. Yet and still, the fact of the matter is that even with the gradual "browning" of the northern hemisphere, none of this really matters if this vastly developing faction of the human family remains gridlocked because of social constraints that have been omnipresent since America's inception. In other words, because of racism, discrimination, and genocidal practices that have and continue to take place, the black male in America has been debased and emasculated to a point where the question of preservation for the future is in serious jeopardy.

Understandably, a feasible question would be what do I mean when I make the claim of the emasculation of the black male? Well, when based on the merit of what the exact words are intended to mean, it is stripping Men of their mental, psychological, and aesthetic components. It is as decreed in the Willie Lynch Letter on how to make a slave, the usurping of manhood and manliness that subsequently results in a state of total dependence by way of infantilizing both the biological and psychological aspects of the adult male. Therefore, in a system that foments economic strife and struggle for the black male (and perhaps all non-white males for that matter), white men, on the other hand, are not being deprived of their patriarchal duties as heads of households if they so choose to establish a family unit. And while it may also be true that society is changing in a sense that women are becoming more independent and have more maneuverability as far as career and money-earning potential, the sordid and volatile reality of race-relations in which American society was initially based have not changed at all.

In outlining the disparities that exists between white men and black males, the results should not only be obvious but similarly staggering. Hence, under a system of institutional racism/white supremacy, white men are at the top of the socioeconomic ladder while black males are indisputably at the bottom. Moreover, white men collectively are gainfully employed at a much higher rate than their black male counterparts. White men on average live more than half a decade longer than black males; have access to better health care and other subsistent resources; are incarcerated at a staggeringly lower rate, even though, collectively, they commit more crimes categorically; and, individually, are widely perceived as being more of the epitome of acquiring corporate and economic success and achieving the so called "American Dream."

Arguably, from a white, patriarchal and conservative perspective, the American dream is still premised on the idea of mother, father, children, the house, the dog, and the white picket fence, in which the father is still perceived as the backbone of the family unit as well as its primary provider. Now, regardless of whether this is true in the neo-liberal reality of American society, what cannot be disputed, however, is that white men have a much firmer grasp on this reality or endeavor than do black males. On the other hand, in a system of institutional racism/white supremacy that has had a profound effect on the family unit of people of color, boys and young males are still being raised in homes where fathers are disproportionately absent, and single mothers have been left with the tasks of being both providers and developers of young boys in a patriarchal yet racist society.

One of the obvious problems, among many to be revealed throughout the course of this book, is that this task is not only ostensibly overwhelming but also goes against the grain of the natural order of things in a (supposed) civil society. For this reason, it should be clear that the progenitors and practitioners of institutional racism/white supremacy projected from the onset the catastrophic end results and are presently fully aware of the manifestation of social conditions that have and continue to widen the gap of inequality between blacks and whites.

Similar to the process of man-breaking and slave-making, the process of institutional racism/white supremacy at some point has to reach an end as envisioned by its purpose and means. In other words, it would not be a process if there was not some end result that is expected to occur at some point or time. The mystique of black people as a whole in American society is that by all appearances they have withstood the tumult, rigors, and evils of institutional racism. That somehow Martin Luther King's vision and dream of the former sons and daughters of slaves being able to claim equal status and having entitlements to the same rights and privileges as their once slave masters has been fulfilled. Indeed, black people are still functional in some capacity, at least in regards to the ability to survive. An important question, however, is what toll—either consciously or subconsciously, hidden or revealed—has manifested as a direct result of centuries of physical and psychological servitude and captivity? It has been theorized that there are only two counter responses to captivity of any sort: acceptance or rejection.

Despite those who fought and sacrificed their lives for civil rights in this country, the black male, and black folk as a whole, have always in some manner accepted their inferior status, albeit either completely willingly or somewhat grudgingly. Even famed author and scholar James Baldwin, in his seminal work *The Fire Next Time*, described black victims of racisms penchant for making peace with mediocrity due to their subhuman and substandard conditions.[2] Accordingly, Posttraumatic Slave Disorder has been theorized as a mental condition that is premised on how the residual effects of chattel slavery have manifested into behavioral patterns and maladaptive forms of social conditioning that have ensued either consciously or unconsciously as a result of years of systematic mistreatment and deprivation, due to years of discrimination and harsh and oppressive conditions. Therefore, the institution of racism/white supremacy that I am addressing and that is postulated in theories of posttraumatic slave disorder was contrived and implemented to condition its victims to function as inferiors, both mentally and physically. So, when manhood is erroneously juxtaposed with an absence of manliness, or the ability to function as a self-sufficient, productive member of a society that is supposedly free from its past of imposing the shackles and restraints of discrimination and race-related social impediments is both circumvented and proven to be an outright lie, it is unquestionably the result of the desired effect of tearing down a man to that of something other than a man.

Defacing Masculinity

*"If you can't stop people from doing it to
you then maybe you deserve to have it done!"*
—ANONYMOUS

In 2009, Morehouse College, an all-black institution in Atlanta, Ga., enacted an eleven rule dress code in which rule #9 stipulated a ban on the male students' wearing women's clothing, due to several students' noticeable habit of cross-dressing.[3] In an effort to promote and impose what the university deemed as attire that is appropriate for its male student body, clothing such as dresses, tunics, skirts, and high-heels were in stark violation of the rule.[4] Thus, it is important to note that over the years there have been gradually expanding numbers of gay black males in every community, town, and major cities across the country. The irony, then, as well as a little bit of controversy that ensued as a result of this enactment is that Morehouse, despite historically being considered as a reputable all-black college, has also in certain degrees been considered as a haven for black America's gay elite. Perhaps, whereas freedom of expression—which epitomizes homosexuality in this society—is encouraged, it has always been viewed with aspersion and ire in the black community. Because of this, we can further deduce the disastrous effects that the stripping of manhood and manliness has caused in communities that covet these particular traits and characteristics; primarily because they have been essential to generational perseverance and preservation, as well as survival.

For the past several generations, the black male in America—who has been the most persistent target of institutional racism/white supremacy—has attempted to compensate the effects of this system by excelling in sports and entertainment, with the latter allowing the opportunities of unimpeded and unmeshed self-creativity and expression. On the other hand, sports is an entity that is widely considered as being the pinnacle of manliness and masculinity in a society that reveres such attributes and characteristics, particularly when they are maximally displayed by white men. In other words, being a man, despite social conditions that dictate otherwise is the apex of the ability to procure survival necessities and assure familial, communal, and ethnic survival. For this reason, homosexuality has been viewed from the black community as a perversion and affliction that white men have been dubiously rewarded, perhaps even being perceived as reprisal the white man's domination of the global landscape that has been dutifully bequeathed by a higher power or spiritual entity. In fact, it could be argued that there was a time when the word faggot was uttered that it was specifically geared and directed towards white men, as connotations of the word were so vile and vehement in the black community that to refer to another black person as such would guarantee a violent response. Well, nowadays, it could be argued that the term is neither race nor gender-specific, although still offensive nonetheless.

Regardless, it should be noted that the incidents of cross-dressing reportedly taken place at Morehouse College was only specific to a handful of students, just as it should be made clear that my claim here is certainly not to imply that being gay automatically implies an absence of manhood or manliness. In fact, my argument is more geared towards the idea that it is not gayness that precludes this possibility; instead, it is the institution of racism/white supremacy that does so with maximum proficiency. Thus, the bigger picture is that due to the institution of racism/white supremacy, that is the real culprit of effeminizing the black male, this epidemic has arguably become so prevalent outside of the confines of Morehouse that not only is there an exponential growth of gay black males across the country, but more telling is the possibility that even being gay is no longer sufficient; hence, the torrent of transgendered and transsexual black males. Consequently, young boys, adolescents, and adult black males who have and continue to be the victims of racism and social isolation in this society are finding that there is more dignity and social acceptance in being a black female than there is in being a black male—being that the condition of being black is in itself, inescapable.

Along with being one of the premiere institutions of learning for young black males, Morehouse has also been labeled as a haven for young black homosexuals. So, when considering that black males in this country make up only 4% of college enrollment nationwide,[5] what is also disturbing is the fact that the values that are being reinforced by administrators at Morehouse, for the purpose of inculcating not only success and individual productivity at an all-black and all male institution are being obstructed by critics who claim that the rules being imposed there are "intolerant" and "homophobic." An important question then, especially when considering the dearth of black males in colleges nationwide, yet young and old black males disproportionately comprise the highest incarceration rate of any ethnic group, is why is it that such a reputable and prestigious institution of learning that is geared strictly towards the success of young black males has an equally prominent reputation of being a cesspool for the transgendered and those who engage in homosexual behavior? Perhaps, the answer lies in the notion that the city of

Atlanta itself is a Mecca for black homosexuality, as the overall culture of the city could account for the widely held consensus, whether true or false, of wanton homosexual practices and cross-dressing predilections taking place there.

Another point to consider is that perhaps it could be that Oprah Winfrey, who because of her legendary and loose-pocketed generosity has been called the greatest black philanthropist in history,[6] making several exorbitant contributions to Morehouse and making the claim that "when you empower a Morehouse 'man' you empower the world,"[7] either adds credence to the institution's historic pedagogic resume or is mere biased rhetoric from one of both white and black America's most beloved celebrity and pecuniary goliaths. Either perspective, however, is in addition to her having the subliminal title of one of the country's premier closeted lesbians. Nevertheless, the point that I am trying to make is that this is an example of how the trait of manhood and characteristic of manliness are being gradually and systematically transmuted into effeminized psychological and physiological functioning. For this reason, I would assert that the process of emasculating the male figure that is seen as a potential threat can reap an end result that comes in various forms. Or, perhaps to be more accurate is a process that works in various stages. Therefore, circumventing one's ability to think, act, function, and live on his own merit and recognizance indeed strips one of the ability to call himself a man; in addition to depriving one of the benefits and privileges that come with true freedom, unimpeded access to resources, and an unobstructed pursuit of one's goals, dreams, and aspirations. What follows is despondence and helplessness as the result of conditions that seem not only overwhelming but also completely unavoidable.

Based on this assessment, I will make the claim that the process of emasculating the male subject from the core of his very nature can render the victim dependent on his captors as a means of survival for both he and his family. Lastly, as Stockholm syndrome predicates, the emasculated male not only accepts his victimization but also gradually learns to both love and identify with his captors. As a result, if the precepts of institutional racism/white supremacy stipulate that there can be only one dominant male figure in a society that has thrived, as well as profited, from racial dissension and divisions that are largely based on a premise of racial and cultural superiority then, certainly, the subordinate or subjugated group is psychologically as well as physically resigned to its condition. Or, better yet, the subordinate or subjugated group is minimized to a degree in which the males may be deserved of the title of "boy" as opposed to being a man, at least in terms of social functioning.

Where's the Dress?

"…give me those high-heeled shoes.
Where's the dress—we'll be money-making fools."[8]
—MOE BANDY & JOE STAMPLEY *WHERE'S THE DRESS*

For certain, the United States, like most western nations, has embraced the practices of homosexuality as a part of its culture. Evidence of this claim is the gradual legalization of same-sexed marriages state by state throughout the country. It is as a result of this that the gradual stripping and extracting of manhood and manliness—evidenced by the rapidly declining social condition of the black male, as well a growing epidemic of black male homosexuals, transsexuals, and cross-dressers—is made possible by a systematic undertaking being utilized under the auspices that it is more effective to effeminize those who are assigned to a collective group that has historically been subjected to harsh treatment and inhumane conditions. Hence, the prospect of encouraging, teaching, and training the black male to confront the evils of discrimination and oppression as Men has clearly been curtailed by an efficient, code-specific system that was created to ensure that one racial group remains superior over the other, as well as one that was coordinated very meticulously and efficiently to make sure that things remain that way.

Consequently, the reference to culture is of great significance, especially if cultural dictates are juxtaposed with adverse and sordid social conditioning that is both culturally as well as individually destructive. Presently, Tyler Perry is America's foremost contemporary black filmmaker who, despite his sudden ascent to prodigious Hollywood fame and notoriety, has also been candid about his troubled past and childhood that consisted of physical, sexual, and emotional abuse. Despite this, Perry has succeeded in amassing a half a billion dollar industry for a slew of financially successful films and television shows that he has produced, starred in, and directed. Additionally, he has established himself as a walking conglomerate and a symbol of power and success within the black community. However, it is also of extreme importance to point out that Mr. Perry's true reputation, as well as success, lies in is his affinity for dressing up in women's clothing and playing the character of a stereotypical, boisterous, ignorant, fat, and buffoonish black female—appropriately named Madea.

In spite of Tyler Perry's acclaim and apparent ability to make highly profitable films, his portrayal of the character Madea has ostensibly been his claim to fame. Perry, who mostly employs obscure black actors for his mostly black-made and produced films and television shows, as a result has established a large following and thumbs up consensus from both black film goers and black mainstream aficionados. Essentially, what this means is that Perry's proclivity for dressing up as a female, in addition to rumors that Perry, similarly to Winfrey, is a closeted homosexual indicates acceptance of Perry's program and brand (not to mention the fact that Perry and Winfrey are also close friends and business partners, as most are probably already aware). This appears to be the case despite being done within the confines of a subculture whose males have historically and continue to be deprived of basic civil liberties and human rights. Moreover, Perry has managed to acquire this level of success appropriately in a society where the masculinity of black males has always been questioned, rejected, or viewed with absolute condemnation to a point that the campaign to destroy and separate the black male from these attributes remains pervasive.

When We Become Men

———

Similarly, in the early 1970s one of the first ground-breaking shows starring a black entertainer was the Flip Wilson show. Not only was it unprecedented in terms of a person of color having his own show, but it was also one of the highest rated and mostly watched shows among both black and white audiences. The show also is mostly known and celebrated for the character Geraldine, a sassy, wise-cracking black female that was portrayed by Wilson. Over the years that have since followed, nearly every major and visible black entertainer has donned a dress and simulated being a female as a means to deliver a dose of drama, comedy, or some measure of entertainment. With the exception of Denzel Washington and Morgan Freeman (probably due to the latter's age), notable actors and entertainers such as Ving Rhames, Wesley Snipes, Jamie Foxx, Chris Tucker, Terry Crews, Martin Lawrence, Wayans Brothers, and Eddie Murphy have all at some point in their respective careers played characters where they were dressed up as a female or have taken public photos dressed in this manner. In fact, in addition to Tyler Perry, Lawrence and Murphy and the Wayans Brothers have created franchises based on their proclivity to dress in female garb on film.

Few would argue that despite America's open—although in many ways grudging—acceptance of homosexuality and femininity among males, the attributes that are highly regarded and revered in men are extreme forms of fearlessness, virility, and incomparable masculinity. Obviously, this is not to imply that all black males who are the relentless targets of a racist society, as a direct response have put on dresses and high-heeled shoes. However, the social practices and rituals that had at some point promoted manhood and masculinity have been gradually dissipating to a point where it has become a crisis and major deterrent to survival for future generations of black people, particularly black males. Indeed, many might dismiss high-profile entertainers' desires to dress in female garb as nothing more than mere entertainment; however, even if that is the case, what should also be kept in mind is that Sylvester Stallone, Arnold Schwarzeneggar, Steven Seagal, Matt Damon, Tom Cruise, Bruce Willis, and the rest of Hollywood's leading white elite (with the exception of the late Robin Williams, *Mrs. Doubtfire*) have never been captured on film in women's clothing. And even if they had the implication would be entirely different. Again, white men are obviously not victims of racism/white supremacy, and therefore have never had their masculinity challenged, discredited, or questioned.

The allure of Black Hollywood and the appeal of white Men and White culture

> *"It's always a place for a black coon or buffoon in Hollywood....come this way; we've got a job for you!"*
> —STANLEY CROUCH

Despondence due to one's repressed condition, dependence on one's captors for survival, and eventual identification and resignation of captive status are just a few of the end results of stripping men of their ascribed manhood and manliness. Few entities in American society are more effective in this endeavor than Hollywood—America's premier film, television, and entertainment juggernaut—as well as popular culture and mainstream media. And despite this claim, making another that pertains to some of the famous black entertainers previously mentioned as examples of the emasculation process at its most advanced and efficient stage could still be written off as complete hogwash, especially in a so-called colorblind, post racial society. That on the contrary, these "men" are representations of the epitome of black success; men who have achieved in spite of REAL harsh, racist, and oppressive conditions that have kept many people of color destitute and disparate and continues to do so.

Another feasible argument could be that there are a slew of white comedians, notwithstanding the previously mentioned Robin Williams, who have also put on a dress to deliver their own respective brand of comedy and drama. And that the previously mentioned black entertainers, many of whom work specifically within the confines of comedy and comedic expression, are merely doing what it is that they do best, fomenting perhaps an unfair comparison to white actors whose reputations rest specifically on being action heroes. And although this may to be true to a certain extent, consider however the fact that in Hollywood there are no hardcore action heroes who are black to compare to hardcore action heroes who are white. In fact, some of the names mentioned, such as Wesley Snipes, Jamie Foxx, and Ving Rhames have played action-oriented roles, although not nearly to the same degree of success or consistency as their tough guy white counterparts. Essentially, what this means is that in Hollywood, being black and being tough are not at all exclusive from also being effeminate; and that it is the black male, irrespective of genre, who is more inclined to play roles pretending to be his mother, his aunt, or his grandmother.

A question then that should be posed as a result is, at what cost have these famous black males succeeded, and not only as it relates to them individually but to the masses of black Americans whom, by and large, are perceived as a cumbersome monolithic cluster and who are not worthy of individual acknowledgement or acceptance? Consequently, acceptance and admiration for the accomplishments and successes of the aforementioned, as well as others who have achieved an equal amount of kudos and social standing and who have set a higher standard to live by is an insinuation that integrity, morality, and responsibility come with a price tag. Or, perhaps these attributions can be bartered given the right set of circumstances—wealth, privilege, power, and prestige. Accordingly, the proposition then becomes would you put on a dress for the right price? Or, better yet, would you conduct yourself inappropriately and act in a stereotypical and culturally self-debasing manner for the purposes of entertainment, despite how truly talented and enterprising many of these individuals actually are?

Take for example that in the early part of the 20th century, a black entertainer who would go by the moniker of Stepin Fetchit became the first black millionaire in Hollywood as well as the first black character actor to receive a screen credit. All of this was accomplished by way of the entertainer's portrayal of a lazy, slothful, slow-tongued, and dull-witted black buffoon who, consequently, emblazoned stereotypes of black males that were widely perceived as real and as an accurate assessment of the characteristics of black males during this particular time period (not to imply that the times and the perceptions have changed, because they certainly have not). And similar to the drubbing of character and disavowal of integrity and respect that is taking place among today's gifted black entertainers, the irony as well as the tragedy in all of this is that Stepin Fetchit, born Lincoln Perry, was a highly literate and intelligent individual who frequently wrote articles and publications for a major newspaper—*The Chicago Defender.*

Clearly, the conditioning that has taken place and continues to take place by means of institutional racism/white supremacy has subsequently resulted in the gradual effacing of individual self-esteem that ultimately serves as a domino effect—trickling down to a collective deprivation of solidarity and cultural pride. As a result, decadent behaviors such as crime and unsafe sexual practices that are largely responsible for the gradually increasing HIV/AIDS epidemic in the black community, as well as disproportionate levels of children born to both unwed and teen mothers and absentee fathers are unrelenting themes in the lives of a disproportionate number of black people as a whole in America. Thus, the inverted animus and disdain directed towards those who are representatives of mass victimization of the American social order, that ultimately results in the decimation and destitution of black and urban communities is unquestionably most telling. However, these things are not only the result of indecent, decadent, malfeasant behavior but also the ubiquitous use of self-debasing terms such as the word *nigger*.

———

While as a graduate student at New York University, I had a conversation with a middle-aged black female immediately following an open *mic* session on the platform at Union Square. During our conversation, she stated that she too was a graduate of NYU and was currently a practicing attorney. And when it was her turn to speak on the microphone she gave a riveting and passionate delivery on the importance of, primarily black males, but also black folk in general taking responsibility for their own conditions and independently reclaiming their own families and communities. She then proceeded to tear into two other young black male participants for their ostentatious and blatant use of the word nigger while showcasing their lyrical rap skills and spoken-word prowess on the open mic. After her passionate diatribe on the microphone and during her conversation with me, she expounded on her objection to not only the words cultural significance as a whole but also her mortification on the prevalence of its use among black males. It is important to note that this conversation that started around 10:30 p.m. ended at 5:30 in the morning. It should also be pointed out that I agreed with her argument on what is now commonly referred to as the "N" word and how its overuse within the black community can be deemed by some as counterproductive to its collective, cultural advancement. In fact, my personal assessment of the word nigger and its common usage among black folk, especially young blacks, is that it is emblematic of our inferiority complex due to centuries of subhuman conditioning.

It is without question unconscionable when considering that not only did slave owners and masters refer to their black slaves as niggers, but over the course of time black people frequently began to refer to other blacks as niggers. And even more shocking is that presently you have black celebrities, such as rapper Jay Z, make a claim that present-day prolocutors of black culture, such as himself, transmogrified the term from its historic negative into a contemporary endearing positive. Yet, contradictorily, as well as tragically, when black males slaughter each other on drug-fueled and crime-ridden streets, it is common to hear the utterance of "die nigger, die" once the trigger is squeezed or a knife is pulled. Nonetheless, what immediately became clear to me was that although this particular black female claimed to be all in favor of black people consummating dependence on white people's outright apathy in regards to the plight of black children, families, and communities, and pseudo assistance in the efforts of black folks' collective advancement, she seemed to be unclear as to how this was going be accomplished independently by black folk or what were the necessary steps to make this happen—other than "silly," misinformed black males refraining from their use of the word nigger. What also became immediately apparent as the conversation progressed was that the idea of black people accomplishing such a task by way of loving each other first and foremost—which entailed reclaiming responsibility not only in their communities but love for culture ,self, and offspring— was not exactly what this particular black female had in mind.

In fact, the conversation took an unexpected turn, as she was surprisingly candid in regards to her fetish for random sexual encounters with rich and successful white men. Moreover, she lauded other black females for their pursuit of these same sexual liaisons because of what she deemed as an epidemic surge of gay black males (a point that I am obviously in total agreement), in addition to those black males who socially and economically fall short of making suitable mates for single, successful black females. It was during this conversation that it had dawned on me that what I was experiencing was the ballyhooing of an educated, successful black female who was torn between immersing herself in a "white is right" mantra and code of ethics, while at the same time looking at her own black self in the mirror and attempting to find some value and meaning to not only her own existence but that of those who look like her and also share her culture, heritage, and skin color.

It has often been stated that a lack of knowledge of history renders those who are ignorant susceptible to repeat it. During slavery, white men tortured, burned, and mutilated black males and raided slave quarters to rape their feeble and powerless black female captives. Because of the clandestine methods of institutional racism/white supremacy, which has rendered black people as a whole completely dumbfounded to conditions that have affected them as a result, the erroneous alternative has been to turn the finger inward and hold the victims of institutional racism/white supremacy accountable for the systematic and strategic practices of the victimizers. Hence, this book is about the effeminizing of the black male due to his constantly being victimized by a system of racism and oppression, and the devolution of black culture that is gradually taking place as a result of the aforementioned system of racism/white supremacy, as well as the black male's being effeminized due to constant racial suffrage. Furthermore, and unsurprisingly, it was my engaging in a conversation with a black female that drove these points home. In other words, what I am saying is that even though the black male in America is still a victim of the same racial animus and disdain that enslaved his ancestors and that caused a cataclysm of spilled blood for centuries, there are, nonetheless, black females who willingly seek out white men for lascivious sexual encounters, same as there are black males who either seek out white women or make themselves available to them for the same purposes.

What had also become apparent during this conversation was that perhaps it takes an astute and intelligent black female to gauge the cultural insignificance and social impotence of the black male. And, perhaps, because of such perceived weakness and impotence, a feasible tradeoff is a willingness and desire to engage in coitus relations that, at least by the admission of this one black female in particular, have absolutely nothing at all to do with legitimate and healthy relationships. Therefore, a reasonable question then is whether or not a black female engaging in sexual relations and/or sexual play with a white man unhealthy? Or, better still, is the decision of two human beings, irrespective of ethnicity or color, mutually deciding to partake in such an activity illegitimate? These are perhaps the questions that one might ask. However, in a highly racist society that is driven by a white supremacist mindset, surely one should and/or can understand the importance of such questions.

I will detail more of my thoughts of the potential harm of interracial courtships throughout the remainder of this book; analyses that are based on my personal theory as well as those of others. Yet despite such claims, I am fully aware of the predicament of the black female under such an unjust system. And it is because of this awareness that what I had concluded from my conversation with this particular black female was the emotionally-laced spewing of someone who was able to appropriately discern manhood and manliness from those who socially, culturally, and emotionally function as boys as opposed to Men in this society. Perhaps this also explains her maternal predilection to admonish and excoriate black "boys" as opposed to young black "men" in regards to the use of what she perceived as inappropriate language and cultural expression. Ironically, and despite centuries of racism and discriminatory practices, this distinction was made in comparison to those who have unimpeded power and prestige and consequently are deserved of among the many of their distinctive titles the designation of REAL Men. Incidentally, a feasible conclusion to the verbal exchange that I had with this particular female is that any impromptu discussion on matters of race, power, and even cultural sensibilities in this society can render only one conclusion: "to the victor goes the spoils"; the victor(s) of course being white men. And clearly, the spoils from this black female's point of view were her sexual willingness and availability, as well as what should be the same willingness, availability, and lascivious desires of other black females in regards to the victors or seeming victors in an on-going war for racial, cultural, and ethnic supremacy.

Two

Divide and Conquer and the Color Complex Theory:

Imagery & Perception

"Denial of racism is what keeps America sick!"
—Joy DeGruy

It should be obvious that the claim of emasculating the black male by way of America's practices of racism/white supremacy runs much deeper than just putting high-profile black persons in skirts and dresses. However, the point is to convey that victims of debasement and disavowed humility cannot claim to be men if the historic victimizers and practitioners of institutional racism/white supremacy determine levels of employment, socio-economic empowerment, and images that are to be showcased in the realms of mass and social media and entertainment. This is not to downplay the importance of entertainment in American society, as well as globally, considering that annually various forms of entertainment, e.g. sports, television, and theatre amass ungodly amounts of revenue. Nevertheless, it is my intention to raise awareness to the exploitation or, for the purposes of my argument, *Blaxploitation* of black people—male and female—as a means to acquire such revenues.

I once heard it explicitly expressed from the perspective of a white racist that if there is a need to keep black people in existence, then that need is strictly for the purposes of entertainment (or, as this person put it, "entertaining Us"). When considering that whites are now enveloped in the reality that they have to compete with blacks and other people of color for jobs, housing, and other necessities for subsistence, this fact undoubtedly stokes the fires of racial strife and continues to polarize this society by race and racial discrimination. Even more profound is that many black people—who as victims of institutional racism and the American social order—don't seem to possess the wherewithal to both fully understand and ameliorate their oppressive and harsh circumstances.

Blaxploitation (which will be discussed much more in depth in one of the later chapters), one of the more salient rejoinders over the last half century due to the results of socioeconomic disempowerment and social and cultural gridlock, was a form of black expression—artistically and politically—that was either never fully deemed considerable or at least objectively analyzed in terms of its social and cultural impact. What's more is that perhaps at some point the genre had been minimized to a degree to where even the resentment or upheaval of those who were more socially and culturally critical of it would not have made much of a difference either way. Take for instance B-level black comedian Renaldo Reye's assertion on the documentary *TV in Black: First 50 years* that the term Blaxploitation, which essentially is a depreciatory jab at the works of mostly black independent films during the era immediately following civil rights, was not correct. That in fact, according to Mr. Reye, the term should have more appropriately been called "black employment."

I once wrote a master's thesis on Blaxploitation films. And with the research acquired I, at the time, found it exceedingly difficult to believe that the dream of racial unity that Martin Luther King had in mind for the descendants of former slaves was to cultivate an image of black criminals—pimps, contract killers, cocaine and heroin pushers, and womanizing and philandering ghetto Romeos—who, at the same time and during this same era, lacked the ability to father their own offspring and hold down legitimate employment to support their families (hence, true ART imitating real LIFE). And while certainly not all black films that were made during the late 60s and early 70s glamorized this sort of imagery, the majority of them in fact did. Therefore, for every black film such as *The Spook that sat by the Door*—one of the first political black films of its kind—there were several films that depicted black male figures who operated on the fringes of law and social decorum, and as a result of such depictions were perceived as the sort of ghetto Gorgeous George's and wayward heroes that Mr. Reye, himself, attempts to personify in his own comedic eccentricities.

Another perspective is how political disenfranchisement and being devoid of socioeconomic power reduces human beings to the barest minimum of existence; thus, leaving those who are victims of such pitfalls completely dependent on a historically racist system, as well as deprived of the ability to present themselves in a manner that is worthy of national admiration and global respect. Because of this assertion, it would behoove Reynaldo Reye and other supporters of black debauchery and buffoonery to ask themselves, despite some truth to the claim of black entertainers finding employment in the entertainment industry, at what expense is this employment to be met? (It would also be fitting for Mr. Reye to be made aware that slavery was "black employment" as well) Indeed, for several generations, black victims of institutional racism/white supremacy have set trends in the culture of entertainment that remain (somewhat) significant to this day. Nonetheless, in Hollywood-made movies and independent films, people of color—especially black males—remain grossly misrepresented and exploited.

Black Bastardizing

"I am a Man!"

As racial conditions have worsened, the perspective of the black male in terms of how to address racism and deal with racial issues has not alternatively gotten better. In fact, as conditions have gotten worse it seems that his perspective (at least in terms of rationality) has similarly deteriorated. For instance, Tyler Perry's contemporary portrayal of Madea has taken the past success of Geraldine, mentioned in the previous chapter, to new and unperceived as well as unprecedented heights. Also, when excluding the successes of black entertainers—Hip Hop (rap) artists and black males who excel in most franchise sports—other black males and black people as a whole in this society can be deduced as coming in either one of two ways: criminals and socioeconomic underachievers—made possible primarily because of social and economic disadvantage. Or, as bible-totting, overly religious zealots who have become desensitized to their own actual and adverse social conditions because of a willingness to immerse in scripture and biblical theology that have in no way assuaged the suffering that blacks have and continue to face as a result of the system of racism/white supremacy. In assessing the latter, the main problem has been the failure to analyze and understand how the initial purpose of the indoctrinating of African slaves to Christianity was to delude and pacify them for conditions and subjugation created by man that the same God they so ardently worship would find not only condemnable but irredeemable.

In a society of which the foundation is stabilized on the grounds of institutional racism/white supremacy, any argument or theory of the black male and black people being provided "work" to foster and engender racial stereotypes is not only foolish but is also a form of ethnic and cultural *menticide*. Frankly speaking, there are human beings, although trapped biologically in an adult male and female body, are rendered unable to function as Men and Women because of conditions that they appear to be either completely unaware of or are in gross denial about such realizations. Consequently, because of this ignorance or lack of understanding and ability to properly decode their subjugated condition, there are many black males and black females who speak, act, and function as a boy and as a girl (or both in regards to each gender) as opposed to that of a Man or as a Woman. Besides, during the times of chattel slavery leading up to Jim Crow, were these not the debasing terms that black males and black females were constantly called or referred to?

What should be clear is that any victim of institutional racism/white supremacy who demonstrates a willingness to cultivate racial stereotypes and imageries that are designed to denigrate his or her own ethnic group is an example of a disenchanted member of that particular group, who has been systematically beaten down by a stigma of worthlessness, meaninglessness, and racial inferiority. Subsequently, an attitude that posits a necessity for survival by any means necessary becomes obligatory—although not exactly in the same manner as what the slain civil rights leader Malcolm X had in mind when he made the claim "by any means necessary" a staple in the lexicon of American culture.

What should also be clear is that being enamored by the dominant culture and architects of slavery and institutional racism/white supremacy, to the point of a compulsive willingness to intermingle, mix blood, and intermarry when the opportunity presents itself is just as obligatory as the need for basic survival, especially when one is part of a collective group that has suffered centuries of systematic oppression and mistreatment. As Stockholm syndrome dictates, captives of slavery and servitude not only gradually learn to identify with their captors but also learn to love them as well. Even when considering cultural trends and where American popular mainstream culture as a whole appears to be headed, what is painfully obvious is that there are a great many blacks—both male and female—who both love and revere those who represent the dominant culture. And as a result of this love and reverence, these black individuals merely exist as functional beings who seek in life to build courtships and alliances with those of the dominant culture as a means to preserve individual, social, and economic survival and maneuverability.

Simply put, I believe that there are many black people—again, both male and female—who have found it to be of economic and social disadvantage to be ascribed to a racial and ethnic classification that is widely perceived as a cursed and dysfunctional and bastard race. And, consequently, these individuals embark on a cultural and mental escape from this classification, despite not being able to escape the external condition of blackness. Without question, this is an endeavor that is pursued by many who seek to escape the clutches and identification of being black in a country in which "white is right" is both the subconscious and conscious reality, despite the rapidly declining numbers of white people not only in this society but across the globe.

Under the Siege of Inferiority and Exploitation

In revisiting some of the theories of Neely Fuller, another one of his claims is that racism and white supremacy have made black people as a whole in America a "silly" and "pitiful" people. Perhaps it is these traits that have rendered the black male incapable of protecting the black female and his offspring. Moreover, perhaps these are the characteristics that have unmotivated the black male to safeguard his ethnic pride and identity and use such attributes to safeguard his home and strengthen his respective culture and community. Indeed, one of the most prominent end results of institutional racism/white supremacy is the total destruction of the black family, as well as the utter decay and disjunction of black communities.

A further assessment is that although the black male in America has proven by way of centuries of chattel servitude and utter domination of every major franchise sport in this country to be physically strong, he has nevertheless been exploited and used by white culture for its own political and financial gains. What this essentially means is that whether financially (e.g., sports and entertainment) or culturally (i.e., stereotypes of being cowardly and lazy), the black male is apparently viewed in this society as a stalwart and as an impediment to his own cultural progress and advancement; thus, making it feasible for whites to either support or relent in opposing the institution of racism/white supremacy, and rendering the black male as nothing more than collateral damage for the purposes of societal and national advancement.

Being susceptible to this systematic process of oppression and exploitation renders black males in American society incapable of being protectors of their wives, children, and communities. As a result, ingratiation into the dominant culture and a mental and cultural disconnect from one's own grouping has and continues to remain the first step in ascending the latter of collective worthlessness and insignificance—at least in regards to individual survival and self-preservation. It must also be understood that overt racism as opposed to covert racism does not truly render a difference between the two. In fact, they are the same in terms of the means being justified by the end results. The difference, however, are the strategies and methods employed from which these ends are expected to be met. For example, during times of chattel slavery and the reconstruction era that followed the abolishment of slavery, black males were often brutalized and/or killed outright. Consequently, black females were that much more vulnerable to rape, brutalization, and outright murder, themselves. Under the current system though, the brutal and blatant tactics utilized to annihilate the black male and the black family have been replaced by a system that is designed to make it appear as if black males are either completely unwilling to step up to the challenges of manhood and manliness, or are devoid of the ability to be protectors of not only themselves but their families and communities as well.

Francis Cress-Welsing, author of the *Isis Papers: Keys to the Colors*, made the claim in her groundbreaking work that when the black male and black female concertedly wage the struggle against racism/white supremacy as a means of procuring collective social justice, only then will they acquire the certainty of remaining united. Moreover, she hypothesized that only by way of fighting these forces will such institutions (and ideology) fail to succeed in driving the black male and black female apart. [9] However, due to the efficiency of the institution of racism/white supremacy, it is common for both the black male and black female to find that they are at odds over money, marital and common law infidelity, household instability and, lastly, discord in regards to assessing and dismantling the institution of racism/white supremacy.

Because of such a projected outcome that is gradually becoming a stark realization, the growing epidemic of interracial marriages and courtships taking place under the penumbra of a still inexorably racist society is both psychologically as well as culturally catastrophic. And although a feasible (or at least common) argument could be made that true love should be devoid of race, color, or ethnic categorization, the facts however indicate that because of the bifurcation of the races and the institution of racism that ensues as a result, black males and black females have been exploited purely on the basis of sexual stereotypes and exploitation (Just watch contemporary television shows and big-budget and independently made films depicting relations between blacks and whites).

In a hedonistic society that engenders sexual exploitation on the basis of color, gender, and ethnicity, the black male is certainly no exception. Long before the porn industry became a multibillion dollar conglomerate, black males were customarily identified for their perceived sexual prowess rather than their intellectual capacity. And similar to how the porn industry is saturated with black males and black females—disproportionately copulating with white women and white men—society in general continues to showcase the black male for any and everything but his intelligence and ingenuity. This form of exploitation/Blaxploitation, however, is nothing new. In fact, we have seen this several times before, and not just in America but in other nations that are noted for propensities geared towards such abuse.

For instance, within the past few years, HBO's *Real Sports with Bryant Gumbel* did an expose on a massive black ex-football player from the United States who relocated to Japan, where he gained widespread notoriety as a King Kong-like sideshow attraction. This obviously entailed dressing in ape-like clothing, eating bananas, and causing complete carnage and mayhem (the universal perception of how black males are expected to behave whether dressed up in monkey attire or not). Additionally, in the United Kingdom, former heavyweight boxing champion Frank Bruno, a gargantuan of a male and unquestionably the epitome of the historical big, strong "black buck," was a much beloved heroic-like figure, not because he was a good boxer (which he was not at all, only winning the heavyweight title once and failing at his first defense of it) but because of his fetish for white women, white culture, and disavowal of blackness and his own black identity. And, unsurprisingly, once his mediocre career ended, he was more laughed at than laughed with, and more mocked than admired, which subsequently caused his institutionalization and treatment for postpartum depression and bipolar disorder. And of course there is, and always has been, good ole American racism and exploitation. Examples are obviously endless; however, for the sake of remaining both tact and thorough, how about Vogue magazine's March 24, 2008 cover of LeBron James impersonating King Kong, same as the example previously mentioned. The difference here though is that on the magazine's cover (the first time the magazine had ever put a black male on its cover, by the way), James has a basketball in one arm and a white woman in the other; racist innuendo that is clearly indicative of America's continual preoccupation with the same "beauty and the beast" imagery that resulted in the making of D.W. Griffith's *Birth of a Nation*, as well as the ubiquitous although erroneous belief that black males were in the past and continue to be sexual predators and annihilators of white women.

Because of this example alone, even the United States, a country that can now boast the unprecedented feat of having a two-term black president—who by the way just so happens to be married to a black female—has never truly valued or been inclined to respect black intelligence (just look at the distorting of black history both nationally and globally). On the other hand, America continues to demonstrate a willingness to play on contrived and sordid racial stereotypes, regardless of the fact that in the previously mentioned example, similar to the president, LeBron James just so happens to be a black male who is married to a black female, yet is on the cover of a major magazine caressing a white woman.

Just as posttraumatic slave syndrome has had a profound effect on the descendants of former slaves in this society, the practitioners as well as those who endorse institutional racism/white supremacy have also suffered from the effects of slavery. For instance, during the times before the inoculation of reconstruction, leading up to the civil rights movement of the 1960s, blacks were not permitted to learn to read or write. For this reason, the same element of fear that could lead to the murder of a black male or a black female seeking to learn to read or write still lingers in the fears of whites who find the thought of blacks obtaining the same degree of literacy and professionalism as themselves utterly disdainful. Consequently, the endeavor of either socially eschewing or denigrating highly intelligent black males has maintained as much if not more importance now than it had back then, or at any other time in the country's history. Or, better yet, the numbers of educated blacks that are permitted a public forum is steadfastly kept to a minimum. Nevertheless, examples to confirm how history does truly have a tendency to repeat itself, particularly if meant to safeguard a certain cause, are exceedingly difficult to dispute. I once read how the character Stimey from the *Our Gang* series, aka *The Little Rascals*, received such limited dialogue because producers of the show had concluded that the young actor, whose real name was Matthew Beard, was too articulate and well-spoken for that particular role.

The Black Audition

The point to all of this is to emphasize the importance of reinforcing stereotypes in a system of institutional racism/white supremacy as a means to disparage and malign those who are biologically and culturally linked to a certain ethnic group, especially if the overall goal is to dehumanize and debase the targeted group. And the most damaging way to attack an entire group is to debase and malign the males of that particular group. Indeed, stripping the males of the targeted group of their ascribed manhood, and weakening their value and self-worth can only ensure cultural disarray and eventual collapse. As a result, any means designed to depict the black male in American society as not only craven and incompetent but, even more disturbing, effeminate (and in a dress), most certainly produces discord among the male and female of the targeted group, as well as ensures a gross disruption of the family unit and communal setting.

It is because of the powerless condition of those who were former slaves and chattel burden-bearers that courtships with those who are representative of the dominant group is foreseen as ensuring validation and a measure of self-worth that could not be established with conspicuous and unabated identification with those of the oppressed group. Yet, sadly, and strangely profound, even to this day and perhaps even more so than in any previous time in the past, images of benign and benevolent courtships of the black male and black female is a prospect that is completely eschewed by mainstream media and popular culture in American society. It is as if any impression or expressions of amorous black on black relations is indicative of being anti-white or brazenly opposed to the status quo, as well as counterproductive to the plan and process of the annihilation of the black male.

Because of this assessment—regardless of whether one chooses to take it or leave it—I will reemphasize the claim that interracial relations in a conspicuously racist society is a de facto condition of menticide, as well as the psychological damage that has manifested as a result of slavery and the implanting of the seeds of racial inferiority. As a result, the massive campaign of promoting black and white courtships, while promoting images of healthy black on black relationships is almost non-existent or is gradually leading up to a point where it is as taboo as white on black relations once were, is completely illogical. One of the worst aspects of racism in American society is that black people as a whole—who are overwhelmingly the victims of racism—have allowed themselves to be victimized because of conditions of internal racial differences or, more appropriately, racial indifferences. If the black male and black female could be unanimous in truly understanding their condition in a racist society, perhaps there could be an equally harmonious consensus as to how to resolve the racist practices in which both are invariably victimized.

Comparable to how overt brutality during the times of slavery completely destroyed the black family and the courtship between the black male and black female, more contemporary covert forms of racism have symbolically caused ethnic as well as gender conflicts between the two. And due to the fact that whites have complete control of mainstream media outlets—exercising taut scrutiny of the dissemination of any and all information and enforcing equally rigid cultural interdictions— attempts at making null and void amorous ties and affection shared between blacks is commonplace. Therefore, regardless of the supposed "browning" of America, those who exercise institutional racism/white supremacy define courtships with former slaves in this society, as well as decide how whites benefit or gain from these courtships. So, when I speak of the "black audition," negative images reinforced by Hollywood— one of the most racist edifices in modern existence—comes to mind. However, to lay blame squarely on the shoulders of white racists who run an institutional system with a long history of false representation and exploitation would be inaccurate as well as socially unacceptable.

The real truth is that stereotypes exist because the collective group that is on the receiving end of these stereotypes has allowed them to exist. Unfortunately, associations to dietary fetishes such as fried chicken and watermelon can only be deduced as mere defamations that have been superimposed on blacks simply on the basis of being black. Certainly, such an endeavor can only be surmised as an unreachable condition of racist practices. However, the actions of those who are assigned to the stigmatized group do indeed account for something. In other words, black people as a whole reinforcing negative stereotypes that are attributed to them simply as a means of individual social and economic advancement, similar to interracial marriages and courtships, are continual examples of *tragic arrangements,* where the onus and culpability falls squarely on the shoulders of black people for failing to abate these practices and negative associations, especially in an exceedingly racist and oppressive society. For example, after Divine Brown, born Estella Marie Thompson, was arrested with British actor Hugh Grant for performing oral sex on the actor, she appeared to have become an instant media sensation overnight, appearing in countless numbers of television interviews, newspaper articles, as well as becoming an international porn celebrity. Hence, to echo the famous catchphrase of Don King, the notorious boxing promoter whose reputation for shadiness and deceit is as notorious as his bouffant hairstyle, "only in America" can an indigent, uneducated, single mother become a millionaire because of her illicit and unlawful coitus encounter with a white celebrity who sought her services as a prostitute.

The fact that there are many who achieve academic and corporate success, yet are circumscribed to underpaid jobs and dead end careers is testament to the fact that in America, not only is one free to be a freak but such hedonistic predilections and illegal improprieties can be exorbitantly profitable. This is especially true if you are a person of color and, due to this fact, have been involuntarily assigned to an ethnic group that has been labeled with a tag of incivility, decadence, and immorality purely on the basis of color. Perhaps there are many who would agree that the most effective way to destroy either the physical or psychological being of a racial group is to first strip them of humanity and then put on display to the world their uncivilized nature, propensities, and weakened cultural condition. And when the mask of civility has been removed, the targeted end result is complete indifference or culpability as to what happens to or becomes of the targeted group. After all, was this not the tactic that Hitler employed on the Jews during the Holocaust to foment his endeavor to see their collective destruction?

The purpose of either falsely endorsing (victimizer) or willingly embracing (victim) interracial courtships is to put on both a national and global platform black peoples' disdain and disunion towards and among each other. Furthermore, this strategy is combined with the pseudo attempt to both put on display and legitimize white peoples' acceptance of their former slaves and present racial victims as a means to civilize them and boost their social standing. Yet on the other hand, the reinforcing and showcasing of negative racial stereotypes only continues to disparage and objectify the females of the oppressed and victimized group and emasculate and caricaturize the males. Unsurprisingly, as a result of this effort, the most persecuted and consistently scrutinized and sought out are those who refuse to accept their conditions and yield to a status quo that dictates inferiority and absence of manhood and manliness. On the other hand, an amalgamation of the outright hard-headed or the pitifully misinformed, many of whom have both explicitly and implicitly conformed to the mass innuendo of decadence and lack of cultural self-worth are embraced and illumined on the cultural landscape.

Amazingly, even in an era of America's first black president (which is gradually proving to not necessarily be such a good thing in terms of black folk's collective advancement), the individuals it appears that are the faces of black America, as well as those who are delegated to either be the voice or act out characters and images on behalf of black folk, is highly questionable. In other words, for every Divine Brown, whose lifestyle is respected as audacious and bold, or Eddie Murphy and Tyler Perry whose characterizations are celebrated and revered, there is a Reynaldo Reye or a Monique who claim that at the end of the day—for better or worse—this is unquestionably a sign of progress.

White privilege and Black passive resistance

I once had a conversation with a black female associate about my frustrations with the treatment, or mistreatment, of black employees at the company that I was working for at the time, as well as the mistreatment of black people within the corporate landscape of America in general. I also had expressed to this particular female my concern that the basis of this (mis)treatment was, as I saw it at the time, due to a lack of white bosses and overseers' acceptance of their black workers as individuals rather than as some trite monolithic mass—whom Tyler Perry and other opportunistic blacks who act as proprietors of black culture—incessantly attempt to portray all black folk as being. Successful and attractive, this female had begun to share with me how she managed to acquire success and stay under the radar for years because of her ability to blend in and, as she put it, "act white." Surprisingly, this is what she proposed that I seek to become efficient at as a means to mitigate my frustrations while working in a white corporate system.

W.E.B. Dubois dubbed this bipolar-type avoidance of reality and self-imposed conditioning as "double consciousness." This observation can be concluded as an attempt to juxtapose two divergent states of consciousness: One conscious state being swathed in the reality of a physiological condition that is inescapable; the other, a metaphysical construct that is steeped in surrealism. This perspective and subsequent survival mechanism has arguably become all-too common for the black male in today's corporate system. This is especially true when considering the present state of consciousness of the black female, as well as those whom, regardless of gender, attempt to deny racism but are transparently race-conscious. In other words, the physiological as well as psychological constraints that have been imposed as a result of white racist innuendo, as well as racist and discriminatory practices, has overwhelmingly deemed blackness or having black skin as a curse, inferior, and less than human since the first ships landed in America, herding black human beings to these shores to be conditioned and treated as subhuman laborers and burden-bearers. On the other hand, the surrealism as alluded to is nothing more than pathological and dysfunctional theater, endeavoring to transmogrify blackness into a state of mind. Thus, you are only as black as you think, feel, or act, implying that there exist an alternative that will allow one to reject or disavow this condition or conscious state at any given time.

One of the more troublesome aspects of being on the receiving end of institutional racism/white supremacy is the widely held belief that any form of discrimination towards blacks in general is not the result of institutional and systemic practices. Instead, such actions are deemed as isolated incidents that blacks encounter on random occasions by individuals who are falsely perceived as a dying breed of the misguided in society, who choose to cling on to and covet societal values and mores that are now widely perceived as repugnant, dated, and immoral in terms of both a national and global point of view. It is as if racism, when it is discussed, is perceived as some intangible relic that is still out there somewhere but yet is out of reach, and the farther out it spreads the more it dissipates and loses any force or relevance. This perspective is indeed tragic given that it is a gross distortion of the true realities that exists globally as well as in western society.

Institutional racism/white supremacy is not only real but is a palpable force in the lives of people of color, all over the globe but particularly in the western hemisphere. Moreover, the practitioners of racism/white supremacy, who seek to debunk racist ideology and practices continue to benefit and thrive on the seeds of racial hatred and bigotry that was planted by their ancestors. So, regardless of the projected browning of America based on its supposed growing diversity, it is still white people in this society who control every social and economic aspect of it. It is white people in this society who invariably purport images that are designed to conclude that white people and the cultural norms and factors that they endorse and sanction are all that matter and are relevant.

It is because of this ethnocentric prose as well as the continued manifestation of social practices that the only color that can still be painted in America, as well as globally, is white. Thus, compounding westernized global domination of resources and wealth are ubiquitous images of the intellectual, physical, and sexual superiority of white men and white women. Major motion pictures are frequently made permeating white people with the ability to clone other human beings, reanimate dinosaurs, develop and employ sophisticated technology to stave off alien incursions, as well as annihilate rogue nations of people of color who are (supposedly) hell-bent on decimating western culture and values. As previously mentioned, the black male has disproportionately dominated every major franchise sport, yet venues to purport and promote incomparable white male virility and masculinity remain omnipresent. For instance, the city of Philadelphia has a rich and grandiose history of producing champion-caliber black prize-fighters whose successful careers have helped magnify and enhance the appeal of the sport of Boxing. However, it is the statue of Rocky Balboa, a fictional character purported in the 1976 academy award-winning film of a down and out white loser who gets a shot at the (black) heavyweight champion that towers magnanimously in the square of the city's historic downtown district. This was made possible irrespective of the Joe Fraziers, Tim Witherspoons, Bernard Hopkins, Harold Johnsons, Meldrick Taylors and a slew of other great fighters that the fighting city currently has, has had in the past, and continues to produce.

While it is a commonly held belief that not all white people are racists, the claim, however, that all racists are white people is difficult to dispute. With that said, the concomitant factor of Sylvester Stallone and the *Rocky* films becoming an iconic brand, during and post the Frank Rizzo era in Philadelphia is indicative of another prime example that confirms America as still the global preeminent institution of racism/white supremacy and repressive practices towards blacks and other people of color. Hence, regardless of the above claim of whom or which white folk are racist as opposed to those who are not, the fact of the matter is that the lone problem in the world is the institution of racism/white supremacy.

And since white people control the system, essentially, the problem then is white people. Nonetheless, a great deal of the culpability lies with the black male as the premiere victim of institutional racism/white supremacy, considering that it is he whom continues to allow himself to be duped and brainwashed into believing that the abhorrent conditions the he and black folk as a whole are besieged by are not the result of the machinations crafted and utilized by whites for the sake of western and global domination. Yet on the other hand, not to sound contradictory, the black male is not solely responsible for his current predicament, nor is he to blame for past misdeeds perpetrated against him (e.g., chattel slavery). I can recall viewing *Rocky* III (or it might have been part II) at the movie theatre as a young boy and, being obviously devoid of race-consciousness, rooted and cheered for the film's protagonist. Today, however, I often wonder and ask myself, how many black folk are still rooting and cheering for Rocky as opposed to rooting and cheering for the "black guy?"

Still, the solution alone is not getting representatives of the power structure to admit to their racist practices. On the contrary, the goal should be victims of institutional racism/white supremacy coming up with effective solutions as to how to neutralize such practices. Undeniably, white people sit at the helm of wealth and privilege in this country because of slavery—then and now —that has weakened blacks as a collective group, as well as ensuing racism and the seeds of inferiority that has kept the masses of black people as a whole, victims of wanton discrimination and systematic group oppression. Yet when zeroing in on and thoroughly analyzing the word "privilege," it is privilege that seemingly has been consigned to white people and white people only that has displaced any notions of malfeasant racism. The problem with this notion is its flowed logic that, with the proper approach and focus, can be thoroughly dissected.

Any notion or claim of white privilege is not only erroneous but deceptive in that it connotes that white people stumbled onto power and privilege fortuitously rather than by force, a force that has been maintained and continues to this day. Also, it is the conditioning that stems from institutional racism and racist practices—from those who claim to be the fortuitous beneficiaries of privilege—that has reduced the black male in America to conditions and circumstances that have rendered him a functional inferior, and has deprived him of the intrinsic attributes that nature bestowed for purposes of preservation and survival. As a result, the indelible stereotypes that are omnipresent, the pursuit of cross-racial courtships, and the ineluctable images and depictions of the black male being reduced to dissolution and effeminacy—traits and characteristics that are antithetical to his TRUE nature—are symptomatic of the cultural and racial weaknesses and dependence that are highly scrutinized and exploited in an institutionally racist and repressive system. It is because of the unchanging and continual potency of institutional racism/white supremacy that the black male has either resigned himself to inferior status by willfully accepting and embracing the precepts of racial inferiority. Or, have black folk in general physically and psychologically attempted to blend in and ingratiate themselves into the dominant culture, as if the last leg of survival is to homogenize the races rather than continue to exist side by side with their oppressors?

It is necessary that I again reemphasize that this book is about the failures, the weakening, and effeminizing of the black male in a racist society. Plainly speaking, however, it is the failure of both the black male and black female to recognize the massive epidemic of black menticide that is destroying black people as a whole; a factor that is highly indicative of the burgeoning numbers of the foolhardy and disillusioned who believe that what is now taking place before them are signs of irrefutable progress that are accompanied by unprecedented rewards and incentives. Tragically, this appears to be the more plausible rationale, rather than the alternative collective effort of one day through mutual understanding, perseverance, and hard work, making such fallacious nonsense a palpable reality. It is because of this failure to understand and act on such common logic that black females have yet to reach the essence of true womanhood, and black males remain boys instead of Men.

Three

GANGSTERS & THUGS:

The d/evolution of the urban Black Male
since the days of chattel slavery

It is difficult to dispute that America is not only a racist society but is arguably the prototype and epitome of a racially disharmonized culture that breeds dissension between various ethnic groups, based on the universal system of institutional racism/white supremacy more so than any other nation on the face of the earth. Yet what is abhorrently deceptive and iniquitous about racism in America are the messages that are disseminated to the world that it is the epicenter of racial tolerance and benign race relations that are indicative of America's creed of "land of the free and home of the brave." Furthermore, and as a result of this deception, the black male in American society seems to think that his condition is far better than those of black people anywhere else in global society.

In this chapter I will attempt to not only disprove such beliefs and call into question any pseudo claims that are to the contrary of my supposition, but also incorporate many excerpts from the Willie

Lynch doctrine of how to make a slave and parallel such theories and practices on how it applies to those who, to this day, possess a slave mentality (i.e., posttraumatic slave syndrome which will be discussed more in depth in chapter 5) as predicated by the doctrine. And, how the doctrine applies to those who continue to gradually devolve as opposed to evolving under the banner of institutional racism/white supremacy which, speciously, is said to no longer be a social crisis under the pretext of post-racialism. Nowhere, and certainly not in regards to any other group of people, can this simple truth be more obvious than the condition and/or conditioning of young urban black males, presently America's most loathed and relentless target for exploitation, as well as expedient removal and extermination. But before going there, per se, let's briefly explore some attributing factors. For starters, the problem is that the denial of racism does not at all mean that it is not there or does not exist. In truth, the pains of oppression and discrimination cannot be suppressed. As a result, that pain and frustration is inverted and, consequently, major social and cultural dysfunctions are manifested. With that being said, the well-oiled machine of institutional racism/white supremacy has been diverted by the sensationalizing of isolated incidents of racial attacks and epithets perpetrated by high-profile white celebrities and public figures.

More surprising is that these racial tirades and insults are invariably followed by the proclamation of not being racist or fueled by racial animus, despite how incendiary or blatant the remarks. For instance, when radio personality Don Imus made insulting racial remarks towards female members of Rutgers University's basketball team, he was given a few months hiatus, in which his time off was mostly delayed as a result of contract renegotiations. Moreover, Imus never fully acknowledged any wrong-doing, citing that he did not find his choice of words offensive because they were taken right out of the pages of his targeted victims' own cultural vernacular and modes of communication.

The Usual Suspects

"Instill fear, distrust, and envy for purposes of control"[10]
—WILLIE LYNCH

It is with analyses offered in this chapter that I will again emphasize that one of the conditions of institutional racism/white supremacy is gradually stripping its victims of their ethnocentric pride and cultural self-esteem, as well as collective and individual self-worth. Additionally, in referencing the Willie Lynch letter and its manuscript on how to make a slave, one of its methods is the instilling of fear, distrust, and envy for the purposes of control. So when combining the pretext of slavery and years of institutional racism, what has manifested as a result is the destruction of manhood and manliness and instead producing human beings with the stature of men but with the mentality and mindset of boys; and, in staying on par with the on-going and gradually expanding crisis, becoming more and more endowed with the mentality and mindset of girls as well.

True manhood, as defined by my transposing its literal definition, entails instilling the values of cultural solidarity, pride, love for family and community, and the desire to do for self. However, what happens as a result of the absence of cultivating manhood and manliness is the sowing of the seeds of discontent and self-hatred. This is what Don Imus sought to exploit. His explanation of referring to the females on Rutgers basketball team as "nappy-headed ho's" was based on his assertion that this method of communication is prevalent in Hip Hop and Rap culture, which is largely comprised of young urban black and brown males.

Without question, it is hard to justify the meaning or intent of certain hip hop tracks and songs, in which the lyrics are as follows: "every other city we go/ every other video/ no matter where I go/ I see the same ho's." Yet on the other hand, unless you are purged by racial bias, such lyrics do not define all of Hip Hop music, and it would be foolish to think otherwise. Additionally, adopting this ploy as an excuse to justify a tirade fueled by racial hostility is even more preposterous. Nevertheless, the gangster and thug bravado that had already shaped the overall impression and veneer of the genre as well as the culture of Hip Hop was magnified that much more, and was successfully used as a scapegoat for the brazen practices and promulgation of racial discord and dogma.

Because of America's institutional system of racism/white supremacy perpetrated against the black male, and black people as a whole, a myriad of social dysfunctions and improprieties have surfaced. In addition to external forces that have ravaged black communities and urban ghettoes nationwide, frustrations and cultural disarray and disunity were inverted rather than projected outward. Disproportionate levels of crime and urban violence were a consequence of the sordid realities that plagued urban communities following the civil rights movement of the 1960s. Thus, young urban dwellers who were forced to face the reality of corporate disfranchisement and an economic lock-out, contrived other vehicles necessary for acquiring the basic necessities of subsistence as a direct response to external forces and demons that solidified urban impoverishment. Moreover, actions and behaviors fostered to enhance and broaden masculinity, a knee-jerk response engendered for compensation due to the diminished capacity of manhood and manliness that racial repression invariably creates, became obligatory for survival.

Hip Hop music/culture, which was the intended scapegoat for Don Imus's racial assault, was crafted for the purposes of providing not only social and economic prosperity but also exaggerated manliness and social cadences based on hyper-masculine themes. And despite the multibillion dollar juggernaut that Hip Hop has become, and the countless numbers of talented individuals who have emerged based on its omnipotent cultural and global influence, the mystique of the genre is that of a collage of roving and burgeoning bands of urban miscreants and incorrigible provocateurs of violence and mayhem, who use the music as a platform for social acceptance (street credibility) and economic overindulgence. So instead of an ingenious, creative form of social and musical expression, engineered by young, gifted, and brilliant artists and thespians, the music is associated with self-titled and self-made *gangsters* and *thugs*.

The Thug Code

"Being a fool is a basic ingredient to the maintenance of slavery"[11]
—WILLIE LYNCH

Despite the supposed increase of the so-called black middle class (which is really only a "politically correct" yet deceptive way of saying that some black folk make more money than other black folk), there are still a disproportionate number of young males and females and young boys and girls who are ravaged by abject poverty and are restricted to deplorable social conditions. For young urban dwellers the pursuit and acquisition of the so-called "American dream" has been obstructed and compromised by a never ending nightmare. Consequently, the *haves* and *have-nots,* made possible by way of an indiscriminate system of capitalism, and racism, irrefutably make certain that there is a stark contrasting reality between blacks and whites in this country. Furthermore, it cannot be disputed that there is an exorbitant element of crime that exists in black communities in every major city, and that many of the young who are reared in these environments have early exposures to the criminal element and squalid conditions that not only exist but are, in all fairness, superimposed. So, for every one young black male who goes to college or who successfully finds legitimate employment, there are three who are young *thugs* who terrorize their respective communities, prior to succumbing to the inevitable prospect of death, substance abuse, or a lifetime spent in and out of the criminal justice system.

Take for example that in 1992 a young Hip Hop artist emerged out of Oakland, California named Tupac Shakur. In addition to going on to become a cultural icon and perhaps a primary symbol and voice of urban rage and frustration, Shakur would also make popular the thug moniker that has remained a staple in the genre since his violent death in 1996. Yet despite his status and unquestionable talent, the criminal element that would become synonymous in Hip Hop did not start with Shakur's thug moniker or cadence, as this particular artistic and self-manufactured effrontery became a subsidiary or variant of the negative imagery that many of the genre's top-selling and most influential artists were already espousing and promulgating in their lyrics and own respective cadences.

Prior to this movement, and Shakur's popularity, Hip Hop was already tagged as "gansta' rap" by popular mainstream media, which, unsurprisingly, only heightened the genre's already yet gradually burgeoning violent reputation. Interesting, however, is that there was a stark paradox taking place that both thwarted the genre's image and erroneously stigmatized young black males who grew up in the same communities that many of these artists were also born and bred. For instance, in addition to his various talents, Shakur was also perceptibly intelligent and at a young age developed a high degree of literacy. John Potash, author of *The FBI War on Tupac Shakur and Black Leaders*, illustrates how Dr. Michael Eric Dyson in his biographical analysis of Shakur, identified how he was reading PhD level books and manuscripts as early as preadolescence.[12]

Yet it was Shakur's adopted (and not necessarily contrived) thug label that underscored the hyper masculine imagery and bravado that he was trying to establish in attempts to elevate his own status as well as that of the millions of loyal black followers that he would refer to as "thug nation," mainly because these were urban dwellers who, similar to Shakur, lived and shared the experience of being black and oppressed in America. For this reason, Shakur had become nearly a godly figure in urban circles because of his in-your-face aggressive, fiery, and poignant lyrics, in addition to his constant brushes with the law. This arguably rang true in the eyes of a culture that celebrated the image of the *gangster* as masterminds of highly sophisticated, well-crafted, and efficiently operated criminal organizations; characteristics and exploits that historically were not associated with your common black criminal in dilapidated and decaying urban ghettoes. On the other hand, the thug was synonymous with the common local street tough that meandered back and forth throughout his own respective neighborhood and community, and whose improprieties and malfeasant criminal acts were restricted to these settings. In other words, being a thug and relishing in thug imagery was not a rallying cry for proliferation or urban uplift and advancement, but was instead a resignation of weakened and reduced status of impotent and emasculated urban youth, same as the condition and circumstance that the adult black male in American society is restricted to as well.

American Gangsta's

"If the nigger woman is broken, the
offspring is also broken in the early years of development"[13]
—WILLIE LYNCH

Years before Tupac Shakur was both literally and symbolically building a nation of thugs, groups like Los Angeles based N.W.A., short for "niggers with attitude," and Houston's Geto Boys cemented the gangster image in Hip Hop by providing and promulgating lurid depictions of urban blight—the wanton violence, the drugs, the destitution—as well as the maniacal and anarchical urban rebellion that stems from such conditions. The media dubbed this form of urban, artistic expression as "gangsta' rap." Even so, the paradox that would later emerge is that many of these artists are not lawless criminals, nor had they ever at any point in their lives been gangsters or thugs; in fact, far from it. And although it may be true that some young males and females who are either artists or in some manner are associated with the genre have had their brushes with the law, there are many who have simply been instrumental in providing a voice to the disadvantaged and downtrodden in a nation that is unapologetically apathetic to urban blight—surmising these circumstances as the direct result of an ethnic group who lack the civility and dexterity to be able to successfully thrive in a competitive society.

Gangs, and gangsters, did not start with the Hip Hop movement, a fact that only heightens the absurdity of the specious label of gansta' rap, as dubbed by white mainstream media, with the aid of black opportunists such as Dionne Warwick and the late C. Delores Tucker. In fact, urban gangs—factions not associated with Hip Hop culture, at least not artistically—developed in black communities immediately following the civil rights era, and these factions were formulated not for the purposes of killing other blacks as the result of urban warfare, but as splinter revolutionary groups that dove-tailed the social and political ambitions of the militant civil rights organizations of the civil rights era (e.g., Black Panther Party, SNCC, and MOVE). Thus, Chicago's Gangster Disciples, BlackStone Rangers, Conservative Vice lords, as well as L.A.'s Crips and Bloods were not just roving and meandering knife-wielding, purse-snatching miscreants, but instead were community organizing, activist-minded, young revolutionaries in training. It was not until the official collapse of black activism, supplanted by the rise of integrationist-minded dependence, that the manifestations of black-on-black gang violence became a lurid reality in urban ghettos and black communities.

Inevitably, the outright political assassinations and violent deaths of the Fred Hamptons of the civil rights movement, at the hands of an anti-black government gave birth to the Monster Kodys in the "concrete jungles" of America's urban landscape. Consequently, politically strategic and organizational brilliance was supplanted by a new "code of the streets" that was strictly geared towards the NEW urban jungle's inoculation of the OLD creed of survival of the fittest. As stated by author and scholar Haki R. Madhubuti, "rite of passages from boyhood to manhood is left in failed schools, pool halls, gangs, military, and negative influences."[14]

Because of such sentiments, in which I am in total agreement, it is my belief that, again, to quote Don King, "only in America" is it possible for a black male with a genius level IQ to spend most of his life in prison as a direct consequence of this level of brilliance. And it is also my belief that because of the reality of institutional racism/white supremacy in this society, such a fate has nothing at all to do with decisions that one makes as a direct result of that reality. Therefore, similar to Fred Hampton and Monster Kody, the fate of Melvin Williams, regardless of his biological and genetic gifts and endowments, was predetermined strictly as a result of the conditions of race and social class. His story is described in detail in the BET miniseries *American Gangster*, a series documenting the exploits of renowned gangsters and black criminals who were able to build massive criminal enterprises before their subsequent downfalls, which resulted in either incarceration or death.

Nonetheless, and regardless of whether many of the previously mentioned are gangsters or not, I would propose that the beauty of Hip Hop music/culture—including all of its related cultural elements—and the practitioners of the art form who have become highly successful because of its mainstream popularity and acceptance, is that it has allowed an oppressed and disparaged group to both aesthetically and financially rise above the melancholic and grim realities of the urban jungle from which they have been purposefully subjected and exposed. It is hard to argue that Hip Hop music /culture—love it or hate it—has provided a voice as well as pecuniary vitality to those who have been either completely ostracized or have been gridlocked as a result of the discriminatory nature of corporate and economic processes that take place in this society.

Like Capone, Montana, and Noriega

*"You got an all-out prize fight, you wait
'til the fight's over, one guy is left standing,
and that's how you know who won!"*[15]
—AL CAPONE, *THE UNTOUCHABLES*

The conscious world is indeed directly and/or indirectly familiar with the bravado imagery and ubiquitous violence that is purposefully assigned a trajectory that has these menacing personas and the decadent behaviors that accompany these characteristics concentrated in American slums and ghettos. Certainly, thugs and gangsters are highly prevalent and personified in Hip Hop music; however, organized crime, mobs, and serial and mass murderers are also images and characterizations that foretell America's violent proclivities and precede its reputation as the most violent nation in the industrialized world.

But if one so happens to live and function along the periphery of the genre of Hip hop, the images of Tupac Shakur and Eazy E, born Eric Wright, cast a much darker and dismal shadow than the image of, say, Al Capone; even though the latter was much more notorious in terms of his exploits in the annals of crime, murder, and mayhem in America. And although it is true that many of these Hip Hop artists that proclaim gang associations and criminal activity do so to establish the kind of street credibility that will guarantee record sales, there are some however who have criminal records or have been associated with real criminals. As a result, many of these young males, and some females, often continue their criminal exploits and, consequently, are often incarcerated even after their respective rap careers have taken off.

What is a common theme as far as the lyrical prose of most of these artists is that they encapsulate the depravity and uncertainty of street life and street culture as a means to display to the world and to their listeners, the day to day toil and rigor of survival and what it takes to survive in environments where certain death at a young age is as much a part of reality than is anything else. As a result, pseudo forms of masculinity and maladaptive behaviors that are identified with manhood and/or manliness are contrived to ensure the proverbial survival of the fittest. And because of the fact that many young urban black males are locked out of the socioeconomic process, not only is some form of the underground economy essential to guarantee survival but also fully embraced and glorified as an inextricable part of 'hood life and the thug and gangster bravado and existence that such circumstances entail. Obviously, poppy fields and marijuana plants are not indigenous to ghettos or urban communities, nor are they grown in the backyards and front lawns of the people who inhabit these communities. Yet these communities are overwhelmingly overrun by the selling and abusing of narcotics. Why?

Despite the bombastic and concerted celebration of the nation's first black president, in addition to the intelligence and ingenuity that many of these young males and females possess, the visage of Tony Montana, made famous from the notorious 1983 film *Scarface*, and Al Capone are the images that are highly scrutinized and glorified and often pursued; primarily because these young urban inhabitants have a palpable connection with realities of life that clearly are a world away from the so called American dream that is advertised and made to appear as easy to acquire or obtain. Therefore, for compensatory means, the images of thugs and gangsters, although not uniquely contrived but instead adopted, became staples in urban communities and Hip Hop music/culture as a means to ostentatiously flaunt manhood and manliness that is otherwise conspicuously absent; particularly being that black people as a whole do not control the socio-economic infrastructure or resources in their own neighborhoods and communities. It is because of this reason that the gangster and thug image and bravado became so synonymous and relevant in urban culture that many of the premiere Hip Hop artists gave themselves names, surnames, and titles based off of famous gangsters and men who cultivated massive criminal empires. The fact that some artists adopted monikers such as Capone, Noriega, Gotti, Escobar, and Ricky Ross should come as no surprise, but should instead be viewed as staples in a form of music where the superfluous and over exaggerated veneer of masculinity is as tantamount to the billions of dollars of revenue that the genre accrues yearly, stateside and abroad.

So, when taking a page from the Don Imus tirade, the justification is based on the widespread self-indulgence that is not only prevalent but culturally celebrated in both the music and urban enclaves where many of the viewers and fans and participants of the genre have themselves been born and bred. And despite the exceptionally creative and brilliant minds that have emerged from the genre, there are equally as many who by way of their lyrics espouse their sexual conquest of black females—commonly referred to as bitches and ho's in the genre—and who verbalize lurid tales of criminal exploits, imbue their manliness with lyrical expose's of the sizes of their penises, and subscribe to violence and murder at the slightest provocation. Now before I go any further with this assessment, it must be stated that I am not at all in favor of censorship of any sort. I will, however, point out a stark problem that is far too underrepresented or spoken of in the genre. It was the late rapper Heavy D, born Dwight Myers, who once provided his analysis of the state of Hip Hop music, pointing out that the negative elements that exist in the music do not make the music bad as a whole.

Despite how simplistic yet straightforward, I still look back with profundity at the prophetic impact of that claim, as clearly the figureheads and music and studio executives have in all appearances embarked on a push towards advertising and selling the negative aspects that the late rapper conceded do exist; consequently, making the music in its totality look bad and to be viewed with scorn and derision. Also, Hip Hop antagonists, by all appearances, specialize in making the art form susceptible to exploitation for the purposes of adding fuel to the racial animus that exists between black and white and rich and poor in a society that from its inception has sought to exploit and demean both, or at least ALL. This has mostly been accomplished by a dumbing down of the content of the music, as well as a heightening and emblazoning of material excesses and highfaluting, flamboyant styles of living. Clearly, modes and methods of representation that are geared towards posturing and effrontery that is in direct contrast with the true realities of the day to day lives of urban youth and the majority of black people.

Prior to the gangster and thug movement, Hip Hop was an art form with a concentration on the purity and craft of the music. Moreover, the culture of Hip Hop was comprised of several elements: break-dancing, graffiti art, emceeing (actual delivery of lyrics), and deejaying—providing beats to the lyrics via turntables that were designed to spin old rhythm and blues and disco records. During the late 1980s leading up to the early 90s, the music was nearly dominated by artists who were making socially conscious music with strong political references. The content of most of the lyrics at this time offered sweeping indictments of America's treatment of people of color, particularly those who inhabited the inner city. Some of the lyrical oratory by certain artists was so powerful and brazen that it was analogous to the anti-American, anarchic rhetoric that was reminiscent of the radical expressions of the 1960s during the struggle for civil rights.

However, this particular facet of the genre was not able to sustain itself, and its displacement by the more decadent form of lyrical expression that would later become known as gangsta' rap is another example of how economically base and impotent black males in this society are—failing to even control the edifices and conglomerates in which their brand of self-expression is created, packaged, and distributed. More telling is that while groups such as Public Enemy and Poor Righteous Teachers fizzled out because of the emergence of the more aggressive and violent forms of lyrical expression, artists such as Ice Cube, Queen Latifah, Common, Ice-T, and Onyx were, from all appearances, bought out by the powers that be of the corporate media and mainstream marketing machines. As a result, the seizing of Hip Hop portended many of these artists trading in their microphones for roles in Hollywood films, in which most of the roles that were offered were those of hooligans, chronic substance abusers, and societal deviants, the kind of sordid and stereotypical images that many of these artists at certain stages in their careers were trying to debunk.

"Made Nigga's"

"To be a fortune 500 CEO it took Rap"[16]
—NAS, YA'LL MY NIGGAS

Thugs and gangsters are unfortunately what human beings who were born to be Men have been reduced to because of the *process of inferiorization,* and the system of institutional racism/white supremacy, indiscriminately designed to obstruct the natural progression from boys to men. So when considering Neely Fuller's proclamation of racism's primary goal of ensuring that there is only one man that exists in (global) society, becoming a gangster or thug could arguably be deduced as not only being essential to survival but also considered as a feasible tradeoff for the resignation of consciously and unconsciously being aware of an inferior status and weakened position that the black male in America has been circumscribed. If close attention is paid, it should not at all be surprising that some Hip Hop artists would rather be thugs or criminals or embrace a lawless lifestyle that is on the fringes of societal standards of decorum or propriety, as the alternative simply entails one's status to either that of tokenism—selling out and ingratiating oneself into the perils of mainstream control and exploitation—or being restricted to a life spent working for meager wages and earnings that are devoid of the perks and benefits of necessities such as adequate healthcare.

A feasible deduction of what would certainly follow as a result is the hastening of a shortened lifespan and the assured preservation of a permanent underclass. In other words, the gangster or thug has for all intents and purposes and, according to Mr. Madhubuti, become a rite of passage, despite the dangers and risks that are assured and inextricably linked to this very existence. Similar to how Hip Hop artists adopted monikers and titles of mobsters and notorious gangsters, kids in urban ghettos, who respect these artists and aspire to be artists themselves, deify and revere those whose criminal exploits and activities were and are still legendary in their neighborhoods and communities; accordingly, referring to them as real "og's" and "ghetto stars," and, ironically, the more depraved and brazen their crimes the larger their profiles and statuses.

In fact, so legendary and infamous were some of the criminal careers of many of these ghetto stars that in 2007, Black Entertainment Television launched a series called *American Gangster*. Not to be confused with the movie of the same title that would follow a year or so later, the series showcased enterprising and ingenious young black males who were able to amass fortunes by building sophisticated criminal empires and organizations. Yet the mystique of the show is its depictions of the variations of the character and mannerisms that set the tone and defined how effective or ineffective these urban criminals' exploits were, or how violent and depraved their actions that largely defined their status and indelible appeal to youth who either witnessed first-hand their activities or were informed by way of ghetto tales and fables. In other words, for every "monster" Kody Scott, aka Sanyika Shakur, who is highly regarded and respected for his depravity and brutality, there is a Guy Fisher, who, although equally as lethal, was widely noted for his strategic and logistical brilliance in the drug trade, as well as for his charm in social settings, and poise under fire and scrutiny.

Despite his own extreme articulateness, brilliant mind, and imposing stature, Monster Kody, because of his inability to hurdle the travails of imprisonment and frequent incarceration was never able to make the transition that is indicative of emerging from a state of dependence, powerlessness, communal and self-debasement to resourcefulness, maneuverability, and self-sufficiency, i.e., true manhood; a factor that I will once again make the claim that the institutional system of racism/white supremacy invariably and effectively denies. Nonetheless, further analysis of the cultural and social factors that produce the Monster Kodys, Melvin Williams, Tupack Shakurs, and Guy Fishers in black communities are but a mere portion of the overall systemic process of emasculating the black male that I will attempt to explore and unveil in this book—hopefully shedding more insight on the circumventing of being born as boys but living and dying as Men in *Amerikkka*.

Four

ANGELS & DEMONS:

Organized religion's role in black passivity and effeminacy

"The White Man's Heaven is a Black Man's Hell"
—LOUIS FARRAKHAN

When it comes to the concept and/or ideology of heaven and hell, for many, hell is right here on earth. And if there is any solace to be elicited from this claim, it is also the belief that there is a better place once this life of suffering and degradation has run its course. Take for example the academy award nominated 1985 film *The Color Purple*, where the main protagonist and the film's most poignant character, Celie, played by Whoopi Goldberg, passionately states, "this life be over soon; heaven last always!" What should also be mentioned is that *The Color Purple* is a film that is largely considered by a very prominent contingent of blacks to be an indelible piece of cinematic perfection as well as a pivotal piece of history for black people, particularly the black female. Also, it is heart-wrenching and emotionally-tugging soliloquies such as the previously mentioned statement that are perhaps proof as to why. Yet despite how heartfelt or heart wrenching, the question that should be posed is whether or not such a statement is in fact true? And if it is, how, why, and says who, despite what black victims of institutional racism/white supremacy have been conditioned to believe is true?

Or better yet, a more telling question should be whether it is at all surprising that members of the most visibly and psychologically damaged and oppressed collective group of people are the most ardent and fervent endorsers of such a theory and/or system of belief? Perhaps it is because the so called American dream has been more of a cultural nightmare that the knee-jerk response is to—as the song from gospel group Sounds of Blackness so aptly exhorts—"keep your head to the sky" becomes obligatory as a mental escape from the tangible and palpable suffering that black people as a whole have to endure on a day to day basis, and not just here in America but anywhere black people can be found on the planet. Equally palatable is the belief that it is black people's piety and religious dogma that has made it possible for them to not only survive but also remain culturally connected. If this point of view has any leg of credibility, then another key question would be whether or not this demonstration of religious piety and zeal affects black people and white people in the same manner? Furthermore, how has the embracing of western-style religion served blacks amid a cataclysm of social injustice and cultural unrest? And if it has indeed hindered the collective advancement of black people as a whole then how has this taken place and at what cost? And if this is the case then what has to be done or what changes need to be implemented?

America and the Negro spiritual(s)

"Forget this Judeo-Christian bullshit. The people that taught us virtue are the very ones who enslaved us baby!"[17]
—DAVID JASON, *DEEP COVER*

Despite America's creed that (supposedly) entitles one to liberties and freedom of worship, America is nonetheless a predominantly Christian nation. And unsurprisingly, a great majority of black people in this society are Christian. In fact, major cultural components for blacks in America are rooted in Christianity and all of its precepts and (conditional) sanctions. So much so, in fact, that it has been suggested that blacks are much more passionate and enthusiastic Christians than are whites, and subscribe to its tenets more willingly than whites ever have done or could ever imagine doing. True or not, the fact that black people have since clamored and held sacrosanct for many generations a religion that was superimposed on them by their captors and subsequent slave masters and owners has not at all elevated the status of black people, especially that of the black male who, again, is not only America's primary target for racial persecution but also the main focus of this book.

So how has organized religion in this society, particularly Christianity, affected the black male — western societies most loathed and targeted victim? All told, despite the majority of black folk in general in American society who worship in various denominations that derive from Christianity and the principles that it champions, there are many who have long felt that Christianity is a "slave" religion that was forced upon African slaves as a means to pacify and keep them in mental bondage and, arguably, has primarily been the biggest hindrance to the advancement of black people under the direct and continual assault of racism/white supremacy. So, in regards to the black male—who because of his victim status is clearly no exception— if Christianity, along with the practices of institutional racism/white supremacy, has been unabatedly effective in keeping black folk as a whole psychologically (and physically) incapacitated, this has indeed been the fate of the black male as well. And, certainly, in any ethnic group or culture in which the males are weak and vulnerable, then that group as a whole is equally as vulnerable and weak.

Similar to most black males and black people in this society, I had to endure years of exposure to the religion of Christianity—its principles and practices—and forced to attend services on Sunday morning, Sunday afternoon, and evening services on Wednesday. However, unlike many, I was not as easily psychologically ensnared by the doctrine and manners of both action and words that others who seemed to embrace the religion often display. In fact, I had issues with the teachings and questioned its validity at a very young age; especially when, similar to most curious children, I would ask certain questions and would not only fail to get valid answers but was admonished not to inquire about such things. For those who are familiar with these gag-order tactics of the Christian creed probably already know where I am going with this, and can perhaps relate to similar inquiries that were prohibitive no no's. Therefore, what I had come to learn about Christianity in western society is that questions such as what color was Jesus, where people of color originate, and what is their relationship to Jesus and/or God, often elicited answers that were either grossly distorted and misinterpreted or deemed as irrelevant. Unsurprisingly, those same distortions and inaccurate images of Jesus can presently be seen in the homes and in churches of both whites and blacks, and on the screens of major motion pictures, and can be met with the same obduracy and dismissal of his physical, biological, and cultural attributes.

Another noticeable staple in the black church was black folk going into emotional frenzies—gyrating, convulsing, and gesticulating as if possessed by some invading demon or spirit. Again, those who are privy to the practices of the black church understand that these actions are the result of one catching the Holy Ghost or Holy Spirit. Regardless however of what exactly it is or what it is called, one thing that I knew for sure was that this does not happen in white churches, and white people certainly do not worship in such a manner. And, of course, the dumbfounding nature of this is that white people supposedly worship the same God, albeit with different physical and emotional reactions.

What was the basis of this? Of course the answer would come to me as a result of the natural progression and maturation from preadolescence to adulthood, in which it would become apparent that white people do not have to endure the day to day suffering of racial oppression and subjugation as do their black counterparts (victims). In other words, white people are not the victims of institutional racism/ white supremacy, same as they were never subjected to centuries of chattel servitude as slaves in this country. In further assessing and analyzing the phenomena of such extreme and ostentatious measures and methods of worship, what would also become clear to me is that such acts of worship are a mental and psychosomatic escape, exhorted from an overzealous and mystical fervor that is scientifically identical to the altering mood and mental capacity that can take effect as the result of the use of a very potent narcotic.

Dr. Frances Cress-Welsing describes this condition in her book *The Isis Papers: Keys to the Colors* as a direct neurological response due to conditioning that is caused by racism/white supremacy, perpetuated against non-whites by those who are categorized as white for the means of whites' preserving genetic survival due to their condition as being genetically inferior to black people.[18] Her theory also suggest that because of their defective genetic condition, which causes an inability to produce variations of melanoma, the system of white supremacy was contrived to control, vis-à-vis destroy the reproductive ability and capacity of people of color across the globe.[19]

As a direct result of institutional racism/ white supremacy, the black male in America suffers from disproportionate rates of unemployment, as the black rate of unemployment due to the recession that followed the Bush administration is nearly double that of whites. Incarceration rates for blacks, particularly black males is astronomical, as black people in general constitute roughly 13% of America's population but black males account for 60% of the prison population.[20] Additionally, black people as a whole make up 13% of substance abusers, consequently constituting 55% of narcotics convictions.[21] Moreover, due to the unwavering conditions of systemic oppression and socioeconomic subjugation, statistics purport an alarming growing number of mental illness and psychological disorders for black people in general. According to the U.S.

Department of Health and Human Services Office of Minority Services, blacks are twenty times more likely to report having severe psychological distress and conditions than do whites.[22]

These facts and figures are unquestionably not indicative of a nation that has put aside its deplorable racist past, as clearly such statistics do not foretell a benign and positive outlook for the future of the black male or black folk as a whole in this society. Also, these facts certainly do not portend that black is superior to white, whether genetically or socially. Consequently, similar to the black female, the black male will call on Jesus as a means to mitigate or ameliorate his terrestrial suffering at the hands of racists and white supremacists. Ultimately, this is one of the reasons why the black male in American society remains weak and emasculated; moreover, this is also a suitable reason why the black male is attempting to be more physically and psychologically commensurate to his black female counterpart. And finally, what the weakness and gradual effeminizing of the black male implies is the continual destruction and evisceration of black communities, and the continual disarray and disjointedness of those who inhabit these communities and who suffer as victims. In light of such facts and/or claim, I do not perceive such ominous signs as racial progress or brotherly union in the name of a common God; instead, I call it the continual laying of the blueprint for inevitable cultural genocide, irrespective of and regardless of what God it is that black victims of institutional racism/white supremacy fall on their knees and call upon!

Another obvious sign of a lack of progress is that there are too many black males and black people who are resistant to challenging the status quo and, because of this, do not consider these societal ills and subsequent dysfunctions the result of the conditions of institutional racism that is driven by a white supremacist mindset or mentality. Instead, such societal ills and social and cultural dysfunctions are widely perceived as a fulfillment of prophecy of the existence of terrestrial inferiors as taught by the oppressors of black people, via Christian doctrine and philosophy. Thus, this willful and voluntary identification with the oppressor and acquiescence to his or her pre-scriptions of social rank and stratification of ethnocentric superiority has rendered the impotent and burgeoning effeminized black male as a willing participant in his own demise, as well as the demise of the ethnic group that he is biologically and culturally ascribed. In other words, because of black folk as a whole having to accept their terres-trial inferior status and functioning under the conditions of institu-tional racism that is perpetrated by whites, basking and immersing in religious doctrine that supposedly postulates racial egalitarianism as well as purity is a psychological release valve, regardless of who super-imposed and spoon-fed these values and teachings to them. All things considered, analogous to the general public that is constantly being indoctrinated via film and television, depictions of black males as buf-foons, criminals, clowns, and spineless cowards and sissies, the black male himself has been indoctrinated to identification with the oppres-sor by willingly accepting western values, culture, social and cultural practices, and even white people's religion.

For instance, and as mentioned in the previous chapter, Tyler Perry is a black male who is perhaps the most notable and visible black enter-tainer on the planet. Yet what makes Perry a liability as far as the point that I am attempting to make is both his propensity and efficacy in painting a distorted picture of blacks as a bible-toting, "hallelujaherin'," monolith, whose overall concerns in life are gossiping and consum-ing chitterlings (or chitt'lins) and pig ears at family gatherings and get-togethers. So, when considering his own status as a black male, his abstract failure of creating character studies via film that encompass the true reality of the black male, as well as the multiplicity of lifestyle prac-tices and beliefs of ALL black people, as opposed to his zeal for crafting stories showcasing the travails of black males that are inextricably woven in stereotypes—buffoonery and/ or debauchery— does not deflect neg-ativism but instead feed into the black male's widely perceived societal weakness and insignificance.

How a Religion that avows eternal life created dead souls

In Hoc Signo Vinces – In this Sign you will conquer
—Constantine, Roman Emperor

Similar to prisons that house a disproportionate number of black males and young boys of color, the church too is a big business in America; as the only true religion in this country is the worship of the "almighty dollar," period. And sadly, similar to the haves and have-nots reality for many that American capitalism and racism ascertains, black people as a whole , despite being the most salient and persistent victims of racism and, as a result, rank dead last on the economic totem pole are the church's most reliable and dependable benefactors. Even more tragic is that it is the black male's participation in the unwavering devotion to the church, irresperrive of the nature in which Christianity was imposed and the discriminatory and racially prejudiced doctrine that Christianity promotes, that has undoubtedly made the black male in America the poster-child for how not to combat social injustices and the chief contributing cause to his fate as the country's premier functional inferior, as well as its most ardent target for discrimination and oppression. Even in a nation that postulates the separation of church and state to ensure sociopolitical power that would be in direct conflict with the tenets of religion that it endorses wholesale and claims to live by, being a Christian is still a badge of honor that symbolizes power and conquest. While Christianity for the black male and black people, only equates and solidifies sociopolitical and economic vulnerability and powerlessness. Hence, the ardent fervor and frightening demonstrations of devotion and faith that are demonstrated in black churches, with the black male commonly at the helm of the church either as pastor, deacon, reverend, or minister, is a direct response to social and cultural restraints that have been superimposed by those who represent the dominant culture, and who practice racism/white supremacy.

So, as there is a condition of the separation of church and state, there can be no separation of racism and the tenets of the bible that are proposed by those who crafted the institutional system of racism/white supremacy, and those who allow themselves to be spoon-fed those tenets and accept them as true. It is said that the most segregated hour in America takes place during Sunday, the day of collective, cultural worship. Yet the obvious paradox is that victims of the practices of any form of segregation accept the specious claim that God views all people with egalitarian and unprejudiced eyes, and loves all equally as his "children." Certainly, the deplorable conditions of the black male and the discriminatory and oppressive practices that are still perpetrated towards blacks in general belie this pseudo belief. Nevertheless, many victims of institutional racism/white supremacy hold onto these beliefs, largely because of historical and traditional value and ramifications, and also because there have been no other feasible and palpable solutions to the conditions that continue to afflict people of color on a national as well as global scale. As the aggressive Black Nationalist's movement of the 60s waned, the passive embrace of Christianity not only persisted but quite possibly intensified. But then so have racism, discrimination, and injustice, making it clear that a massive merger to so called brotherhood, imposed by Christian precepts and ideology, has not worked.

And why hasn't it? My answer would be that it is because of discrepancies and spurious precepts that could but have yet to be elicited from the bible if decoded and interpreted properly and impartially. Without question, the bible's lack of proper and suitable interpretation has not empowered the black male, nor has it provided him with palpable representation as to who he truly is and where he fits on the world stage in terms of biblical and historical value. Instead, it has inculcated the belief of his being the biological male representative of a bastard people who are the subordinates of the so called chosen people whom, as a result, the subordinate group is subjected to a life of servitude and insurmountable suffering. And because of the servitude and suffering that ensues, victims of such suffrage are only to be rewarded in the aftermath of this dreadful existence if they go along with the program and play by its insidious rules.

What should be clear in regards to the assessment that is being offered thus far is an inability to speak candidly and truthfully in a system that is engendered and empowered by institutional racism/white supremacy, especially for those who are the victims and are accordingly circumscribed due to that balance of power. The problem also is that the black male in American society, lest he be ostracized or killed (e.g., Louis Farrakhan, Malcolm X), cannot speak so freely as to both address and redress the problems of race and religion in this society. Therefore, when considering one of the bible's supposed disclaimer of serving two masters, clearly, victims of Americanized institutional racism/white supremacy violate those tenets. And so it is that the biggest contradiction for the black male in regards to religion is to spurn the very essence and true nature and characteristics of a people that he grossly covets to be like and equal to, as well as ingratiating his very existence to currying and gaining the coveted group's favor. In other words, you cannot denounce God being *white* if you both willingly and grudgingly clamor to be white yourself, fueled by the notion that "white is right," hence superior.

As Dr. Cress-Welsing speaks of black people's form of worship as a spontaneous mass-psychosis that is the direct result of extreme forms of oppression; Frantz Fanon, in his book *Black Skin, White Masks* calls this a development of various forms of neurosis that is due to an inferiority complex and a desire to be white.[23] However, we can be certain that at some time in history, black people on the planet as a whole did not fortuitously stumble upon white people (or, to be more precise, white people stumbled upon them) and were smitten by the beauty of their skin. In fact, this is far from the truth. And according to Fanon, the inferiority complex that he spoke of only took place after being colonized and indoctrinated to certain beliefs and ideologies by the captors of black people. Subsequently, an invariable concomitant of neurological and social dysfunction continues to plague American society, and continues to reduce the status of black people, particularly the status of the black male.

It's the God in Me!

"I don't know what God is, but I do know what he isn't"
—*JORDAN MAXWELL*

Institutional racism/white supremacy has a retrograding effect of maintaining powerlessness and helplessness out of human beings who from birth are ascribed and entitled to a natural transition from boyhood to manhood. In addition to a slew of other traits of manhood and manliness that, because of institutional racism/ white supremacy leaves black males in general devoid of such traits, men, for instance, tell the truth and are not afraid of the consequences of doing so. A boy, however, will lie and/ or kowtow to avoid the consequences of his actions, and will cower in a corner because of the perceived consequences of telling a lie, opposite the actions of a man who will stand tall after telling the truth. It is because of this claim that black males such as Malcolm X, Martin Luther King Jr., and Marcus Garvey are historical black figures that had and continue to receive varying degrees of praise in the black community for their willingness to tell the truth and live by principles that derived from those truths. Also, it is because these individuals met either untimely ends or lived their last days as outcasts that perhaps the marks and traits of true manhood and manliness have practically become nonexistent.

Tragically, the black male in American society does not tell his sons and daughters the truth. If he did there would be no question as to the real issues of both race and religion in this society. The fact of the matter is that under the conditions of institutional racism/white supremacy, two masters do indeed have to be served in order to barter and lobby for survival. For instance, to this day, I ask black Christians to describe Jesus's physical appearance and they cannot (or perhaps will not) give me a precise description (other than provide the brief, rudimentary description as illustrated in bible texts). What I have concluded as a result of this failure is that this cowardice and/or gross ignorance is not the result of not telling the truth because of whether or not one wants to but more or less a situation of not telling the truth because one cannot do so, at least not without consequences. In addition to the fact that there are many who simply do not know the truth yet perplexingly boast their Christian ties and virtues.

———

There was a time however when black people, collectively, and who represented every crook and cranny of the planet were not so confused about religion; primarily, because of the fact that there was an extensive period throughout the annals of history that black people as a whole were not bound by the restrictions that institutional racism/white supremacy imposes. Similar to how self-sufficiency for black people existed in Africa prior to the transatlantic slave trade, so too did clarity and purpose of worship.

Unlike what is largely believed by many, Christianity did not start in Africa; nor did it have salient roots in Africa prior to the advent of organized religion, in which Christianity is the archetype of such manners of worship. Historically speaking, how could it have salient roots in Africa? Similar to how the images of Jesus, or Christ, (it should be noted that Christ is a title and not a name) that have been bombarded on the world as being a white man with blonde hair and blue eyes are historically inaccurate, so too is the fallacious claim that He was a Christian. In fact, presently there are religious historians and theologians—of all creeds and nationalities—who have themselves raise the important question as to whether or not Jesus actually existed at all! Consider that for a moment.

For those who are not so bound by traditional conventions or duped by false theological representation, as well as conditioning, the facts should be clear that there is no record that Christianity even existed during the times that are documented that Jesus walked the earth and performed his good deeds and works. Therefore, if according to western theology, Jesus was the embodiment of Christianity or would later come to be its chief entity, then how is it numerically possible that Christianity had its origins in a region where civilization began, and Christianity was never even thought about or heard of? This is *tricknology* that those who came to understand the evils of institutional racism/white supremacy were speaking of. How globally, black people as a whole have been deceived and subsequently subjugated by a religion that rather than empower spiritually has instead been used to pacify and weaken individually, socially, and culturally; and, in which the physical and psychological restraints remain intact and seemingly unbreakable to this day.

Even scientific studies confirm that human beings who possessed various levels of melanin were the first who ever existed on planet earth. Therefore, in the region that is known as Africa, many of these primogenitors of humanity were not Christians nor did they worship an entity known as Jesus or Christ. Instead, they were primordial and pastoral peoples that were comprised of hunter and gatherer societies. Yet despite this, there are many whom have made the claim that Christianity has salient roots in Africa, a region that is overwhelmingly comprised of people of color. And even more contradictory is that it is white-Euro imperialism and hegemony that to this day boast of an image of Jesus that is unmistakably European; unequivocally, a perplexing illogicality of both biblical and historical value of the world's most celebrated and embraced form of organized religion. And, obviously, one that is still steeped in distinctions based on color, caste, culture, and RACE. Nonetheless, the main point of the aforementioned claim is that many of these primordial beings practiced what is now known as animism or animistic worship that put them as one with several elements of nature. However, it cannot be ruled out that other forms of worship that are mostly ascribed to ancient civilizations or are believed to be indigenous to people of color across the globe are perhaps more credible than any claims of Christianity being the religion that served as the chief precept or blueprint in terms of the constructing of civilization. But on the other hand, what Christianity can be credited for is setting the framework for the introduction of organized religion as a whole, even though religions or customs such as Hinduism and Buddhism predate Christianity. Even so, because I am mostly concentrating on the issues that affect western culture and society, Christianity is principle in terms of this discourse.

Similar to my analysis, there are many who see loopholes in the doctrine of Christianity, in addition to its visible methods of politically, economically, culturally, and spiritually pacifying and disfranchising members of the darker-hued global family. For instance, It has also been proven by sociological research and studies that Australian aboriginals, who are historically totemic, have over the recent years engaged in a significant exodus to the Islamic faith; quite possibly seeing it as a religion that, unlike Christianity, culturally empowers and enlightens rather than one that maintains socioeconomic and political powerlessness and cultural constraints. Although it must be pointed out that the Islamic faith, same as Christianity, is more political than spiritual, and is more organized than individually based. And strangely enough, as well as absurdly, it is western do-gooders who flock in droves to predominately Muslim countries to demonize patriarchal leadership with claims of the malicious subjugating of women in these societies, irrespective of the fact that black males and females in America suffer from similar if not worse forms of oppression and discriminatory practices. It is therefore my assertion that the reason the black male in America has become such an easy prey and target of Americanized institutional racism/white supremacy is because of his willingness to embrace certain pseudo beliefs and idiosyncratic cultural practices based on confusion to racism, its practices, and exactly how institutional racism/white supremacy works. Also, it is the failure to see how obvious misinterpretations once decoded properly have sowed the seeds of confusion, vulnerability and, consequently, continues to lay down the foundation for the black male's ethnic and cultural demise.

Evidently, institutionalized racism has not only kept the black male subjugated and has incapacitated black people as a whole, but also has ensured their failed understanding of the mechanisms that are designed to ascertain this endeavor. I can recall hearing an advertisement for a local church on a radio station in Kansas City, Missouri that exhorted worshippers to come on the assurance of stellar worship because at this particular place of worship, "only Jesus matters!" Only Jesus? Oh! How is this possible being that Jesus is a part of a (supposed) indelible trifecta (trinity)? According to Christian theology, is not God both the architect and father of the son—Jesus? Therefore, where do the contributions of the Father come into play?

The answer is that this is an example of the mass confusion and failure to decipher facts from outright lies that has allowed the mechanisms and practices of white supremacy and the institutional structure of racism to remain intact. How can you debunk an ideology that posits racial superiority and supremacy if it has not been collectively challenged or at least the basis of the ideology called into question? Furthermore, who are the minds that crafted such a mythology, and for what purpose?

In Christian theology, the entity known as Satan or the devil is not only known to exist but is also the antithesis of God and the archetype of evil-doing and ultimate endorser of wicked and hedonistic virtues. Who is the Devil, and what does he look like? And more importantly, what is His role in the construction of institutional racism/white supremacy that has kept the black male down for centuries, and has quite possibly caused his seemingly permanent emasculation as well as subsequent effeminacy?

The Devil made Me do it

"Let him that hath understanding count
the number of the Beast, for it is the number of a man"
—REVELATIONS 13:18

It is foolish to believe that in a world that is comprised of good and (extreme) evil, one entity that is both instilling and reinforcing the actions and practices of good is a palpable and material being in flesh, and the other that is inculcating and encouraging the practices of evil is some sort of apparition that is more a figment of human being's worst fears and failures than anything else. Yet this is what many believe. And as a result, those who are the driving forces of all that is wrong and morally corrupt with society are perceived as doing so based on their own free will, free of the moral obligations and precepts that the Judeo Christian doctrine dictates. On the other hand, the good that is perpetuated in society is done so at the divine intervention of Jesus, who is the embodiment of all that is good, and whose deeds— past and present—influence those who are practitioners of benign deeds and benevolence and who claim that those good deeds are done on Jesus's behalf and as a result of such profound influence.

The Chinese yin- yang theory, meaning shadow and light, postulates how opposing forces are intertwined, and though interdependent are not mutually exclusive in the natural world. In other words, shadow and light, which are meta-physical manifestations, cannot exist without one or the other. And while good and evil are not physical dualities but are more perceptual in terms of analysis, both concepts, whether perceptual or real, clearly exists in the world. Thus, the paradox is the pseudo theological claim that one's virtue and subsequent good deeds that coincide are orchestrated and instilled from the primogenitor of good who is a material being; on the other hand, there are behaviors that are influenced by an immaterial being whose only roots apparently stem from traits and characteristics that are harbored in the deepest and lowest rungs of human fears and the primal forces that compel certain actions. It is written that man was created in God's image and of his likeness. In Christian theology, Jesus, who is perceived as God, has been documented for his very earthly existence by way of his exploits while on earth. So how is it then that his natural nemesis is not himself a material being of palpable flesh?

There are many religions that have a belief in the existence of Satan or some evil entity whose role and purpose is the opposite of the purported role and purpose of God. With the exception of Judaism, which has no reported or documented belief in Satan or the Devil, there are plenty of other theological doctrines that theorize an evil being who once was in the favor of God before an eventual fall from grace for either apostasy, jealousy, or flat out betrayal. Perhaps it is the Jewish religion's absence of the belief in a biblical and ancient evil entity that has caused many who have espoused anti-Semitic rhetoric to surmise members of the Jewish faith as the embodiment of evil and practitioners of evil acts that are illustrated as opposite of Godliness as purported in biblical literature. Nevertheless, Christianity is no exception in its belief in the Devil or Satan.

According to Christian theology, the world is engulfed and plagued by sin because of the Devil's trickery of Eve in the form of a serpent in the Garden of Eden, which, is conjointly referred to as the "original sin." However, unlike the palatable and historical documentation of the existence of Jesus, the bible depicts the Devil as an apparitional figure for the purposes of enhancing and illuming allegorical tales that are designed to engender beliefs in individuals' falling from grace based on their own free will. In other words, the Devil is inside us, as are the iniquitous proclivities, acts, and deeds that are associated with his mythical status. Therefore, similar to when I ask black Christians about the origins of Christ and cannot get a cogent answer, the end result is no different when asked about the Devil's origin, as well as a visual of his true being and very nature. Clearly, it is not just black Christians but people of color from all of the corresponding Abrahamic religions who believe that Jesus was a human being. However, there appears to be no consensus or uniformity of the existence of Satan or the Devil, as belief systems vary. One thing to be certain however is that the inability to decipher the truth is because of the fact that most black Christians (or black people in general) are engulfed in a maelstrom of European concepts and ideologies, which is strikingly profound when considering what both Europeans and their conceptions of Christianity have done to black people, and not only in America but worldwide. And contrary to what many will try to argue, Christianity does not have roots in Africa, and it certainly did not begin there.

In fact, the real truth in regards to Christianity is that it is a pagan religion that was conceived based on accounts of the ethnic practices and cultural ideologies of the early and rural traditions and practices of the Greeks, Romans, and Jews. Before it became known as what it is today, Christianity was based on the theological and lifestyle practices of primitive European factions. Hence, these practices, historically accounted for as being a form of pagan worship, were cemented by the pre-Christian practices of Germans, Scandinavians, and other Anglo-Saxon peoples. It was not until the global conquest-endeavors of the Roman emperor Constantine Constantinople that the rest of the vast and largely colored world was indoctrinated with Christianity and its practices. Consequently, who I believe are the last and the most significant victims of this historical campaign are black people who inhabit the shores of North America, particularly the socially weak and impotent black male. This is not to imply that Christianity is not practiced in Africa, Asia, India, and the South Americas, or anywhere else in the colored world. The only difference however is that in the aforementioned regions they still have sole propriety of their culture and aesthetic roots and ties and, arguably, the males in these regions still play a pivotal role in these societies, as well as their respective communities. However, it is on the shores of North America that the black male has been completely robbed of his historical roots, ties, and natural state of being.

Yet there are many who have surmised these misdeeds as some sort of merit or badge of honor to be associated and identified with their captors and oppressors, rather than viewing this as an outrage of astronomical proportions, and as one of the worst acts of social and civil disobedience in the annals of global history, and failing to live the rest of their dying days to see that such an injustice is meted out and dealt with appropriately. In other words, if black folk are so deeply religious, and believe whole-heartedly in the "vengeful" God they worship, then why not spend every day of their lives praying that God either destroy their oppressors and sworn enemies or provide them with the strength, knowledge, and courage to fulfil such a task on their own?

Is the crime of kidnapping hundreds of millions of slaves off the coast of Africa and inflicting on them hundreds of years of slavery, maiming, torture, and murder not the Devil's work? If not, then arguably it must have been an act and continued actions that could easily be perceived as devilish. Who then is the Devil, and what has been his purpose on the planet, if he indeed even exist? It is because of mind-altering articles of belief such as Christianity that not only the black male but black folk in general discredit their own cultural ties and aesthetic roots, yet have alternatively chosen to embrace those of their oppressors. More disturbing is that this is done amid a gross failure to acknowledge the ramifications of what has been done in the past, what continues to be done in the present, and the dismal projection that the future portends while still stuck in the clutches of institutional racism and under the banner and precepts of white supremacy.

The Beast within

"*Now who is able to make war with the Beast?*"[24]
—Paris, *Bush Killa*'

This is not racist's rhetoric, or "reverse racism," as many no doubt will attempt to surmise; nor is this sacrilegious overture. It is, however, an attempt at a thorough examination in order to ascertain fact from fiction, put uncertainties into proper perspective, and clear the smoke of pervasive confusion. Most importantly, it is an attempt to analyze and ascertain westernized religion's effect on the black male, and how organized religion subsequently contributed to his becoming the system of racism/white supremacy's most constant and hapless victim. With that being said, consider for instance how religious scholars and theologians have analyzed and decoded the passage in Revelations of the whore that sits upon many waters, in a scarlet colored robe and arrayed in precious stones and pearls with a gold chalice that is filled with all of the filth and abominations of the earth; thus, having identified this great whore as being the pope of Rome. And without question, the Pope is the most powerful living representative and face of the Christian religion. Therefore, both a pivotal and obvious question to be asked is when was there a time in the annals of the history of human beings that a black male or any person of color was the pope?

Is the Devil, whomever the Devil may be, responsible for the black male's plight in America and fall from grace in regards to his place in human history? Or has it been the indiscriminate system of racism/white supremacy, leaving the idea or concept of the Devil preposterous and completely without merit? According to the doctrine of the oft-maligned Nation of Islam, the Devil is not an entity that is shrouded in mysticism or what they refer to as "spookism." In fact, their theory posits that the Devil is the same person who crafted the ideology, concept, and mechanisms of the societal ill that has been called the number one and most salient health problem in America as well as across the globe. Moreover, the Devil, according to NOI ideology, could arguably be perceived as the same living being that bombed the 16th St. Baptist church in Birmingham, Alabama in 1963 that destroyed the lives of four little black girls; thus, in doing so, crossing the boundaries of civility and functioning that is based on integrity and moral value, as Sunday worship in a country that prides itself on Christian values and ethics should have been respected and held as sacred. Now, in today's world the overwhelming consensus is that times have undoubtedly changed since those precious little girls had their lives violently snuffed out by white racists. And because of this fact such an analysis is beyond preposterous. Or is it? Keep in mind that recently a psychopathic racist was just found innocent of any wrong-doing (by white people) for stalking and snuffing the life out of another black child; an act fueled by the same racial disdain and animus that was demonstrated by the aforementioned murderers in 1963 who—whether devils or not—certainly acted as such.

A feasible segue to the previously mentioned claim would be the NOI's theory that contrary to Christian doctrine and theology, the Devil, similar to Jesus, is himself a Man. And he is given this designation based on deeds and crimes committed against humanity both past and present. Also, just as Christian doctrine purports that the Devil's existence and reign on earth is based on allegorical tales and anecdotes that represent an individual crisis and subsequent fall from grace due to an abject failure of crisis management, the Book of Wisdom contradicts this hypothesis. Instead, it points out specific endeavors and goals that the Devil is resolute to fulfill; goals such as bringing death to the world based on his hatred and enmity towards humanity. As stated earlier, the bible is of extreme, invaluable quality if it can be interpreted properly. Hence, what is between the lines are truisms that are essential to understanding both past and present conditions; particularly if one wants to decode the conditions of institutional racism/white supremacy, and the subsequent damage that has been caused not only to the black male in America but black people across the globe as well.

Revelation 13:18 is aptly subtitled John of Patmos. Now, in understanding the passage of revelation 13:18, again it says "let him that hath understanding count the number of the beast, as it is the number of a man." So, in revisiting the beliefs of the Nation of Islam, their theory presupposes that if Jesus, who is the chief deity and object of worship in Christian theology, is a man made of flesh then so too is his arch nemesis—Satan or the Devil.

Similar to criticisms of the doctrine and theology of Christianity, the theories of the NOI can be lambasted as pseudo-scientific and mere conjecture. However, the differences arguably lie in the perceived, palpable impact both have had on the black male in America. In other words, when considering that American society (or to be more specific, black America) did produce Martin Luther King Jr., whose mission and purpose was deeply rooted in Christian theology, it must also be taken into consideration that the NOI produced Malcolm X—a once common thief, pimp (well, he is widely perceived as a pimp being that he was a driver for an escort service), substance abuser, and ex-felon. In addition, the argument could easily go that while Christianity has been a primary mechanism to keeping the black male emasculated and confused, the NOI has an impressive record of reshaping the lives and consciousness of many black ex-offenders in America, same as it had done with Malcolm X. Thus, The NOI's age-old rhetoric is that of Christianity being a slave religion, designed the keep the victims of institutional racism/white supremacy "deaf, dumb, and blind" to their real circumstances and predicament.

The theological tenets of western culture dictate that the number 666 is associated with evil and gross anathema. Consider then that the black male suffers at the hands of white racists who run the institution of racism/white supremacy because he is perceived as being inferior and therefore deserved of such mistreatment and systematic abuse. Consequently, another pivotal question is whether or not the two previous statements are in any way intertwined? With that in mind, what is also interesting, as pointed out by Dr. Welsing, is that presently white people make up less than one-tenth of the global population, yet white supremacy is predicated on the remaining ninety percent of the world's people of color being genetically inferior. Nonetheless, it has been the actions that have taken place in America over the past 400 or so years that requires further analysis. In light of that, I would argue that the actions that have been perpetrated against black people in this country since the inception of slavery are definitely not normal, nor are they consistent with the precepts and tenets of Christian theology if we are to rule out any other claims. But whether it is perceived as reality or conjecture, the coveted ends justified by means that are irrefutable carries a lot of merit and credibility.

We need Jesus!

"Jesus is not white! He's 'cablinasian' like Tiger Woods, and you're getting on my last nerve!"[25]
—TERRI JONES, BARBERSHOP

The above passage is taken from the urban drama/comedy *Barbershop*, a film that even though it received positive reviews and featured a talented pool of black actors, was lambasted from black leaders, film critics, and cultural historians for its insensitive approach of denigrating the ambitions and purported personal travails of historical black leaders and key figures in the struggle for civil rights. The most notable of these civil rights activists being Martin Luther King Jr. and Rosa Parks. Yet, incredulously, while two of the most prominent figures of the civil rights movement were the primary targets of the questionable and controversial dialogue delineated in the film, Tiger Woods, the golf celebrity who has no identification with ANY aspect of the black community, and who also coined the term "cablinasian" to, in all honesty, disavow his identification with being black was mentioned in a gratifying association with Jesus. Now, consider that for a moment.

What I find interesting about this particular observation, and one that I will expound a bit shortly, is that during the decade that preceded the attacks of September 11, 2001, black churches were being burned in droves in the southern region of the country. Yet the (supposed) attack on America by males of brown hue, and who were described as being anti-American, clearly may have restored some vigor for romanticizing both cultural and religious ties with the dominant culture. However, this feat did not change the conditions of the black male in America nor did it diminish the scourge of racism and discriminatory practices that black folk as a whole are subjected to on a daily basis, just as it did not reconstruct the background of the most segregated hour that takes place every Sunday. How else is it possible that black females flock to churches in droves every Sunday to romanticize their courtship and amorous ideations with a god whose global description is one of European ilk? More telling is that more than likely it is a black male who is in the role of buffer, proxy, and/or mediator facilitating this romanticism between the material and fleshy black female and the immaterial, symbolic deity/god—who is universally perceived as white.

My reply would be that it is because of the embracing of white standards, aesthetics, religion, and the discrediting of self and other black folk, that such actions are not only exhorted but principally defines the conditions and circumstances of contemporary black people in American society. I would also assert that this is not the case because black people are innately predisposed to revel in self-hate, but rather is indicative of black people's being socialized to do so because of the tenets of institutional racism/white supremacy that have engulfed black existence, social functioning, and train of thought for so long that any good that is exclusively associated with black is widely perceived as being anti-white. Dr. Salim Faraji, an Africana Studies professor with California State University, Dominquez Hill's, in an Our Weekly article entitled "On the Trail of the African American Roots in Christianity," stated that "Europeanization of religion has, over the years, conditioned the black mind to accept inferiority and view the western world as the apex of human civilization and culture."[26] Perhaps it is because of such a claim that rich and successful blacks such as Tiger Woods believe that they can sell or barter their black identity. Furthermore, it because of the discriminatory endeavors of Hollywood that it is made possible for other blacks—male and female—to not only appreciate and endorse Wood's eschewing of his color but also associate his appearance and virtue to be like that of the Christian world's sole deity for doing so (arguably, the pinnacle of self-hate).

The purposes of entertainment of any sort are either to distract or prevent its consumers and viewers from thinking critically and intelligently in regards to real issues. More tragic is that the deception and lies that have been spoon-fed and consumed by black people as a whole are tantamount to the effectiveness of feeding lies to and manipulating a child. Indeed, if a lie is told enough times, at some point that lie will be perceived as truth, regardless of palpable facts that state otherwise. Thus, it is the failure of the black male in a racist society to shirk and rebuke the lies and untruths of his oppressor and instead proactively inculcating to his own—including the young—the obligatory need to disavow the practices and mores—religious or otherwise—of the oppressor that has and continues to keep the black male, the black female, and black children in both physical and psychological bondage. The problem then is not that black folk in general have "too much damn religion"; it is instead a widespread belief that a religious ideology that was bestowed by the captors of black people for the purposes of preserving chattel slavery will ultimately disentangle them from earthly psychological and physical bondage. For this reason, it is primarily because of such failures that former chattel slaves remain contemporary dysfunctional slaves, and the black male in this society can only be categorized as male in the biological context. And with present societal trends, at some point even that fact is subject to change. However, what is clear is that the transition from boys to men has been an incontestable failure!

Five

POSTTRAUMATIC SLAVE SYNDROME/ MENT(ICIDE)ALITY:

Analyzing and dissecting the Slave Mind

*"There is no in between, you are either free
or you're a slave. There is no such thing as
second-class citizenship!"*
—H. RAPP BROWN

It has been said that self-preservation is the first law of the nature of man, or any living creature for that matter. If this is true, then what happens when a collective group of people—human beings—abort this invaluable principle? Or better yet, what is the end result when in order to ensure self-preservation, a people gravitate toward actions that constitute racial, cultural, and ethnic suicide? The answer is that such are the actions of a people who, due to psychological trauma as the result of centuries of enslavement, possess the *slave mind*. Or, perhaps in being more clinical, such are the actions of a people who suffer from a disorder theorized as *Posttraumatic Slave Syndrome*.

Posttraumatic Slave Syndrome, or PTSS, posits that the institution of racism/white supremacy perpetuates injury inflicted on blacks and other non-white peoples due a belief of black inferiority, or any condition of functional inferiority that is afflicted on any person if that person is not a white person (nonwhite) in a racist society. Nearly five hundred years ago, black people were brought to the shores of the Americas for the purposes of chattel slavery. Since that time, black people as a whole have simply been a massive collective clinging on to survival, but without clear or efficient methods as to how to go about maintaining that survival or demonstrating a joint effort that would make certain that self-preservation is assured. Obviously, this is easier said than done when the same conditions that brought black folk to these shores still exists, even if not in the same overt and barbaric form. Nonetheless, even the more subtle methods of institutional racism/white supremacy that are still intact and acted upon to ensure that black people—former slaves—are left wanton, confused, disjointed, and deeply entrenched in self-hatred are indicative of posttraumatic slave syndrome. Therefore, globally speaking, posttraumatic Slave Syndrome also predicates that there is either a grudging or disposed consensus that being white in a racist society is both right and, therefore, superior.

We see evidence of this claim in the abhorrent conditions of black people as a whole in America, as well as worldwide. Furthermore, we see evidence of this in the proliferation of interracial marriages and courtships, which I will discuss throughout the course of this chapter; also, evidence made clear by excessive resources and monies that are spent to accommodate European standards of beauty (e.g., monies spent on hair weave products, skin lightening procedures, and hair and eye coloring); and a complete willingness to become immersed in culture and aesthetics that are catered to white people and are not at all designed to imbue and enhance the qualities of a multi-racial mixture which, contradictorily, is what America is becoming more and more.

It was Frantz Fanon's assertion in his book *The Wretched of the Earth* that racists and racism creates social and functional inferiors, and that blacks feel inferior to whites by the process of colonization.[27] Undeniably, it is a different dynamic that is and has been taking place in America since the country's inception—one that was deeply rooted in the concept and practice of slavery. And while it is true that Europeans did in fact systematically wipe out Native American tribes who were indigenous to this land, black people as a whole are not native and therefore were not colonized here. However, their embattled brothers and sisters on the continent of their homeland are still in recovery from their being invaded and subsequently, as well as similarly, were placed in captivity and bondage—both psychologically and socioeconomically. In other words, slavery, whether transporting victims for the purposes of bondage and captivity, or colonization resulting from an incursion on one's native land yielded the same catastrophic results and, in the case of black people in America—especially the black male—seemingly irreparable damage.

While embattled blacks of Africa have fought tooth and nail to reclaim their land, culture, and independence, and ethnocentric pride, black people in America seem to revel in their second-class status, as if doing so is either by way ignorance and foolishness that is beyond comprehension or is pertinent to their overall survival. Prior to the presidential inauguration of the nation's first black president, the most salient identification of black people in the western world was by way of the vehicle of entertainment (e.g., music, comedy, and sports). And because politics and economics were, at one point, considered either too far out of scope or null in void of the black experience in America, entertainers and celebrities such as Michael Jackson, Bill Cosby, and Oprah Winfrey became cultural iconic figures as well as the faces of black America. It should not be overlooked however that there have been in the past as well as the present, black intellectuals and civil rights activists who were on the front lines of the fight for the eradication of institutional racism, and who both fought and died for the cultural advancement of black people.

When assessing the profound effects of PTSS due to the condition of institutional racism/white supremacy, and considering the plight of say, Michael Jackson, many could (and have) argue that his life as well as his tragic demise was simply a case of someone who was marred in his own issues and gradually succumbed to his own internal demons. However, I would argue that the troubles of Michael Jackson were the result of something much more severe, as well as sinister; a dynamic that implies that there is something wrong with something and not necessarily someone. A mechanism that is so indiscriminate in terms of mental health functioning and social conditioning that even the filthy rich and most successful of black people are far from being immune to the social conditions and constraints that are imposed as a result of oppression and double-standards that are determined by color and ethnicity. Consequently, the acquisition of material and monetary gain is completely insignificant (just look at the scandal that Bill Cosby is swathed in presently).

For instance, one of many racist and white supremacists mantras presupposes that if you give a white man a million dollars he is called a millionaire, but if you give a black man a million dollars he is called "a nigger with a million dollars." Yet despite such statements—whether true or not—what is true however is that it is the continuing acceptance and embracing of the values that are superimposed by the dominant culture that renders black victims of institutional racism/white supremacy unable to assess, understand, and improve their conditions. As a result, it is the ambition to curry favor and ingratiate these superimposed values and mores and parley these indecencies and indiscretions into those of the dominant culture, by steadfastly putting on display a complete reluctance to challenge the conditions that renders black people as a whole vulnerable to racism, discrimination, double standards, and preconceived notions of who black people really are, and what it is that they truly want (or need).

The Slave mentality: "where did we get this Mind?"

"Have you forgotten that once we were
brought here, we were robbed of our name,

robbed of our language? We lost our religion, our culture, our God; and many of us by the way we act, we even lost our minds!"
—Khalid Abdul Muhammad

In 1996, at a Ku Klux Klan rally in Ann Arbor, Michigan, a black woman hurled herself on top of a Klan member to prevent him from being beaten by anti-Klan demonstrators. The reasons for her actions were never fully ascertained, other than the fact that she claimed to be an anti-Ku Klux Klan protestor. What was certain is that many members of the press lauded her for her actions, proclaiming that she was a paragon of Dr. King's dream, and an example of what all Americans should aspire to being. In the preceding chapter, I illustrated certain theories of black people's predilection to Christian views and ideologies. One of the more salient tenets of the bible is to love your enemy. Perhaps this is what this particular black female, whose name is Keisha Thomas, was doing.

Malcolm X, the slain civil rights leader of the 1960s, called this mentality and course of action the result of having what he coined the "slave mind." Furthermore, it was Malcolm's brilliant articulation of the distinction between the *field Negro* and the *house Negro* that lent credibility to this claim. According to Malcolm, those blacks who possess the slave mind harbor more of the mentality of the house Negro and, consequently, are the ones who are more prone to giving whites a pass for their mistreatment and racist tendencies towards blacks, and all non-whites; are more susceptible to sleeping with white women and white men; are more apt to conforming to European standards of beauty and aesthetics (e.g., frying and straightening the hair and engaging in the use of skin-bleaching crèmes and cosmetics); and are more prone to engaging in unsafe and high-risked behaviors that are more endemic to westernized standards and norms of behavior (e.g., promiscuity, especially interracial promiscuity, and engaging in tobacco and alcohol use and other illegal narcotics and substances). Additionally, according to Malcolm's theory, the house negro loved his master more than he loved himself, and, as a result, would question the field Negro's endeavors to escape the clutches of his master and the conditions of slavery and servitude. It should come as no surprise then that the insurrectionist's ambitions of Gabriel Prosser, Denmark Vessey, and Nat Turner were either completely thwarted or compromised because of slaves who lived in the master's house and believed that they had a rapport with their captors and, because of these beliefs, blew the whistle on many ensuing slave rebellions.

When mulling over the legitimacy of theories purporting the ramifications and effects of possessing the slave mind, or suffering from the disorder of posttraumatic slave syndrome, what should be clear is that under the unjust system of racism/white supremacy, black people as a whole have been duped and indoctrinated to love their enemies; yet it is the lack of proper interpretation and contexts that renders black people not only victims but the perfect victims. Ignorance of the knowledge of self, as well as common knowledge and principle of being black in a society which is bifurcated by color that is so simple and obvious that even a child could understand, have deprived black people of the truth and the courage to see the truth as it is. But, incredulously, the truth is either relative in terms or perception or is completely ambiguous when it comes to a people who are, as it has often been stated, the victims of "the greatest crime in human history."

It has also been stated that the way to defeat a people is to get them to destroy themselves by dividing the ranks among them. Certainly, the ranks are more than divided. Actually, they are in complete disarray. What is then left for blacks is the embracing of things that are antithetical to understanding and eradicating their primary condition, and to instead imbue benign and benevolent qualities in those who either don't have their best interests or seek to be representatives and proxies for black people's causes but have absolutely no control over their own dysfunctions and internal demons.

For example, the first day of the New Year of 2013, Black Entertainment Television or BET, had an all-day marathon of Tyler Perry films. What this fact denotes is that while black people (especially blacks in America) are the most despised, vilified, and debased people on the planet, instead of starting off the new year with a new-found direction and sense of purpose for improving conditions by countering such preconceived notions and rebuking associations to such fallacious imagery, the alternative for black folk in this society is to immerse themselves in the same negative associations and support of those who put on display the imagery and stereotypes that make mockery and demean the very existence of black people; rather than uplift, unite, and socially and culturally empower blacks, both here in these United States and across the globe.

Admittedly, I have deliberately revisited some examples pointed out earlier in this book because, as I see it, it can only be fruitful and beneficial to identify simple truisms in an attempt to thwart the proliferation of gross ignorance. On that note, one of the main problems is to treat slavery—and the racist and white supremacist mindset that gave birth to slavery, and is the principle cause of the suffering of black people to this day—as if it is some remnant of the past, when clearly the residual effects and damage that were caused are evident in the mentality, actions, and deficiencies of former slaves and contemporary victims of institutional racism/white supremacy. This is the slave mind that Malcolm X theorized. And this is posttraumatic slave syndrome that many social scientists have hypothesized as being perhaps the most salient detriment to the well-being of black people—ethnically, culturally, psychologically, and socio-politically and economically—as a whole. Therefore, to delude oneself into believing that racism and the white supremacist mindset that are far from being mutually exclusive yet, by overwhelming consensus, do not exist is equivalent to handing a knife to a sworn enemy and then stretching your neck for that enemy to slit your throat.

Take for instance that within the past couple of years, a black female meteorologist in Louisiana was fired from her position after responding to a white viewer who criticized her for having a short, natural hairstyle. Her response was a mere assertion that as a black female, she was comfortable with her features as well as her cultural heritage. In other words, embracing and loving what is black and is associated with being black is considered as being anti-white in a racist society that is fueled by a white supremacists mindset. Furthermore, what is viewed as being too ethnic is uncomfortable to a point to where it causes antagonism and arouses disdain in the person who is threatened by ethnic and cultural diversity due to that same white supremacist mentality; a fact made more plausible by comedian Paul Mooney's assertion that if your hair is relaxed white people are relaxed, but if your hair is nappy white people "ain't" happy. Yet the only castigation meted out was not to the person who ignited the racial firestorm in a so called post-racist society, but to the woman who simply expressed her right to be whom and what she is and to be content in doing so.

Color-blind Society...?

"This generation isn't racist!"
—Jay Z

We as society are familiar with the argument or claim that we are now in the midst of a color-blind, post-racial society. And, of course, what can be more supportive of this claim than the fact that there is a two-term black president. Or, perhaps we as society are privy to the more obscure claim that classism is just as salient an issue than any discrimination or prejudice that is based on color or ethnicity, if not more so. Well, the aforementioned anecdote regarding the black female meteorologist belies such claims, as does the recent uproar regarding a Cheerios commercial that showcases a mixed-raced child in a biracial family setting (basically confirming that the majority of white people in America still do not want to see the advertising of interracial couples in a family setting, especially if the paternal figure of the household is black).

More telling is the fact that, as actor Samuel L. Jackson put it, "it is open season on young black males," as a slew of incidents have purported black children either being shot dead by police or by racist good ole' boys with conspicuous hero complexes and an even more noticeable bloodlust to slaughter black people—particularly black boys. In fact, it has been expressed by both white and black social critics that Barack Obama's presidency has only worsened race relations, subsequently arousing white people to be more outwardly racist. Perhaps it is because of such widespread beliefs that none of the murderers of these young black children were found guilty of any wrongdoing in courts of law throughout the country. For these reasons, those so-called liberal white do-gooders, who espouse that we are in a color-blind, post-racist society are either outright tricksters or suffer from delusions of grandeur. And, without question, people of color who endorse such idiocy are either completely ensnared by the slave mind or suffer from an acute form of posttraumatic slave syndrome. Or, maybe, a little bit of both.

———

In 2010, a black female phoned in to Dr. Laura Schlesinger's syndicated radio talk show to receive advice on how to deal with her white husband's friends and relatives making racial remarks and obscenities in her presence and her husband not intervening or speaking up on her behalf. What followed was a tirade and barrage of racial epithets from Dr. Laura, who then punctuated her claim by asserting that if a person of color (actually her use of words was somewhere along the lines of people who have melanin) is going to be sensitive to racial epithets, then that person should not marry a white person, in addition to other incendiary racists remarks that she felt compelled to make. Dr. Laura would subsequently announce a hiatus from her radio show, stating her disgust with an inability to exercise her right to free speech.

I mention this to confirm my claim of the ubiquitous nature of racism in America—both institutional and preferential. Moreover, I mention this to assert another claim of the slave mentality that is so deeply engrained in the victims of institutional racism/ white supremacy, that it would compel a black person to get advice on issues of overt racism and racist practices from another white person in a highly toxic and racist society. In other words, when scratching the surface, the message clearly conveyed from Dr. Laura was that she, along with the friends and relatives of the caller's white husband, have a right to be racists if they so choose to be, and as long as it falls under the banner of free speech they should have the right to do so with absolute impunity; same as the actions that were devoid of consequences and made permissible to the aforementioned racists murderers of black children, not to mention regardless of whether they committed these murderous acts while plain-clothed or in uniform (evidently when it comes to killing black children it doesn't matter).

Nonetheless, the banner of the blame does not lie completely with the Laura Schlesinger's of the world (because she is right: she does have a right to be racist, as long as she, and other racists, understand that that same right extends to those who choose to call her out as such after the fact), as the intent here is to point out that it is the possessor of the slave mind that will either write all of the aforementioned incidents off as isolated acts of mere prejudice that has no bearing on the entire collective of black people, or dismiss the matter of race entirely. Again, it is the slave mind that would compel a black female who is married to a white man to seek out advice on how to address a conflict concerning race and racism from a white woman that she has no personal ties to in a society that is still highly acidic and racist, not to mention who also was revealed to be an avid racist! And in the case of the previously discussed meteorologist, it would be an isolated incident of racial prejudice being exacted only if the comment had been made and the meteorologist's response rendered no penalty for doing so. However, the fact that this black female was fired clearly and irrefutably points out that the wheels of institutional racism/white supremacy continue to spin and disrupt the livelihood and well-being of black people—male and female.

This is irrefutable evidence as to how the slave mind as described by Malcolm X reaches far beyond the plantation and the cotton fields and is years removed from chattel servitude. To be more specific, it is an inferiority mind state that renders one unable to see his or her true value, as well as collective self-worth based on their true historical standing in global society. Moreover, it is the affliction of posttraumatic slave syndrome that precludes victims of institutional racism/white supremacy from asking the simple question of how black people as a whole can effectively attack the system and formulate the obvious answer as being one that requires the usage of basic proactive strategies and measures. For instance, if one black person is persecuted and victimized by institutional racism/white supremacy and egregious acts of prejudice, then all black people should bear the brunt of that same victimization. What this means is that if a black female is fired from a prime time network because of her responding to criticisms regarding the texture of her hair, then there should not have been a single black individual in Baton Rouge watching the television network that was responsible from that day forward. Unequivocally, the edifice of mainstream America would undergo a radical transformation if its black victims of institutional racism/white supremacy uniformly stop supporting programs and other means of entertainment/exploitation that are not pertinent to their causes and real issues and, perhaps more telling, depicts black people in a negative fashion, as do the majority of these reality television programs, movies, talk shows, etc. According to Dr. Welsing, if black people were to collectively come together for a common cause and display love and affection towards one another, the edifice of racism/white supremacy would collapse within twenty-four hours.

The safe Negro/acceptable
Black: The plus side to Posttraumatic Slave Syndrome

"Failing is a very common thing in our society;
the unique thing is success!"
—JOHN THOMPSON

One of the many problems of institutional racism/white supremacy is that it strips its victims of the need or desire to be comfortable in their own skin and be proud of who they are as human beings. This is particularly true of black male victims who gallivant and circumambulate in a racist society. As stated earlier, knowledge of self is not only self-empowering but also a proclamation of the importance of being connected culturally, communally, and spiritually to those who look like you, come from where you come from, and endure similar life circumstances and experiences. However, it is because black males have for centuries been subjected to an oppressive, white supremacist system that the expectations for survival have been manifested by thoughts and actions that are typical as opposed to atypical (in this case practical), and that are less-threatening as opposed to adversarial to the unjust status quo. As a result, this is the upside of the slave mind, or, if you will, the positive symptom or more acceptable condition of posttraumatic slave syndrome. In other words, black males in America are accepted for being overly-friendly, effeminate, passive, and non-threatening. On the other hand, they are vilified, eschewed, and brutalized for displaying a façade that is overly manly, masculine, and virtuous (telling the truth), which for all intent and purposes is really nothing more than an instinctive reaction to deeply rooted and palpable oppression.

Another simple fact is that in order for a black male in America to be considered safe, although not accepted or fully appreciated, he must exude the passive-aggressive spirit of Martin Luther King rather than the "give us what we are due" non-negotiable prose of Malcolm X. Arguably, it was not until the election of Barack Obama that the intellectual capacity and capabilities of achievement that was long considered beyond the scope of the black male was put on display to the world, via Obama's unprecedented accomplishment. But even that extraordinary feat did not completely invalidate the widely preconceived notion of the black male, or cause the white establishment to accept the black male on the merit and terms of his own unique individuality. For what it is worth,

Obama s mannerisms and façade play right into the notion of the non-threatening black male, as widely perceived by white America. Hence, he is considered safe and agreeable to white people, and a paragon of the ultimate success and beacon of hope to blacks.

Even in 2014, roughly ten years after Obama was put on the global stage outside of his home state of Illinois, there are still plenty of white people who feign a con implying that they either do not know their own black victims or are perplexed by some black peoples' ability to maneuver around the parameters and proscriptions of institutional racism/white supremacy that white people, themselves, constructed and continue to practice. I call it a con because, as far as my analysis, white people are indeed all too familiar with *black exceptionalism;* hence, an appropriate term for the purposes of the case being brought forth here that was reintroduced to the consciousness of society by Michelle Alexander in her book *The New Jim Crow: Mass incarceration in the age of colorblindness.28* Clearly, and with the aid of individual's such as Tyler Perry, white people have in the past and still perceive black people as being a typical and mundane monolithic group of people, who dangle on a precipice of minute success and tumultuous, continual failure. For instance, and as Al Sharpton so astutely pointed out, not only is Obama not the first black person to attend and successfully complete his studies at Harvard, but W.E.B. Dubois accomplished the same feat back in the later part of the nineteenth century, as have scores of other blacks since that time. Yet it was Obama's resume and credentials that were treated as both profound and unprecedented to a point that they helped lead him all the way to the front steps of the white house.

What is the point of the previously mentioned? Well, the answer is that in America—global society's premiere bastion of racial and cultural angst and civil and social disequilibrium—fairy tales (as Bill Clinton mentioned prior to Obama's first-term election) do not exist, and everything, including the election of the country's first non-white president, is predetermined. Nevertheless, it is also my contention that the black male has simply resigned himself to accepting whatever it is his former slave masters have given or show a willingness to give, regardless of whether or not such gratuity is beneficial to the black male's advancement or detrimental to his survival and/or well-being. This is why when I speak of the failure of becoming true Men or being considered as Men in a racist society, I am referring specifically to the black male in America. Certainly, Jewish men, in contrast, and who are categorized as white, learned from their own holocaust, and orchestrated a propitious collective stance in route to cultural and socioeconomic empowerment. Black males, however, have failed in this endeavor. A fact that cannot be disputed by the obvious conditions that the black male is in; how black people as a whole are portrayed and exploited by mainstream and cultural media, as well as black people's penchant to intermarry and intermingle with other races; therefore, ingratiating themselves into the cultural domicile of others while rebuffing and eschewing their own people, heritage, and culture. Indeed, it is the act of gravitating towards self-hatred in the face of institutional racism/white supremacy, and not institutional racism/white supremacy itself that is gradually leading to the cultural demise of black people—particularly the black male—today.

Homunculi

"Yessir, I please to aim and aim to please!"[29]
—MALCOLM LITTLE, *MALCOM X*

One black scholar and social critic made the claim that historically, black people have been tolerated by white people for the purpose of serving three functions. First, to satisfy the conditions of menial labor and underemployment, which is essentially what chattel slavery was all about. Second, entertain white people. Third, either be available to whites for the purposes of mistreatment or act as confidants and proxies that white people can confide in for issues that are solely pertinent to white people and white people only. It is no accident that Hollywood and various other media outlets that are driven by the need for entertainment, vis-à-vis exploitation, often put forth portrayals and images that showcase the black male or black female, if either are showcased at all, as the friend or pal of the main white character or protagonist. Unsurprisingly, these black individuals/confidants have no stories of their own, and their feelings and sensibilities are dismissed for the purposes of purporting white people's pains, feelings, experiences, and existential well-being as the only human emotions and qualities that are meaningful.

In contemporary mainstream America, there is a burgeoning trend that is geared towards portrayals of amorous ties and courtships between white men and black females. And in order for this new trend to be credible or effective in any way, the rare depictions of black male and black female relations are either for the purposes of purporting the dissension and dysfunctions that exist between the two or such relations are completely eschewed in mainstream culture. Thus, white men and their conquest of both the white woman and the black female should not be surprising in a society whose white supremacists endeavors and motives are for the purposes of imbuing white men with incomparable qualities—intellectually, sexually, and culturally. In other words, in a racist society, the existence of black people as a whole is only relevant hence, allowed, if it suits or serves the purposes of white people—whatever that purpose or those needs may be.

Cisco Streetlove, in his book *Yesterday's Shame: the Atlanta Child Murders*, states that these actions are driven by white people's belief that black people are not real people such as themselves, but are instead deemed as "homunculi."[30] Homunculi, as defined, are mere variations of human organisms that have been crafted or created to suit the needs and purposes of their creators. Now, before this claim is written off as either frivolous or egregious, it should be noted that it was Frantz Fanon who also made the assertion that to white men, the black "man" is not perceived as a man but a new kind of man that has no resemblance to himself. Moreover, the theory of homunculi is premised on a myriad of racial connotations. While chimerical in theory, the description of homunculi having large hands, large lips, and massive genitals, engenders racial stereotypes that were derived from a society that steadfastly and persistently postulates racial distinctions.

The fact of the matter is that black people as a whole in America, since the days of suffering as chattel slaves and burden-bearers, have and continue to suffer from inhumane conditions, are discriminated against and mistreated strictly on the basis of race and ethnicity, or have been reduced to all three manners of the aforementioned expectations that are superimposed on them from white America. In other words, the theory of homunculi can be deemed as white people taking advantage of the many blacks who are afflicted with the slave mind or who suffer from the ills of posttraumatic slave syndrome. Either way, despite proficiency in certain areas—whatever they may be—surely the black male has risen above and beyond expectations of chattel servitude and cheap labor; particularly considering that America was built on the backs of black labor with absolutely no recompense in return. Moreover, the black male has certainly exceeded expectations as far as entertaining both white people and black folk, yet has been categorically mistreated and continues to be mistreated on a day to day basis. As mentioned earlier, Michael Jackson is perhaps the most prolific entertainer that white America (and the world) has ever seen; however, the perpetual decimating of his character and persona that happened as a result of his personal demons and inner turmoil that, without question, was manifested by conditions of racism/white supremacy, tragically was the cause of his untimely death.

For instance, when Michael Jackson was accused of child molestation it was his friend and biographer, J. Randy Tamboriello, who in attempting to make a case for Jackson's innocence, claimed that Jackson was not seen as a sexual being. He went on to state that Jackson was more widely perceived as asexual. Certainly, the tragedy behind such a claim becomes obvious when considering that in addition to Jackson's talents, he was in fact a human being who possessed the same feelings, pain, sensibilities, and capacity for love and receptivity for love as everyone else. However, the statement that Tamborielli made could easily be interpreted as meaning that Jackson's sole purpose and expectation in life was to strictly be an entertainer, with the apex of his monetary success and global stature contingent on how effective his ability to entertain white people in particular. I will assert that such a claim has substantial merit when considering that it was mostly white people whom Jackson centered himself around and they in turn mostly centered themselves around Jackson—a course of action often employed by white people in regards to certain blacks, whom whites occasionally admire and are captivated by that I call the *pink poodle syndrome*—especially when it comes to rich and successful, high-profile blacks such as Jackson.

Because of bleaching crèmes, ointments, and plastic facial and bodily reconstructions, Jackson s appearance went through a drastic and unpleasant transformation. But despite that, while it cannot be disputed that Jackson was a prolific entertainer, neither can it be dismissed or overlooked that Jackson was in fact born a black male. Hence, the large lips, nose, hands, feet, and genitalia, as well as black dogs and black hens that are associated with the birthing process of homunculi are arguably also subconsciously associated with Jackson, considering that these were many of the physical traits that he, himself, deemed repugnant and disagreeable to white America.

If not homunculi, then clearly some other theory or explanation must exist to justify the condition of the black male in American society as mere fodder and a supplementary human being, compared to the status and social standing of his white counterpart. Some rationale must exist to explain the condition of black males as toadies or being placed several steps behind white men in terms of importance, dexterity, masculinity, and accomplishments. If no such theories or explanations exists and, in a post-racial society, black people as a whole are perceived as having the same opportunities as everyone else, then without question there must be some system in place to obstruct or thwart the prospect of advancement for the black male and for black people as a whole; hence, leveling the playing fields in terms of economics, politics, and entertainment. Some system that is in place to constantly reinforce the notion that black is an inferior state of being as well as existence, and one that has succeeded in convincing the black male that he is but a mere sub-species in western society and, because of this, in order to accomplish or achieve anything—white alliances, white values, and a white code of ethics must be fully embraced.

What should also be certain is that America is a society that endeavors to minimize, denigrate, or make insignificant the black male, the black female, black children, or anything associated with black or blackness, by use of colloquialisms and terms such as "blackmail," blackball," "black sheep," or "blacklist" to insinuate either aberrant behavior or appearance in a family dwelling or social setting. Or, attempt to eschew and discredit accomplishments that fall outside of the parameters and boundaries of what are perceived as "cultural norms." For example, after every major holiday or event in western culture, both major and minor retail outlets and retailers have what is called "black Friday" sales, a corporate and marketing tool designed to sell goods that are marked at a significantly lesser value than the items actual retail cost. Tragically, it is black people who are overwrought with the slave mind that engage in such colloquial-isms and manners of speech and communication. Additionally, it is the affliction of posttraumatic slave syndrome that causes black folk to turn out in excessive numbers to compete and/or cooperate in black Friday sales, despite the objective of saving and spending less money. And it is America, as well as the rest of global society, that scrutinizes such sordid actions in order to assess and determine black people's collective value and cultural self-worth on both a national and global scale.

Another of the several theories of homunculi posits a black hen lay-ing eggs that are then injected with semen that gives life after thirty days, which ironically is longer than black history month—the shortest month of the calendar year. Whether one agrees with this theory or not, what I would forewarn for those who are skeptical to keep in mind is that in western society, the black male has been both reduced and circum-scribed to a subculture that is gradually being engulfed by a racist and white supremacist system that nullifies and makes null and void his true heritage and cultural and global significance. An example of this claim would be subjecting black people as a whole to egregious classifications such as *minorities* and, my favorite, *African Americans.* For this reason, I would argue that these are tactics designed to inculcate the omnipresence of white people—both nationally and globally—when statistically and numerically, they in fact make up a tiny minority on the planet. Yet this is what black folk willingly and elatedly refer to themselves as. This, clearly, is what Malcolm X described as the slave mind, and sadly it is the slave mentality and posttraumatic slave syndrome that causes black people to engage in such self-denigrating and culturally-debasing activities, and willfully identity themselves with such frivolous and specious classifications.

Colored Girls

"Being colored is a metaphysical
dilemma that I haven't conquered yet."[31]
—YASMINE, FOR COLORED GIRLS

The above passage is a soliloquy that was excerpted from the Tyler Perry produced and directed film *For Colored Girls.* For certain, the film was more than just an unnerving proclamation of black females' victimization as a result of black male dysfunction and pathology, but also was an inference of self-deprecating ascriptions and associations of being black in a society that continues to portray itself as omnipotent, benign, and magnanimous—all attributes that are attributed to whiteness. The contradiction, however, is that even in a so-called post-racist society, depictions via film, television, and news media of how the black male or black folk in general is mentally and psychologically regressing rather than moving forward and making the kinds of strides that cultural and social prognosticators claim is what are actually taken place, is not only becoming all too common but the Tyler Perry's of black cinema are highly praised for such thematic and cinematic degeneracy. As a result, it is easy for those who represent the dominant culture to refer to black people as African Americans when they know that black people in America have very little, if any, identification with Africa or Africans other than skin color, in which both people are globally vilified and impugned for that very unchangeable fact. Why? Because the objective of enslaving blacks for the purposes of ownership and servitude was to ensure that there would never be any identification with other blacks, Africa, or Africans.

Carcinogenic skin bleaching creams are also widely distributed in both regions to whiten and lighten black skin. Furthermore, interracial marriages and courtships, while considered conditional by white people, are either highly coveted by blacks or are routinely condoned. Internet dating websites such as *Black Women for White Men* and *Afro Romance* are designed specifically for the purposes of interracial dating and hookups. Although this may seem contradictory for a society that balks in the appearance of being racially and ethnically-neutral, I would argue that the reason being is this is what the institutional system of racism/white supremacy is designed and intended to do—DIVIDE and CONQUER. And, as a result, the more black folk there are who are vulnerable to possessing the slave mind or who are afflicted with posttraumatic slave syndrome, the endeavor of exploitation and creating mass confusion is made that much easier.

It may indeed be true that black females are oft-confronted with the realization that there is a shortage of eligible black males for marriage; consequently, there is a push for single, black, professional, and eligible black females to subscribe to a "white is right" dictum, under the guise of happiness and security that many black females believe that black males are incapable of providing. For instance, sample online MissJia.com and check out her ten reasons why black females should consider partnerships with white men for a sure-fire example of the slave mind at work, as well as a cut and dry indication of the schism that institutional racism/white supremacy has produced in the psychological functioning of black people in terms of how they view and perceive themselves. Or, visit the site of the *Oreo Experience*—a moniker coined by a young black female who shows little compunction of illustrating and espousing her obsessions with white culture, white standards, and white men; again, actions based on the conspicuous absence of a sedative for being deluged in the sickness of posttraumatic slave syndrome, hence possessing a slave mentality.

One question in particular is whether these few examples speak for all black people? Perhaps not, but I only point out these examples because in addition to the growing trend of interracial marriages and the push for the entertainment industry to showcase black female and white male court-ships, there is a tendency to overlook the fact that there is a reason behind these growing trends; reasons that grossly contradict the proclamation of a post-racialized society that is gradually gravitating towards tolerance and embracing of true cultural and aesthetic differences. Accordingly, the pro-prietor of Missjia.com advocates for black female and white male court-ships because it is her belief that white men are better suited to address the financial as well as physical needs of the black female. The black male, on the other hand, according to her, is either ill-equipped or "too ghetto" for such a task. Moreover, the Oreo Experience simply prefers white men because she finds the distinction of skin-whiteness appealing; in addition to her claim that very few black males live in the part of town where she resides (what better way to assume whiteness and white identity than to live in predominantly white areas and communities).

Regardless of these frivolous and absurd rationales, the truth is that there are many black females who are fooling themselves into thinking that white men in a racist society are conditioned to willfully and honestly give their hearts, dedication, and commitment to them, a prospect that is completely contradictory to the grooming process that takes place in white households; particularly those white households that embrace the ideology and tenets of institutional racism/white supremacy. In fact, in a racist society that is driven by a white supremacist mindset, white males are steadfastly taught to preserve racial purity, and that a little "play" outside of the confounds of what is truly important and held sacred, such as main-taining and preserving racial purity, has nothing at all or at least very little to do with love and commitment. Here is another case in point.

Khalil Baaqi

Long before I read the *Isis Papers: Keys to the Colors*, as a high school student working at a pizza restaurant in Southern Indiana, a young white male coworker would constantly pester me with the idea of, as he put it, "hooking him up with a black chic." When I inquired about his persistence, particularly being that he had a girlfriend who was white like himself and who would often visit him and drop him off and pick him up at the restaurant, his response to me was his father informing him that a white male is not a man until he has engaged in intercourse with a black female or, again, "slept with a black chic."

Interestingly, I was introduced to this white supremacists ideology and racial dogma long before I had even heard of Dr. Francis Cress-Welsing or her book, which, coincidentally would be published a year or so later. Perhaps even more interesting is that at that time it had been a little more than a decade since songs from musicians and bands, such as the Rolling Stone's "some girls," insinuated the oversexed and libidinal nature of black females. For those who would impose a counterargument that these examples are coincidental or are in need of a little more contexts, my reply is, well, not really. Especially when considering that Mick Jagger, who is the lead singer of the Rolling Stones and is a musical icon, fathered an illegitimate child by a black female. Furthermore, years before the release of some Girls, another Rolling Stone's track, entitled "brown sugar," vocalized and celebrated the simulated rape of a young black female. The truth is that not much has changed since those times.

As of the new millennium and, give or take, the decade that preceded it, there is a growing trend of black females' actually marrying white men, perhaps more so than at any other time in the country's history. However, when carefully analyzing and weighing statistics, the reality is that many of these black female/white man arrangements purport black females fairing no better than courtships with black males, in which many black females' claim that the latter is either non-accessible or is steadfastly eschewed under the premise that it is no longer aesthetically or personally pleasing. When considering actual data, a 1999 statistic purports that of 1.2 million interracial marriages during that time, black/white marriages—which includes both black males and black females—did not even constitute one percent.[32]

I can recall a phone conversation that I had years ago with a black female who shared with me her theory of how the ideal mate for a black female is a white man. Again, I say this to point out that this is the state of mind that many in black America have either willingly gravitated towards or have unwillingly fallen victim to: The proclamation of eschewing and harboring disdain and contempt towards her biological and natural partner in humanity and instead juxtaposing herself with a species of Men who were the mass murderers and enslavers of her ancestors and, who to this day, are the orchestrators of a system that ensures either certain death or a life plagued by misery and hardship for black children (I wonder whether black females who are mothers echo such sentiments while their children are shot dead in American streets with no consequences or penalties being imposed on their killers, lest those killers are other black males).

The fact of the matter is that despite increasing rates of interracial marriages—both black male/white woman, black female/white man— the percentages are still minute to a point to unabatedly make the claim that these are mere random unions that are not numerically plausible enough to support an argument for increasing racial tolerance. Additionally, such figures have nothing to do with the realities of institutional racism/white supremacy that affects the black male and other people of color as well. Thus, the jaded, diffusive, incoherent, and self-deprecatory ramblings of those whom when they open their mouths and espouse their mantra of white is right and regurgitate the proclamation of white ethnic superiority, only confirms the efficacy of the spinning wheels of racism/white supremacy—regardless of whether this is done by black people (victims) or white racists (victimizers)—and regardless of whether those who do so are aware of this fact or not. Also, it is the truly ignorant and deluded of black people who should be aware of the subliminal and unspeakable acts that have and continue to take place around them before they assiduously pursue coitus relations with whites and dive head first into their interracial courtships. Perhaps if they were mindful of such potential impediments (to put mildly), then certainly awareness of still being subjugated by a white supremacist system would be quite clear and hard to dispute. What would also be clear is that it is the racist practices that are fueled by this system that would warrant a reprieve for George Zimmerman, after evidence proved that he profiled, stalked, and murdered a black child.

Menticide

> *"I freed a thousand slaves. I could have*
> *freed a thousand more if only they knew they were slaves."*
> —HARRIET TUBMAN

In her 1994 book, black female author Shahrazad Ali asked the pivotal question, *Are you still a slave?* The answer no doubt should be obvious for many when considering the physical aspects of slavery. However, the mental and psychological aspect of whether black folk—victims of racism and racist practices—are still slaves is a question that remains unanswered and requires further analysis, such as what I am attempting to offer with this book. The fact that former slaves and present-day victims of institutional racism/white supremacy are perceived as not being under physical bondage, clearly obstructs the fact that many of the conditions that the black male in America, and black folk in general throughout the world, experience today is the direct result of *menticide*: the mental and psychological destruction and eradication of black people's cultural heritage, aesthetic ties and alliances, and shared love and affection among one another because of those physical and cultural trappings that tie black people as a whole together.

What menticide also entails is black folk's eschewing culture, heritage, and allegiances toward one another for the purposes of supplanting such ties with something else; in other words, the standards, values, and qualities of those who enslaved them over four hundred years ago.

As stated earlier, what black females who seek life partners and intimate companions need to realize, especially before they become too smitten by the idea that these are conditions and needs that presently only white men can accommodate and fulfil, is that white men in a racist society, and one that is driven by a white supremacist mindset, are not groomed to engage in life partnership practices and deep interpersonal relations with them. They must also understand that this is true regardless of whether there is a perceived shortage of black males, or if disdain towards black males completely envelopes their psyches'. Similarly, black males need to aspire to effectively treat the symptoms of posttraumatic slave syndrome that exhorts the urge to get their mitts on a white woman in what they perceive as a free society. In other words, the sexual objectification of black males and black females cannot be excluded or taken for granted in a society in which its racist's ideology coined the inference that one is not a man until he has slept with a black female, or "once you go black you never go back." Also, consider that the Rolling Stone's "some girls," mentioned earlier as a musical expose' of the oversexed and licentious nature of black females, which was released in 1978 has sold an additional six million copies within the last decade.

So in addition to my claim of menticide, in terms of the present condition of the black male in America, the theory that he is perceived as homunculi resurfaces as well, especially when considering that in addition to Hollywood and mainstream cultural media's presentation of the trend of interracial courtships, the porn industry's thirteen billion dollar enterprise is rife with depictions of interracial sex and copulation; factors that clearly point out that the small but gradually increasing numbers of interracial encounters have to be looked at from a different perspective, or at least from both sides of the coin. Hence, the assiduous persistence of the young white kid whom I worked with as a teen having an intimate encounter with a black female was not because he wanted to connect with one on a personal (or maybe even spiritual) level, or learn more about the culture, heritage, and the day-to-day struggles of black people, but instead for use as a tool (homunculi) to enhance his masculine qualities, from which the white supremacists mindset and ideology avows that only black females can aid in achieving.

Ebony & Ivory: Analyzing black/
white marriages and identity deconstruction

It cannot be emphasized enough that that the actions that have been discussed are the direct result of the conditions of slavery that largely affects the black male and black people as a whole to this day, particularly being that the black male is still circumscribed to conditions of Euro-American domination, supremacy, and ways of life. While it is possible that there are situations in which human beings are brought together by a mere common bond, this possibility however is not the case across the board, as the increases in thematic depictions and overall cultural scrutiny that has been placed on interracial marriages and relations are indicative of an entirely different dynamic. Consequently, interracial marriages in America are arguably viewed in two ways: An egalitarian point of view, in which younger Americans favor its practice; or, a conservative perspective that leans more towards endogamy.

According to E. Franklin Frazier, the author of *Black Bourgeoisie*, in redirecting the point for a moment back to black females, it is his claim that if black females were not being raped outright by white slave masters and slave owners, they willingly gave themselves to white men for the purposes of acquiring certain advantages.[33] Thus, they were able to work in the house as opposed to working out in the fields, and because of this their mix-raced children might be entitled to privileges that were not available to pure black slaves. It must be understood that history is not linear but is instead recursive, especially if any of the analyses being offered here is going to make any sense. And according to the common adage, history is bound to at some point repeat itself. For this reason, I would argue that today it is no different. The fact is that both the black male and black female seek out interracial relationships in a highly toxic and racist society to mollify his or her condition, rectify perceived inferior status, and appease their former slave masters. This is also done in order to prove that his or her virtues are similar to those of the dominant culture rather than those of the oppressed. It is nonetheless, for all intent and purposes, the slave mind at work.

It was Frederick Douglas who once made the claim that in order to make a content slave, you needed to make a thoughtless one. How prophetic are the ringing of those words today, considering that many within black circles are content to engage in interracial courtships and marriages in a highly racist and white supremacists minded society without considering the ramifications of doing so. Accordingly, it is completely thoughtless to claim that "love has no color" in a society that places proscriptions on the potential, choices, and achievements of those who have color, and strictly on the basis of being endowed (or stricken, depending on perception) with color. Of course, there are many who may disagree with this claim and instead make the argument that the emasculated black male, as well as all black people, are a free people who are privileged with the right to choose whom they wed and bed, a prospect made possible by *Loving V. Virginia* in 1967 that spearheaded the nullification of anti-miscegenation laws. Nonetheless, what is certain is that there are those who, because they possess the mentality of the orchestrator of missjia.com or the Oreo Experience, lack proper perspective and insight and, consequently, live in a perpetual state of fear and anxiety but do so under the guise of hubris and a pseudo sense of intellectualizing their true reality and condition. As stated earlier, self-preservation is the first law of nature. Therefore, it is only natural to love oneself and love those who share similar traits and circumstances, unless someone or something disrupts this simple process and flow of nature or what is natural.

A plausible reason for this mentality and the subsequent actions that might ensue is that the black male has been brutalized for centuries and bombarded with a philosophy that stipulates black inferiority. As a result, the slave mind or posttraumatic slave syndrome or menticide, or a combination of all, is the direct result of a conditioning process that has been passed down from generation to generation, thus claimed by Kenneth Raymond, author of the article "Do African Americans think like former Slaves?"[34] In other words, if not black, then it must be white, is the self-deluded concept that has consumed the mindset of the Oreo Experience and those who seek courtships and relations with those who are biologically and physiologically the opposite of themselves. More perplexing is that these endeavors are driven by the premise of color blindness as far as it relates to love, yet contradictorily the system of institutional racism/white supremacy was constructed to annihilate, debase, and dehumanize strictly on the basis of color, leaving the prospect of love completely null and void. According to Olomenji, a Chicago-based social worker and author of the article "Menticide, Genocide, and National Vision," this form of menticide is the result of black people indulging in "delusion, denial, and escapism" in attempt to counteract the reality of their existence by imitating whites.[35] Moreover, he asserts how excessive consumption of media and mainstream accessories is a distraction from the reality of dehumanization that those same institutions invariably perpetuate. However, what he refers to as denial and escapism, I, on the other hand, consider as a pernicious form of ethnic and cultural trepidation and reluctance that leads to what I have labeled as black *identity deconstruction.*

———

Black identity deconstruction is a psychological and mental detachment of values, customs, and patterns of thought, perception, and behavior that, historically, have been identified with blackness or affiliated with those who are considered as black. And it is because of this need to disavow oneself from the stigma of blackness or being black that a psychological reconditioning and transmutation to whiteness and acceptance of white values becomes obligatory. Interestingly enough, Dr. Michael Eric Dyson in his book, *Is Bill Cosby Right? Or has the Black Middle Class lost its mind,* offered his own unique assessment of black self-loathing and cultural disavowal, in which these conditions are based on what he describes as "accidental" or "incidental" blackness (Dyson also had a third component, "intentional" blackness, which is more indicative of pro-blackness).[36]

In redirecting back to my previous point however, being black is largely perceived and treated as a coincidental result of gene pool distribution, in which many who have melanin and pigmentation believe that they came up with the short end of the stick, connoting genetic superiority over inferiority, or a deficit that renders one collective group inherently weak and the other inherently powerful. Ironically, in regards to interracial courtships between blacks and whites, I once heard a black community organizer and activist on a talk radio program provide a very intelligent and cogent response when asked to offer his opinion on interracial dating and marriages. To summarize, he asserted that these arrangements would be fine considering the mentality of the black individuals involved. Such as, are they entering these relationships as proud African peoples who are comfortable in their own skins and proud of their culture and heritage. Or, are they entering these relationships as "sub-European negroes," rebuking and rebuffing their culture and heritage and immersing themselves in white values, white standards, and white lifestyle practices.

Whether one agrees with such sentiments or not, it would nonetheless behoove both the black male and black female to not be fooled or lulled into what some contemporary social (or antisocial) activists have coined as *tragic arrangements* (interracial relations in a racist society) by the claim that love has no color. Sure it does! Consequently, those who seek to have exclusive relations and courtships with white people do so for the kind of validation and acceptance that they will never fully or truly receive; just ask Nita Hanson. Furthermore, black males and black females seek out these relations for political power moves and what they perceive as upward mobility in a society that they know both consciously and subconsciously is fueled by race and ethnic and cultural differences, whether they admit to this fact or not.

As the emasculated black male looks upon the world around him, it is completely delusional to try to deny the fact that white people seem to have and control everything; therefore, it is easy to get caught up in a mind state of envy and intrigue without considering how, why, and what process was used for THEM to acquire the power that they indeed possess. Without such forethought and consideration, it is no wonder why black males covet white women and envy the power of white men, as do black females envy white women and covet white men. What other reason could there be behind the billion dollar enterprise of importing weave products from India and other foreign countries, the proliferation of the use of skin bleaching cosmetics, and the purchasing of colored eye contacts and dyes for hair coloration, all for the purposes of either minimizing African features or completely eschewing associations to that of the Negroid classification.

The bottom line is that the black male in America has succumbed to the ubiquitous claim that white is right—therefore superior and dominant—and, consequently, has embraced this claim, regardless of willingly or grudgingly. The problem, however, is the lack of understanding or failed insight to understand that as long as one possesses color and hue in a society that both implicitly and, oft-explicitly, announces and demonstrates its superiority over colored skin and African cultural heritage, then the slave mentality of the individual and, perhaps posttraumatic slave syndrome that affects the group as a whole, is extremely perilous; hence, the dubious nature of colonization of the mind—menticide.

Hopeless Romantics

Science purports irrefutable evidence that the first human beings on record as the primogenitors of human existence looked like those who are the sons and daughters of former slaves and burden bearers of America. Furthermore, they looked like the victims of institutional racism/white supremacy in American society today. Gripped by the affliction of posttraumatic slave syndrome/slave mind that has been conditioned by institutional racism/white supremacy, black folk as a whole immerse themselves in worship and theology that they have failed to properly interpret;

thus, black folk's (particularly black females') romanticism with Jesus and Christian doctrine, all the while rejecting the truth or failing to fully interpret who Jesus truly was and what it is he actually stood for. What is disturbing about this assessment is just as images of Jesus that are omnipresent across the globe are that of a man of European origin and stock, so too is the romanticism in which black people have their strongest psychological rapport and connection with Jesus, particularly being that they wield very little socioeconomic and political power. It is because of this truth that it is easy to understand why black people—black male and black female—are so enamored and infatuated with white people and what it means to be white in western culture and society. After all, according to ubiquitous images, wasn't Jesus himself white?

In retrospectively analyzing the purpose and cataclysmic results of the transatlantic slave trade, it has been determined historically that two types of enslavers came to the west coast of Africa: those who had guns and others who toted bibles (no doubt as their guns were sheathed). Additionally, those with guns came with the purposes of enslaving blacks under the belief that they were inferior, subhuman beings that were only good for serving their white superiors. Those with bibles came for the purposes of inculcating that despite the inferiority and subordinate status of the African, they are still however in favor of Jesus and because of this there is a place reserved for them in the pearly gates. Evidence of this trickery is seen in the present-day culturally-oriented colloquialisms of blacks, such as "you need Jesus." Again, only the slave mind as theorized by Malcolm X and the condition of posttraumatic slave syndrome would prompt such an outcry—connoting that a white man is the black sinners personal and direct salvation—rather than espousing something more culturally empowering and uplifting such as the need for collective freedom and ethnic and cultural liberation, i.e., "let's get free!"

Understand that I am not at all against any form or measure of spiritual or pious virtue, considering that I believe that that is the benefit of freedom of choice and preference in a society that claims to be the paradigm of bequeathing such entitlements. However, if black people as a whole are going to be Christians, then Christianity has to be put into proper perspective and viewed from a different lens and acted upon from an entirely different context and frame of mind; in other words, the TRUTH should be told. And if it is thus deemed as acceptable to have Jesus in one's heart (and life), it is equally important for black folk to live their lives fighting and clamoring for rights and entitlements that Jesus, himself, would have looked upon and embraced as obligatory and non-conditional. In other words, lifting your head to the sky and praying to a historical, biblical figure whose visage is shrouded in mysticism and complete ignorance is not going to liberate a people who immerse themselves in such doctrine and theology from the vantage point of subjugation and physical and mental bondage.

What is also of extreme value and importance is considering that during the times of chattel slavery, black males were labeled as rapist of white woman and suffered the worst of inhumane treatment and brutalization as a result. But a true sense and understanding of history clearly reveals that it was white men who raided slave quarters and raped and brutalized black females. Fast forward four hundred years and you still see crimes purported on television, on film, and in books of black males' supposed predatory inclinations towards white women, despite crime statistics and national victimization surveys that purport otherwise. Yet according to missjia, Oreo Experience, and thousands, perhaps millions, of black females who endorse, post profiles, and peruse interracial websites, pursue black female/white male relations, and write books about the benefits of interracial courtships, it is the benevolence and nobility of white men that should be pursued by today's enterprising black female. Is this not posttraumatic slave syndrome or evidence of the slave mind that is based on systematic conditioning, or is this just a few cases of innate, ingrown stupidity?

Is it not posttraumatic slave syndrome/slave mind that allows the black male, and black people as a whole, to continue to endorse products and view images that are either anti the true reality of black people or have nothing at all to do with the advancement of black people? If so, then it is obligatory to understand that Tyler Perry's films and his lackluster attempts to create images of black people and tell stories concerning the lives of black people are far from avant-garde or the result of some cinematic neo-ingenuity. To be honest, his films quite frankly range from mediocre to "why did I waste my money" to flat out terrible! However, it is because his works far succeed in reinforcing negative images of black males that have both past and present caused their brutalization on the basis of being subhuman, or have ostensibly added credence to the belief that they are innocuous buffoons that he is able to enjoy unprecedented wealth and recognition as a black filmmaker. This simple fact should lead to one simple conclusion: as black males strive to become men in a society that obstructs this endeavor, the message that should be sent loud and clear is that the Tyler Perry's of the world do not and should not speak for black males who have bigger goals and purposes to pursue; goals and purposes that are not skewed by a myopic lens or obscured by egregious racial stereotypes and/or black banality.

As I write this, the buffoonery and exploitation continues in Hollywood and, contradictorily, black folk—particularly black females— continue to flock to churches and movie theatres in droves. Yet outside of the realms of the surreal, the unemployment rate is gradually increasing, as is the incarceration rate that includes both the black male and black female, with the latter representing the fastest growing inmate population. These facts, without question, only further confirms and stigmatizes the criminalization of black people as a whole, particularly black males, who in a racist society are mostly seen as either criminals or clowns. Furthermore, the poverty rate is gradually increasing for black children, mostly because of the continued cultural and collective exposure to symptoms of posttraumatic slave syndrome, failure to completely put to rest the slave mentality, and rapid advances towards menticide; conditions that have kept the black male from crossing the threshold of being a boy to becoming a MAN.

Six

WHITE RACISTS, REVERSE RACISM, AND THE UNCLE TOM SYNDROME

"Every brother ain't a brother,
'cause of color just as well be undercover."[87]
—PUBLIC ENEMY, *WELCOME TO THE TERROR-DOME*

In a society such as American society, steeped in bloodshed, disparity, and social and moral corruption, there is an anything goes mentality that thrives on its inhabitants to both knowingly and unknowingly adhere to tenets that are based on degradation, hedonism, moral turpitude, and inequality. Basically, it is a "get in where you fit in" or get in where you THINK you fit in mentality that precipitates certain lifestyle standards and practices, which appear to be so ubiquitous in western society that it trumps or envelopes any moral code or standards that are tantamount to the proverbial principles of justice and equality for all of its citizens, irrespective of race, gender, class, or ethnicity. America is not just a racist country but is arguably the premiere bastion of racial hatred, unrest, and enmity throughout the world. If this is not true, then what other explanation would there be for the richest, most powerful nation on the planet to be most violent—boasting the highest murder and crime rate across all categories—as well as having the highest incarceration rate of any other industrialized nation?

White people who practice institutional racism/white supremacy know that this is the truth, evidenced not only by the obvious fact of institutional racism/white supremacy, but also by the way white people deal with black people and address blacks that are within close quarters to them. Despite the fact that black people as a whole for centuries have been the victims of the most abhorrent and horrendous crimes and mistreatment, it is white people that have an attitude that it is their black victims who are supposed to kowtow when they come into contact with them; or act in a certain manner, style, or fashion that is comfortable to white people in order for them to deem these blacks as safe or "okay." That's why when dealing with white people in a highly toxic and racist society it, arguably, takes a lifetime for them to like you as a black person or for you as a black person to get their approval. On the other hand, it only takes a minute for them to find fault with you or dislike you, even when they attempt to see past color, and particularly depending on the façade or the demeanor of the black individual.

I can recall as a graduate student, while in a human services course, a young white woman accused me of being a reverse racist when I made the claim that someone who comes from poverty and impoverishment is oft-times more likely to relate to those who come from similar backgrounds and circumstances. This was not surprising to me, particularly in terms of reverse psychology in regards to race. The reason as I see it is because it denotes the residual effects of a racist mentality and a white supremacist ideology that lingers hundreds of years after chattel slavery, despite white people's denial of being racist in a society where racism is still the most telling and salient factor.

In Dr. Jack David Eller's book *Cruel Creeds, Virtuous violence*, he points out how the brutal treatment that was the result of certain role playing in the Stanford Prison Experiments, conducted by Phillip Zambardo, was the result of certain behavioral patterns that were as much situational than they were the result of the individuals involved own, unique personalities.[38] Also, it is peoples' understanding of certain roles that impels them to act accordingly and in concert with those ascribed roles. Indeed, the problem with institutional racism/white supremacy in America is the seemingly collective failure to understand it as a cultural phenomenon that is deeply embedded in the psyche of white people. But erroneously, it is widely perceived as a social impediment that is mostly the result of the preferential actions of the few who choose to go against the grain and norms of societal expectations. As a result, bedding and befriending white people, joining them at the local bar after work or at get-togethers on super bowl Sunday, and attending company soiree's does not at all entail that the sons and daughters of former slave masters, slave owners, and plantation oversees, and who are the direct beneficiaries of the legacy of racial discrimination and oppression, view their contemporary black counterparts/victims as their equals. In fact, they do not!

However, there are some who will tolerate blacks depending on how these blacks strive to relate to white people and assiduously attempt to appease them. In other words, and as pointed out earlier, in order to get in with whites you have to be a black individual who exudes the spirit of Martin Luther King rather than the spirit of Malcolm X. This is especially true if you are a black person with a tendency to display any semblance of conscious values, particularly race-conscious values. Hence, you cannot come at white people as an African that is proud of your culture and heritage without outwardly or inwardly offending them, because in a racist society that is driven by a white supremacist mindset, not only does this illuminate the widely perceived repugnant differences between the two, but more telling, and in terms of a dominant and subordinate duality, it is also widely perceived as being anti-white.

Such analysis is not an attempt to imply that all white people are racist, perhaps there are many (or some) who may not be. However, the adage of not all white people are racist but all racist are white people has validity because it is commensurate with the conditions that continue to exist and affect black people as a direct result of institutional racist ideology, discriminatory practices, and systematic oppression. Ironically, in a society that is still extremely racist, white people, it appears, are more apt to be accepting of ethnic differences as well as demonstrations of pride in those differences than they are of being reminded of their past misdeeds and mistreatment of black people, whether this reminder is exhibited explicitly or implicitly—such as how a black person wears his or her hair and having to defend that right to do so. It is for this reason that the safe negro or the black individual that is welcomed in white people's circles is the one whose actions and mannerisms fall far from placing a mirror in front of white people and forcing them to see the error and evil of their ways—the practice of institutional racism/white supremacy both past and present—as well as forcing them to accept such ethnic and cultural differences.

Racism, Racists, and Reverse Psychology

In revisiting the example of the young white woman who accused me of reverse racism which, as previously implied, is nothing more than a psychological tactic, I would argue that the rationale behind such a course of action was because of what she perceived as my intractability to white compliance, as well as her attempt to displace guilt. Certainly, it is the psychological damage that ensues by the old concept of if you tell a lie enough times and with great frequency, then that lie will eventually be perceived as truth, regardless of actions that belie the claim or evidence that proves otherwise. Thus, to call me a racist, when in fact, I was a broke, black graduate student is to imply that I have control over something that is pivotal in affecting lives or people's well-being when obviously I do not; in fact, when it comes to the white/black dichotomy here in American society, no black person does. With that being said, it must also be understood that in a racist society where one dominant group is bent on controlling the other more subordinate groups (people of black and brown hue), psychological tactics and techniques are invariably employed to not only control the psyche of the masses, but also make it appear as if those who exact such courses of actions are unseen or neutral. This is a tactic by white people that is prevalent in today's so-called post-racist society; a ploy to make it appear as if the practitioners of racism and racist practices is a circumstantial or preferential act, similar to a child who has found his father's gun and now wields it to exert some semblance of authority. Or, some would go so far as to make the claim that the true racists in this society who seek to divide rather than unite is an assemblage of some unseen (well, with the exception of visible black and white entertainers) and clandestine yet omnipotent force that seeks to control everyone, regardless of race or ethnicity.

Today, this chimera is referred to as the "illuminati." And, despite the clear social disadvantages that affect black people as a whole, it is not an issue of race or ethnicity, undoubtedly another psychological tactic that works in the reverse just as well as it does in a linear fashion. Therefore, I would argue that in a racist society that pursues its racist endeavors more covertly, reverse psychology and reverse racism are in fact interchangeable concepts. How so? Well, as expounded on by the earlier example, as well as if you are a person of color that makes a claim of racism as the primary condition that underlines the circumstances of black people, such as the claim that I am making in this book, you can be accused of being a reverse racist.

Evidence of the reverse psychology model can be seen in cartoons that both we as adults watched and our children currently watch in regards to how the "yes you did" and "know I didn't" back and forth banter can be manipulated with the reverse "no you didn't" that is subsequently followed with a "yes I did" response. In the case of black people in America, what started out as "what you are doing to us is wrong" was subsequently followed with a "no it is not" to a "you are right—it WAS wrong,"—then followed with either—"it was wrong but you are forgiven"—or "what wrong are you referring to?" Thus black people's present-day rapport with whites is as follows: True, we were once your slaves but we are not slaves anymore; so all is well. Or, slavery is a reflection of the country's past and past misdeeds, so no one or any particular group should be held accountable. Or, sure, slavery might have existed at some point in time, but I, myself, have never been a slave so the topic is completely irrelevant.

As illustrated in the previous chapter, it is the practice of black people trying to permeate and sync their existence to that of the dominant culture that renders the problems of race idle and unsolved. Certainly, white people are not going to initiate solving the problems of racism or white supremacy; they both invented and practice it! More telling is that at the same time they practice it they claim that it does not exist, and would rather call the black person that has the audacity to speak along the lines of race a rabble-rouser or reverse-racist, rather than take accountability of the conditions that centuries of institution racism and oppression have caused for black people. Consequently, an important question to be asked is that even in an increasingly worsening racist and hostile society, does the blame fall solely on white people; or, can white people in fact be blamed at all for being racist? If not, then who is to blame?

The factors that are associated with institutional racism/white supremacy connote more than just an issue of powerlessness and impotence of the black male, and black people as a whole, to address these issues or ward off these impediments that are designed to suppress the black male's advancement and bamboozle black people in general as to who the real culprits are of institutional racism. In other words, it is this passivity and disinclination that has compelled the black male to offer forgiveness for horrors and mistreatment that white people reluctantly acknowledge that they've ever committed, let alone have ever asked forgiveness for committing. For this reason, it is my claim that the black male continues to be emasculated and marginalized in this society; moreover, the black female thus feels inclined to look for strength and protection in men from other ethnic groups due what she perceives as characteristics that are missing in the black male. It is under the banner of institutional racism/white supremacy that the failure to address the marginalization, socioeconomic weakening, and the collective disjunction between the black male and black female is symptomatic of what I call the *Uncle Tom Syndrome.*

White Man's Nigger:
deconstructing the myth of the Uncle Tom

Obviously, the term Uncle Tom is nothing new to mainstream America and the literate among us. In fact, it has strong historical implications. History purports an Uncle Tom, made famous by Harriet Beecher Stowe's 1852 novel *Uncle Tom's Cabin,* as a person who conducts him (or herself) in a docile, passive, and non-threatening manner to white people. Moreover, these individuals act in manners that denote the impugning or eschewing of their own ethnic group and conduct themselves as if they are more enamored by the standards that are dictated by those who are representative of the dominant culture. Now, keep in mind, this is not to imply that every black individual—male or female—possesses these traits and characteristics. In fact, there are plenty of black folk who are outraged by their situation as well as those of other blacks, and take up actions (even arms) to redress the problems that black people as a whole have historically and continue to face. However, as I pointed out earlier, history is not simply a study of facts from the past; in fact, history is more recursive than it is outdated. Furthermore, a dated term that is seldom used does not and should not automatically exclude or dismiss practices and actions that are just as relevant today as they were in the past. Regardless of what it is that people believe they are entitled to, the fact of the matter is that under a system of institutional racism/ white supremacy, interracial marriages and courtships, black folk being republicans (or supporting any laws or legislative policies that are not conducive to black causes), black folk arguing against or denying the practices of subjugation and oppression towards blacks and people of color as a whole, and white-identified blacks—talking and acting white and embracing white mores and values (and yes, there is such a thing as talking white)—are all symptoms of what I call the *Uncle Tom Syndrome*, and I will be more than happy to explain how and why.

When I think of a modern day Uncle Tom, there are many names that come to mind, some of whom I will address in this chapter, as well as the actions of many that confirm my theory and the historical definition of an Uncle Tom. An example of such actions, however, would be those who are quick to absolve white people of being racist—when they in fact are. Meanwhile, the prospect of proving a case of racism that is perpetrated against black people is an indefatigable task in a society that scoffs at the mere implications of actions motivated by race that are made by black people. In some black circles, common knowledge presupposes that any white person that has to mount a defense of not being a racist for any reason must in fact be a racist. Nevertheless, before I go any further with making a claim of the Uncle Tom syndrome at the expense of the misinformed, foolish, neurotic, or just outright "touched," I would like to delve a little more into the history of the Uncle Tom and how it relates to black people as a whole today.

———

In today's society, there are blacks who will refer to another black individual as an Uncle Tom for reasons that are obvious and some that are a bit asinine. In other words, based on how the term can be used, and at any point or time it can be used, an Uncle Tom arguably has no clear or definitive meaning. Rather, the appellation is more fluid, meaning that individuals may label someone as such based on how they perceive the term, and how it applies to the individual or situation in question. For instance, in the early 1990s film *Waiting to Exhale*, the character played by black actress Angela Basset referred to her husband as an "ass-kissing

Uncle Tom" after the revelation of his longstanding affair with his white secretary. Thus, the implication being that he was not just a cheater, but an Uncle Tom at that, especially being that his scandalous affair was with a white person. Similarly, a black male or black female who work for a company or organization might feel that their black superior's interests that sway more along the lines of corporate or structural interests rather than those of the employees, particularly the black employees, might label the superior an Uncle Tom.

My point is that similar to the discrepancies elicited in the definitive definition of an Uncle Tom during and following the success of Beecher Stowe's novel, the same inconsistencies hold true to this day. In terms of its historical relevance, the actual character of Uncle Tom in Beecher Stowe's novel was inspired by the life of a man named Josiah Henson, who was anything but a pacifist or sycophant in terms of his relations to his white superiors. In fact, it was Beecher Stowe's novel that transposed Henson's real life exploits of arduously fighting for and preserving his freedom to that of a character of servility and Christian non-resistance, of which the novel was criticized. However, to this day, and despite the inconsistencies, Uncle Tom is the moniker bequeathed on any black individual who exudes an attitude of passive resistance to white people, the status quo, or the social order of the times. Moreover, an Uncle Tom is someone who immerses himself in white standards and basks in the cesspool of actions and mores that are commensurate to whites and the realities of white people as it pertains to their maintenance of the social order.

Historical Analysis

*"No matter how much power or
how much money you make, you're always going
to be a 'nigger' in their eyes."*
—SNOOP DOG

To further my claim, or at least put the Uncle Tom theory into a more historical context; basically, an Uncle Tom is a black individual who does not necessarily hate the ethnic group that he (or she) is ascribed, but instead has been forcibly resigned to the idea of white superiority, and thereby acts as a proxy to further propel that notion. Historically speaking, during the times of slavery, most plantations were overrun by an overseer who enlisted the aid of a slave or plantation foreman, whose job was to act as a sort of man at arms as a means to enforce compliance and efficiency in regards to work among the slaves. In other words, the job of the foreman was to keep the Negroes in line. So when I speak of the recursive nature of history, it should not be overlooked that the myth of the Uncle Tom, both past and present, and perhaps a tad misunderstood, is not and should not be completely shrouded in mystery.

Historically, a black slave considered or perceived as an Uncle Tom was not just a pacifist or your average yes-man for the master, but was a slave who had been the most effective in earning the master's trust and was more emotionally connected to his master than say the average slave. Similarly, in breaking down the historical distinction between the field-hand slaves as opposed to the plantation domestics (i.e., field negro and house negro), we can base that distinction by way of the amiable and emotional ties to the master and his family that the house domestics had, as well as the privileges that they in turn received based on those ties; whereas, the field hands were devoid of this connection as well as the privileges that came with it. Cooks, butlers, mammies, housemaids, and coachmen were the plantation domestics that not only worked in the big house but who also had close personal and, in some cases, blood ties to the master and received all of the perks and benefits that such ties entailed. These slaves acted in a certain manner that appeased the master, particularly being that they were better spoken due to access to books, as some house slaves were allowed to read. Needless to say, this benefit was denied the field hand. And as a result of this denial, it was the field slave that was more inclined to rebel, run away, and either lead or participate in slave insurrections, many accounts made famous by the exploits of Nat Turner, Gabriel Prosser, and Denmark Vessey, just to name a few. On the other hand, the slave who resided in the big house spoke, acted, conciliated, and connected in a manner designed to convey to the master complete servility, loyalty, and obsequiousness.

When analyzing the relevance, as well as prevalence, of the Uncle Tom presently, and not just how the term relates to the past, we see evidence of many of these actions and mannerisms that are displayed today by many black people—male and female—in the hopes to curry favor and disarm their white superiors. It is well known within the realms of black existence in America that black people speak in a different manner to white people than they do to other blacks. In other words, talking white, in which I will delve more into shortly, is not a myth or slander but a survival mechanism. Or, similar to the endeavors of the house domestic, a learned pattern of behavior designed to gain additional privileges as well as secure favor and trust from the master and his family. Furthermore, mammies—who epitomized the emotional and personable connection to white people to the apex—confided in the master's wife or mistress in her time of loneliness and isolation, and allowed her breast to be suckled by the progeny of the master and mistress.

The writing of this practice is unquestionably on the wall if one reads between the lines and seeks to understand it. For instance, in contemporary Hollywood, more than likely it is the black female who is oft-portrayed as the confidant of the white female, consummating her availability to the emotional needs and empathetic longings of the white female counterpart. However, the sacrifice or cost is that while accommodating the needs of the white woman, the personal existence as well as the needs of the black female is completely irrelevant, unless she is being portrayed in a coitus relationship with a white man. I cannot emphasize enough the circular nature of history, as well as the validity of the common adage of those who do not know their history being bound to repeat it. In a racist society that is driven by the ideology of white supremacy, it is the needs, feelings, and emotions of white people are what matters and are all that counts. Thus, it is the lack of either historical perspective or complete dismissal of its relevance that support for white supremacy—its ideologies, dictates, and practices—as well as stories and images that underscore the days of overt and untenable conquest for white people, not only is culturally appealing and pleasing but also highly profitable in mainstream society.

Take for example Hollywood films such as *The Help*—a cultural revisiting of pure and pristine white womanhood and white women's relationship to the prototypical black *Aunt Jemimah*. Now, regardless of the so-called historic value that many, including those who deemed the film Oscar worthy, credit the *Help* for providing, the film nonetheless is typical in its depiction of black females not only availing themselves to the issues that affect white womanhood but also emphasizing a clear distinction between the life of a black female as opposed to that of her white female counterpart; thus, confirming the postulated superiority, class, and beauty of the white woman to that of the base, servile, and prosaic qualities and existence of the black female.

The significance of the historical context of the Uncle Tom theory or appellation, even to a point that it outweighs its relevance today, is that its historical value is analogous to the basis in which the term was created. It has to be equally understood that the concept of slavery, in which the term Uncle Tom is simply a byproduct, was crafted by way of the racist and white supremacist mindset of the European male (even though it was a white woman who wrote the novel). Consequently, it is this condition that not only created the very existence of the Uncle Tom but is also the primary cause in which the Uncle Tom's actions are predicated. So, when meticulously analyzing the etiology as well as etymology of the Uncle Tom, I would say that the answer is more contingent upon what the person who might potentially be labeled as an Uncle Tom does, rather than crafting some profile of who deserves the label based on personality and character traits. It should be kept in mind however that the historical analysis of the character in Beecher Stowe's novel is not always consistent with the varying nature of the term, particularly in terms of how it applies today.

Khalil Baaqi

In Harriet Beecher Stowe's novel, Uncle Tom actually forfeited his own life to preserve the sanctity and well-being of three slaves who had succeeded in absconding from their captivity. In today's times, I doubt if a black individual is given such an appellation based on a decision to take a moral stance even when facing the prospect of death for the benefit and well-being of other black folk. In fact, that person would more than likely be labeled as a martyr or crusader for the cause of justice as opposed to injustice, particularly in terms of how it applies to black people and circumstances based on institutional racism/white supremacy. Therefore, those who stood on the frontlines for the cause of justice and equality for the oppressed and downtrodden, many of whom even forfeited their lives, would obviously not qualify for the label of an Uncle Tom, at least not without some excessive penalty towards the person with the gall to assign such a label. Nevertheless, I would say the term is as appropriate and relevant today as it has been at any other time in history based on the actions of not just a few, but many, particularly during this present time where the gradual dissipating and lessening of black male masculinity is manifesting to resounding proportions. In other words, an Uncle Tom can manifest certain behaviors in a myriad of ways. However, in the final analysis, those actions are geared towards the regression of the black male, and black people as a whole. Additionally, those actions are seemingly driven by contempt for being black in a racist society that both explicitly and implicitly postulates white dominance, virtue, and superiority; thus, resulting in a steadfast eschewing of black ethnicity and identity; and aiding and abetting in calling attention to the actions and behaviors, good or bad, of those who classify as non-white. No doubt, it was this same mentality that allowed the house slaves, despite that they too were in bondage, to believe that they were of better stock than their field counterparts. Also, it is this mentality that served as impetus for slaves to act as whistle blowers at the slightest hint of impending slave rebellions.

History does in fact repeat itself, and times have not really changed all that much, and so called dated terms and actions are just as pivotal now as they were in the past. As stated by Alice Walker, the author of the book *The Color Purple*, which was later made into a critically acclaimed major motion picture, "slavery is still very strong in terms of its effects." It should not be a coincidence that there are those blacks who continue to manifest certain behaviors that seem to be in concert and adherence to a principle that the lighter ones skin the more dominant and superior that person is. Furthermore, the lighter one's skin the more legitimate and irrefutable that person's credibility. It is because of the recurring nature of history that this society seems to breed individuals who explicitly, implicitly, consciously, or subconsciously adhere to the tenets of white supremacist ideology. And despite the many accomplishments of many of these persons, the issue of race seems to be the primary factor that is inescapable. For example, it is the conditioning of white superiority and black inferiority that would compel Tiger Woods, despite his incomparable talents, to concoct an unprecedented racial classification designed to draw attention away from the fact that he is considered to be a black person, particularly in a society that immerses itself in color-consciousness. Equally as critical is that despite the prominent factor of race, behavior patterns that constitute as survival mechanisms are often taught. As a result, it was not surprising when Tiger Wood's father, Earl Woods, when asked on the Oprah Winfrey show what race he considered his son to be a part of—his reply, "the human race."

Tragically, this is the result of the conditioning of those who are considered as functional inferiors in a racist society. Moreover, it is a society that approves of this conditioning, hence displays of self-hatred that would prompt a roar of applause of its approval as demonstrated by Oprah Winfrey and her studio audience. And while both the crafty and the foolish continue to applaud in unison, the wheels of racism, hatred, and indignity continue to spin, as Tiger Wood's recent exploits that consisted of scandal and marital infidelity served as a reminder of how truly black he really is, not to mention the fact that racist ideology decrees an entirely different dynamic than just being human. In other words, his lascivious and licentious predilections and fetishes for white women consigned him to that of age-old stereotypes of black males and how they both perceive and covet white women in this society. More telling is that Earl Woods, similar to many who lived by his code of ethics in life, went to his grave not as a man but as a coward, deemed as such because despite what contributions his talented progeny would make to the world of sports, his failure to teach him to love himself and his own first was highly indicative of the path and trajectory that would result in scandal that brought his son more shame and scrutiny than acclaim and adulation; moreover, they were the actions of two individuals—father and son—who possess the slave mind, and are afflicted with the Uncle Tom syndrome.

Hollywood Patsies

There's a sucker born every minute!
—KHALIL BAAQI

Earlier, I mentioned the film *The Help*, and when considering referencing it I asked myself, why would such a film garner the critical acclaim that it received and gross over 200 million dollars at the box office, particularly considering that we as a society are several years deep into the new millennium? Just look at the recent box office success of the Quentin Tarantino film *Django Unchained.* I mean, wouldn't a post-racist society imply that we have laid to rest such past indiscretions and put behind us such cultural differences? My answer is that white people in a racist society continue to take to images and portrayals of black people as coons, slaves, maids, buffoons, and sambos like fish to water. So, no! Those past indiscretions and differences are far from behind us. On the contrary, I would argue that such revisiting—via film—reminds racist whites and those who practice institutional racism/white supremacy of the glory days when it was culturally pleasing and an irrefutable symbol of white superiority and dominance when blacks were forcefully and overtly relegated to serve whites. And to do so not as corporate or socioeconomic equals, such as how some blacks are presently threatening the status quo, but rather as domestics, maids, and willing and docile servants and subordinates.

This only confirms the relevance of historical factors and how it applies to the state of race-relations today. For instance, the transgendered ideations of Tyler Perry that are perpetually delineated across the silver screen have profound significance in a racist society that relishes in Uncle Tomism, black male femininity, and buffoonery. And the more willingness from a black entertainer to engross in such personal and cultural debauchery, the more visible that person becomes and the higher that person's celebrity status is raised. Similarly, there is a strong desire for the dominant culture to establish a trend that enhances the status and images of certain black entertainers, imbuing them with invaluable qualities and putting them at the apex of social pedestals. However, the paradox is that many of these individuals' lives behind the curtain or screen are starkly different and completely antithetical to the values that white people embrace and deem as hallmarks of Judeo-Christian virtues, in which whites also claim that this country is inherently based. In both analyzing and assessing the facts, the truth is that Hollywood and the entertainment industry is saturated with black individuals who arguably fit the Uncle Tom profile; let's examine two in particular.

———

Oprah Winfrey and Tyler Perry who, ironically, are good friends and business associates, are also perhaps the two most powerful black players in mainstream media and popular culture, as well as two of the highest paid. Yet in an overwhelmingly dual liberal and conservative society, the apex or epitome of the American success story is comprised of the husband, wife, the kids, the dog, and the house with the white picket fence in a suburban cesspool that is mostly colored white. On the other hand, institutional racism/white supremacy dictates that the embodiment of black success stems from social and personal dysfunction that blacks in general are categorically associated with, although there are those few who have been able to overcome such stigmas and crises, as evidenced by the success of Winfrey and Perry. Thus, a primary factor for the admiration for such individuals is that they were able to overcome the odds and achieve success despite the tumult of hardships and challenges that would have normally obstructed their path to the top of mainstream success and social deference and acceptance. However, it cannot be overlooked that many of these individuals' lives are in stark contrast to those that lie at the root of red-blooded Americanism, as some of the most successful and celebrated blacks are those who are openly gay or lesbian (e.g., Lee Daniels), whose sexual orientation is either questioned or inconspicuously speculated (e.g., Winfrey, Perry, Just to name a few), whose actions are conspicuously geared towards the complete shunning or denigrating of black values and standards, and who fill in all of the blanks of what a modern day Uncle Tom would look like and whose profiles are commensurate to its legend. I'll explain.

Consider for instance that in the United States a female—irrespective of color or ethnicity—is assaulted every fifteen seconds by a male partner. But in 2009, following the assault of pop singer Rhianna at the hands of her then R&B singer boyfriend Chris Brown, a panel was put together on a special episode of the Oprah Winfrey show that was spearheaded by both Oprah Winfrey and Tyler Perry, adding more sensationalism to the assault and, consequently, making the nineteen year old Brown (that was his age at the time) the poster-child for domestic violence in this county. Certainly, statistics and national crime victim surveys purport domestic violence as a major problem as far as criminal justice in America; however, in the case of Chris Brown, domestic violence was not the primary issue, even though it was deceptively masked as such. Plainly speaking, the issue of race superseded that of domestic violence. Or, depending on how one looks at it, the two components were juxtaposed but only insofar as race, as well as celebrity status combined with race being the more prominent factor.

The British have a saying that negative press and publicity makes for good breakfast. And despite the frequency of domestic assaults in this society—illumined by the fact that around the same time it was reported that a white, highly respected and renowned physician in the northeastern region, battered his wife to within an inch of her life—a young black male of celebrity status acting in a criminal fashion that is commonly associated with black males, whether celebrity or not, becomes the breakfast of champions, so to speak. This is especially true in a society that sensationalizes actions based on ethnic and cultural differences. Yet, incredulously, it took two of the most financially powerful blacks in the industry to draw more attention to this incident, transmuting the notion of *black-on-black crime* to *white-on-black collaborative justice* at the expense of a young black male.

Black President

It's not black America, it's not white
America, it's not red America, it's not yellow America,
but the United States of America
—Barack Obama

In the event that I have been unclear, long-winded, or just flat out wrong on my assessment of the myth of the Uncle Tom, and its relevance to today's dilemma of race and race-relations; I will clarify. My answer is that perhaps I don't know any more than those of you who may be confused. However, what I will attempt to do is draw attention to certain people whose reputations and actions are highly questionable in terms of their commitment, or lack thereof, to aiding in improving the conditions of people that look like them and are inundated by the same deplorable circumstances and conditions. Also, I will attempt to call attention to those persons who demonstrate an apparent apathy and disservice in regards to nullifying the images and misconceptions of black people as a whole in America, being a disjointed collective group of people who wallow in the streams of ignorance, self-loathing, buffoonery, and who put the standards and values of the dominant culture first rather than seeking to preserve their own culture, values, as well as their own collective survival.

I will again argue the validity of the notion of self-preservation being the first law of nature of human beings, as certainly this is the case of all of life's living species that comprise of both humans and animals. So, when there seems to be a growing trend of simply being an American, as opposed to being a black person in America, particularly the endangered black male; and when considering that black is simply seen as, again, *incidental*, by way of the genetic and biological distribution pool, I would argue that the folks who are black and in the public eye and who act as if blackness is purely circumstantial, are the people that concerned victims of institutional racism/white supremacy should either thoroughly scrutinize or collectively disavow themselves from whatever business that has made these individuals the successes that they have become. Particularly if this careful examination leads to the inevitable fact that these manufactured black successes are clearly not on the same page as black folk who seek justice, equality, and complete liberation from institutional racism/white supremacy.

If compelled to ask what does this all mean, and what course of action should subsequently follow? The answer is simple. I have an issue with what I know about Oprah Winfrey, and since what I only know of her is based on what SHE ALLOWS the media to divulge, or what she chooses to reveal, I don't watch her shows, buy books that she recommends, patronize films or plays that she has either produced or aided in financing, or support anything else that she engages in. Similarly, I do not watch Tyler Perry films (well, I have seen a few for research purposes, and have read reviews, compelling me to give my assessment of his work in an earlier chapter), nor do I watch black reality television shows (or any reality television for that matter), or watch movies that invariably depict black actors as secondary or *homunculi* to and for white actors. Additionally, I did not vote for Barack Obama for his campaign for a second term as president. Now, before I am labeled as what it is that I am trying to dissect and analyze, as it relates to the black male and black people in a racist society, it must be said that I certainly did not vote for Mitt Romney either. In fact, I did not vote at all. But with that being said, I understand how even that course of action, or lack thereof, might have Uncle Tom connotations.

Nonetheless, days after the inauguration of Barack Obama's second term as the forty-fourth president of the United States, I called that day not only a historical moment for the country overall, but a day of inconspicuous *coon-fusion* for black people. To put it mildly, I found that particular day to be more tragic than historic. Tragic because I found both perplexing and problematic the fervor, dancing, singing, partying, celebrating, and disproportionate public adoration for a president who, although is black, has not at all explicitly or implicitly demonstrated a desire to change the conditions of black people—particularly the black male—in a country that is extremely racist and oppressive; a condition that he has only subtly addressed. In fact, since he has been in office, Obama has spoken more on a kinship basis and optimistically to whites (remember, he was raised in a white household and by his white grandmother). On the other hand, he has demonstrated a propensity to speaking very harshly and admonishingly to blacks, particularly black males, and what he perceives as a collective failure on a disproportionate level of being adequate fathers and providers for their children (remember, his father played a minute if not completely absent role in his upbringing). This claim only adds credibility to the criticism that Jesse Jackson Sr. made about Obama prior to his first-term election, a criticism in which he was harshly condemned by both blacks and whites. Thus, when I say a day of *coon-fusion*, I am describing what I see as a day of indiscriminate deception, made possible by massive neurosis that is fueled by a fervor that is similar to black church-goers collectively and simultaneous catching the Holy Ghost or Holy Spirit.

Coons, Toms, & Nefarious Politics

Historically speaking, a coon is obviously a pejorative word that has been attributed to black people and black people only, deriving from

133

the baracoons or cages that black people were housed and held captive during the slave trades. Furthermore, and for clarity, it has been hypothesized that many blacks while being held in baracoons were unaware of their condition or what was inevitably in store for them, and the only thing that was left to cling to was an array of hope that something good would eventually come to what was palpably a bad situation. But before I go any further, it has to be understood that the actions of black people—both male and female—are in stark contrast to the actions of those who represent the dominant culture.

White people in America are the practitioners of institutional racism/white supremacy—hence are the purveyors of suffering that accompanies the bifurcation of race and ethnicity. Recently, in a conversation that I had with a former boss, mentor, and educator, he made clear the fact that the black male, and black people as a whole, because of the centuries of racism and oppression that has been endured, identify with suffering; particularly with those of black hue whose suffering only ignited the flames of their desires and exhorted their endeavors to acquire success, such as the Oprah Winfrey's and Tyler Perry's of Black America. This is perhaps the bond that both Oprah Winfrey and Tyler Perry share among each other, as both have revealed their paralleled backgrounds being marred with emotional, sexual, physical abuse, and neglect. And as white people have propelled the status of successful blacks such as Winfrey and Perry, based on the premise that the suffering that they both endured and were able to overcome is a human condition that all should respect and admire, the deference and support shown and displayed by blacks based on such accomplishments are maximized tenfold. Why?

My answer is because the exodus of the black male and black female in American society—which is mired in trials and tribulations—compels most blacks to believe that they own lock, stock, and barrel the exclusive rights and patent to suffering. And, as it is so often the case that deep-seated and deeply-rooted emotions often shrouds rational thought, the fact that black victims are so privy and perspicacious to suffering has consequently rendered an inability to truly see the motives and intent of those whose suffering has only driven them towards self-serving, unilateral gains and ulterior motives. The trick, however, is that this is often accomplished under the guise of humanitarianism and, sometimes, even ethnocentricity and a veneer of favoring strong cultural ties (e.g., Tyler Perry).

More telling is the failure to effectively identify and surmise the motives of those who truly carry power, and who make all the decisions that have a profound effect on the political, economic, and the social framework that sets the tone for the conditions in this society—hence ascribing certain individuals and certain collective groups to certain roles and expectations. As I speak on president Barack Obama, before labeling him anything or offering my opinion of him as an individual or assess his performance in the oval office thus far, it needs to be shared that the argument that has often been made on his behalf is that the majority of blacks, particularly those who voted for him, truly believe that in addition to him being black, his heart is also in the right place. This is especially true in terms of his widely perceived (and deluded) desire to improve the condition of all of America's citizens and not just black people. Therefore, what is essentially taking place when such arguments are made is the grudging acceptance of a power imbalance that ultimately leaves all victims of institutional racism/white supremacy powerless and wanton; even in the case of the first black president, if it is indeed true that his hands are tied, and as a result he can only do so much.

Consequently, it is this same grudging resignation of white supremacy and absolute power that is wielded as a result that I write this to illustrate how black victims of institutional racism/white supremacy in America, function as inferiors because of a collective and excessive acquiescence of their inferior status. Furthermore, the socioeconomic and political maneuverability, as well as the collective and individual upward mobility of blacks is contingent upon whether the powers that be deem it appropriate in terms of time, and whether it is necessary in regards to how it benefits the country as a whole, and not just the advancement of black people. For these reasons, it is white people who decide what type of relationships that they have with blacks if they have a relationship with blacks at all, just as it is more than likely white people who determine whether or not blacks will have jobs or are worthy of having suitable professional careers. And, it is white people who determine for black people other blacks who are worthy of culturally-collective praise and adoration, and whether they are a credit to not only the ubiquitous belief of unimpeded success of any individual—regardless of race, color, or creed—but also a credit to their own ethnic group.

The point that I am making is that black people act in a manner that is in strict accordance with white people's approval. Therefore, "talking white" and embracing white standards are stark realities that is in both the conscious and subconscious psyche of black people, whether they admit to it or not. Yet, paradoxically, speaking broken English or in an inefficient manner that is associated with being "ghetto" is also a stark reality and just as omnipresent in the black community. While on the other hand, talking white is widely regarded as an egregious conscription that is fallaciously consigned to blacks who are intelligent, and the coinciding articulate expression should be viewed as a badge of accomplishment rather than deemed as an attempt to distance oneself from their black identity. However, given the anecdote that was illustrated in an earlier chapter regarding the black female acquaintance, who made the assertion that the most efficient way, as she saw it, for black people to fit in with white people—corporately or socially—was to be more like them; in other words, talk and act like them.

In a society that is bifurcated by race and ethnicity, it is should be of little surprise that those who represent the dominant culture determine whether or not they want to deal with blacks and, if so, dictate the nature of the relationship with them. In other words, if white people choose to deal with black people—whether the basis of that relationship is professional or otherwise—this union is largely based on how that black person relates to white people, and not the other way around. Accordingly, white people who choose to deal with black people do so by way of their associations with what I call the *safe black* or the *pseudo-self-black*. The safe black obviously being the black person that speaks and acts in a manner that lowers white people's defenses, and who is antithetical to the rampant negative images of blacks that far too many white people are exposed to, as well as the black person who embraces Judeo-Christian values and who is complicit with the status quo. Furthermore, whites will deal with this safe black individual because he or she compels them to say (among themselves of course) "he's alright for a black guy" or "she's cute for a black chic," or "I don't see color" when it involves Jerome or Ayesha (especially considering the fact that color or whether one is black is either never omitted from even a complimentary statement or is painstakingly diminished in a racist society).

Similarly, the *pseudo-self-black* implies white people's own willful embrace of the safe black; although correspondingly revealing the deceptive nature and intent behind this course of action, considering that white people are very much aware of both the cultural differences as well as their social standing in relation to blacks. What I am saying is that white people are comfortable when they encounter blacks who speak, think, act, and embrace the same values and cultural norms as themselves; however, at the same time are very much aware of the biological and inherent cultural differences that exist between the two. It is because of this claim that I will further make the argument that white people will never fully embrace black people by way of eschewing the stark and apparent distinctions that are insoluble and unavoidable in a society that is strictly based on ethnic and cultural differences, as Malcolm X made clear in his autobiography, "white people will be with you through thin but never through thick."[39]

One of the impetuses of Barack Obama's ascent to the presidency is because of his being widely perceived as a black man that is agreeable to both white and black America. In other words, he is a *safe black*, mostly made agreeable by his ostensible disposition and stance of eschewing and making null and void the disproportionate population of impoverished, albeit unemployed and underemployed blacks, while steadfastly aligning himself with the middle-class, a designation that epitomizes white America. The fact that he has a white mother and was mostly raised by his white grandmother didn't hurt his case either. Incredulously, in a society that reigns supreme in its indiscriminate mistreatment of people on the basis of race, class, ethnicity, and even gender, the black male has historically and continues to receive the most deplorable and abhorrent racial treatment because the black male has been perceived and described as being the biggest threat to the white middle class.

Yet it is the middle-class whom Obama has sworn his duty and dedication to reach before he has exhausted his tenure as leader of the "free" world. Inexplicably, however, it was black males along with many others who danced in the streets and publicly espoused their support for a president, who although looks like them, has both (subtly) explicitly and demonstratively made clear their insignificance. As a result, there are many, such as Michelle Alexander, author of the book *The New Jim Crow: Mass incarceration in the age of Color-blindness,* who have asserted that Obama's presidency was a smoke screen to hide the true motives of extreme racism and genocidal practices that are particularly directed towards black males. This sort of resistance to the advancement of black causes and disavowal of allegiance to black people as a whole is both loved and respected in a racist society, particularly when considering that white people made certain what type of black male they were putting in office before this historical feat ever took place. Hence, the situation with Rev. Jeremiah Wright has great significance when assessing the true motives and intent behind Obama's rise as president.

As stated earlier, it is safe blacks such as the president who are rewarded for certain resistances. Thus, it is no coincidence that Booker T. Washington, a man who although dedicated his life to the assuredness of the advancement of black people in the fields of education and vocational training, did so by taking the path of least resistance—purposefully lobbying and working towards the advancement of blacks while at the same time trying not to anger or ruffle the feathers of whites. For this passive approach, Washington was the recipient of a myriad of awards and achievements that were unprecedented in regards to black achievement, such as being the first to have his image on a postage stamp. In addition, he was the first black male who was invited to the white house, as well as the first black to have a cruise vessel named in his honor. Furthermore, Jackie Robinson, because of his pro-war façade and mannerisms (even though he was not deployed to duty as a soldier because of a racial incident) and denouncement of a young Cassius Clay due to his position as a conscientious objector of the Vietnam war, was the beneficiary of numerous first for blacks, the most significant being the first black baseball player recruited to be in the major leagues (though, technically, Moses Fleetwood Walker was actually the first black player who was accepted into the majors back in 1884).

The battle cry of a Warrior and the tears of a Clown

"Losing a fight ain't near as bad as hiding from one!"
—EMANUEL STEWARD

The list could go on and on. The point however is that it is no coincidence that many of today's contemporary and most high-profile blacks, particularly black celebrities, are either gay or lesbian—"out of the closet" or *closeted*—have limited educational backgrounds despite their colossal success, and have little or no ties at all to the black community, confirming the notion that if blacks are going to be visible in a racist society then they are carefully hand-picked for the purposes of assuring that they are not the types who will challenge and subsequently change the status quo; primarily, because many lack the chutzpah and background to do so. And regardless of whether they are celebrity or non-celebrity, many blacks are rewarded based purely on their ostentatious predilections of absolute compliance to the program that confirms white values and cultural dominance as the only ones that count and that are worthy of deference and devotion. For every Michael Eric Dyson and Cornell West, popular culture and mainstream society are saturated with clowns and buffoons who can barely put sentences together when attempting to speak on REAL issues that matter to REAL people. Yet these are the people who are given substantial airtime, and are on most major networks. It is perhaps with this assessment that the wheels of posttraumatic slave syndrome take full spin. Hence, the self-hatred that is invariably accompanied by self-destructive behaviors is the result of the incessant bombardment of the implicit treatment of black people, particularly the black male, as an inferior, subhuman species. This fact alone is arguably the catalyst that would compel young urban males to demean not only themselves but also the females whom they are biologically connected for the purpose of procuring profit, wealth, and prestige, such as what is often perceived as the primary condition of Hip hop music/culture.

Another key question would be, if it is not the conditions of race and institutional racism/white supremacy, then what other motivation or reason would suffice a genre and cult-following of young musicians and artists to demean black females? Contradictorily, the façade and demeanor that nearly all of the young males in Hip Hop music display is that of ultra-masculine and virile young warriors. Even early historical and primordial cultures firmly understood that that there is a warrior spirit in all young boys; however, this can only be true if those innate qualities are properly fine-tuned. The problem, then, is that the conditioning of mass inferiority in a racist society has obstructed any efforts at fine-tuning young black boys to becoming young black warriors. And not just warriors for self-serving and self-aggrandizing purposes, but warriors for causes that are pertinent to the uplifting, preservation, and survival of their ethnic group and culture. Thus, in revisiting the myth of the Uncle Tom, and in attempting to analyze its relevance to contemporary crises that are pertinent to the black male and his suffering as a result of institutional racism/white supremacy, it is important to understand that the more general definition of an Uncle Tom is that of one who acts in manners that are in accord to the misconceptions and preconceived notions and the treatment that follows as a result to those who are members of his own race and/or ethnic classification. Furthermore, it is the debunking of their own ethnic identity and, conversely, the clamoring for collective identification with those whom are perceived as the superior caste, regardless of whether this is done consciously or unconsciously (as many can be accused of committing the latter).

In other words, what should be clear as far as a proper assessment of the myth is that it is an individual or collective response to institutional racism/white supremacy. Or, it is both an individual and collective failure, in which certain actions should simply be attributed to certain individuals. However, when considering present conditions, such actions (or failures to act) are relegated to the entire ethnic group of victims of institutional racism/white supremacy, due to a failure to decode and properly eradicate this age-old and unchanging social injustice. Indeed, certain behaviors can be called into question, as they have been in this chapter to emphasize the point of how this myth applies to the impasse of the advancement of the black male and black people as a whole. However, I would essentially skew the evidence that precedes my own hypothesis if I ascertained that the existence of the modern day Uncle Tom is relegated to the actions of only a certain few individuals.

So, for instance, when I point out president Obama's perceived justification to hold black males exclusively liable for the failure to raise their children and be present in the homes that these children are being reared, I believe that it is equally justifiable for black males to hold Obama liable for his propensity to downplay the societal ills and iniquities (I.e., racism and racial discrimination) that obstruct black males' abilities to be providers and be present in their children's lives. But perhaps the bigger picture, however, is the failure for many black males to catch on to and properly question this behavior, and because of this failure the alternative is for them is to celebrate, applaud, and admire an individual solely on the strength that he is black and not by way of his deeds. Therefore, due to the reasons as just described, who is it then that really falls under the banner of the Uncle Tom mystique?

What we do...

In filmmaker Byron Hurt's documentary *I am a Man: Black Masculinity in America,* a question that I found interesting was posed as to why black males hold their penises when they speak or while engaging in conversation. Not being aware that black males do this, or have in the past done this, I would instead make the claim that in a racist society it is the Uncle Tom who symbolically grabs or holds the white man's penis for him (and literally in many cases considering the new trend and dysfunction of the black male). In other words, the black male accomplishes this by being homosexual or transgendered, by frolicking around with his pants sagging, by seeking to exclusively date and marry white women (as well as white men when, again, considering the burgeoning trend of black male pathology and dysfunction), by neglecting his responsibilities to children and family, and by failing to challenge a status quo that has laid out early graves and, along the way, has assured a deplorable and dreadful existence for himself and black people as a whole.

Interestingly, respect is one of the most powerful aphrodisiacs in the black community. Boys and young males have and continue to be killed for it, street gangs and urbanized allegiances have and continue to be formed based solely on the premise of respect—respect for one's reputation as well as respect for the alliances that have been established and in which one seeks to be permanently identified. So, when dissecting the notion of why black males hold their penises when speaking, the idea of respect should be interchangeable with this course of action. Perhaps there is validity to this claim if in fact black males do hold their penises; and if this is the case, it is probably because it is the last substantive thing of value that even institution racism/white supremacy cannot deny them of or separate them from, just as respect is so magnanimous and coveted in black and urban communities, considering that it is virtually non-existent outside of those realms.

Respect, then, is obviously a virtuous character trait that needs to be earned rather than a trait that is forced upon or is taken by force. Paradoxically, while young black males maim and kill for respect, black children are being raised in single-parent and fatherless homes at a rate that is nearly three-times the national average. This is what the world sees. Furthermore, for those who practice institutional racism/white supremacy, this is one of the many adverse characteristics and actions of the oppressed that they want the world to be aware of. It is also obligatory to keep in mind that in Nazi Germany during World War II, the Nazis sent out messages to the world by way of false propaganda and sordid images via film for the purposes of portraying the Jews, as well as other victims (e.g., Gypsies and other ethnic groups of color) of the Nazi's genocidal ambitions, as human waste. Thus, once the Jews were successively perceived as a subhuman collective so base and repugnant that once the Nazis commenced with their murderous campaign, no one would bother or question the intent behind their motives or see the error in such bloodlusts.

Long ago, white people realized who they were and where they stood on the world stage and made a choice as to how they were going to exist in global society. The choice that they made was global conquest under the premise of white supremacy, and death to any group or individual who challenged this ideology. As we move into Black History Month of February—the shortest month of the calendar year—black people in general will almost exclusively immerse themselves in the philosophy and actions of a black male whom even white people claim is worthy of celebration and admiration for his non-violent and passive resistance to institutional racism and oppression. However, during the time that this widely celebrated black individual basked in the philosophy of non-violence and passive resistance and inculcated that black victims of institutional racism/white supremacy do the same, he was deemed by racist whites who were in stark opposition to his stance to be controversial enough to ensure his own violent death by their hands. Yet even in a society in which, as Michael Eric Dyson in his book *Between God and Gangsta Rap* offered his shared analysis of black males gradually becoming more and more of an endangered species,[40] black people as a whole still commit to standing side by side and shoulder to shoulder with those who proclaim an analogous admiration for Dr. King, and his message of nonviolence. The irony however is that in addition to his being killed for displaying all of the qualities for which he was admired, one can traverse every city, county, and state in the country and fail to find a Martin Luther King Jr. drive, lane, or boulevard anywhere in predominantly white neighborhoods.

This fact, among many others, leaves a lot of questions unanswered. It can also be perceived as a glaring contradiction or irony as just mentioned; especially when considering that essentially King's message for non-violence was really more geared towards civilizing and holding up a mirror to white people, perhaps so that they could bear witness to their own monstrous and barbaric ways. The reason being is that certainly it was not black folk who were lynching, burning, beating, water-hosing, and unleashing rabid-toothed canines on white people. It is because of this analysis, as well as others throughout this chapter, that the Uncle Tom mythos is as relevant today as it has been at any other period of time in history; notwithstanding the fact that the character of Uncle Tom was crafted during a time of an omniscient slave and slave master dichotomy. That same, exact dichotomy exists today. And while there are those who would argue against this claim, it is nonetheless hard to overlook that during the times of chattel slavery in the antebellum south, there were many who either did not believe that they were slaves or convinced themselves that there was nothing wrong with serving their white Christian slave masters. What other reason would there or could there have been the thwarting of slave revolts and insurrections?

Even in today's modern era there is a reason why there are many black folk—male or female or boy or girl—who act and conduct themselves in the manner that they do amid the scourge of institutional racism/ white supremacy. Nonetheless, these actions are mostly based on a de facto concomitant: One that is indicative of the exuding of extreme sympathy for blacks and the conditions of other black victims, regardless of how legitimate or frivolous the purpose of relaying that sympathy. The other is a stark unconscious and repressive denial of race and how it affects the day-to-day lives of black people, especially black males. Evidently, the black male and black folk in general, talk and act like white people, and center themselves in places and settings where they can absorb all of the values and mores of whites for the purposes of cultural acceptance, validation, and approval. it is equally important to make note of how many of today's biracial population act, carry themselves, or are cast in roles and positions as if they are agents of change (e.g., Obama), or at least symbols of supposed change between black and white America, which automatically entitles them the natural right to play whatever side of the chessboard that they choose; rather than simply seeing themselves as people of color who should have a natural identification with other people of color in a society that harshly oppresses and discriminates against people based solely on color differences.

When thoroughly analyzing the Uncle Tom myth and the conditions of slavery in which the character is derived, it should also be kept in mind that this is how house slaves and plantation domestics conducted themselves, as many of these domestics were mulattoes whose blood ties were linked directly to that of the masters. Nevertheless, one could argue that there are still strong semblances of culture that black people continue to hold onto and have not yet yielded their grip, even under the conditions of white influence. But even if that were true, I would argue that these actions are in some way associated with the influence of whites and the conditions that they set as a result of white supremacy. For instance, it has always been widely considered that black people practice corporal punishment on their children (in some cases to the extreme), while many white people simply do not exercise this method of parental control or behavioral compliance. Accordingly, we see via film and television how white kids talk and behave in response to the parental conditions that their parents have set; actions and behaviors that arguably are unfathomable in many black households. My take on this perspective is that white people let their children, particularly their teenage children, talk and act in this manner because it is a part of the conditioning process of white supremacy. Hence, it is the sharpening of certain personality traits and characteristics that is indicative of remaining at the top of the social and cultural food chain, and is incumbent upon white kids learning these traits and applying them once they are enmeshed in the outside world as a means to display effective control and maintenance of superiority tactics.

In contrast, black people as a whole spank and beat their children as a means of grooming them to compliance due to norms and expectations that are not just expected in black households, but how such expectations and acquiescent behavior is to be conducted in the presence of white people and in a system that is fueled by the ideology of white supremacy. However, these differences are hidden under a belief of cultural differences, as well as being based on a notion of "white privilege" that has little if anything to do with the repression of the black male, and black people in general. And, consequently, another concomitant takes rapid form. If white people are truly not racist, then the plight and adverse circumstances of the black male is clearly the result of biological and cultural inferiority, upon which the whole impetus behind the system of chattel slavery was based.

It is because the black male is faced with a double whammy in a racist and oppressive society, and one that consist of being black and (disproportionately) poor amid an abundance of wealth and affluence that this adherence is perhaps a matter of life and death, or is a powerful determinant as to whether black children can acquire jobs or wind up in penal institutions with a number stenciled across their chest. And it is because of this inherent necessity for survival that I am not even certain if the Uncle Tom myth essentially applies to anyone—male or female—or whether certain individuals should be labeled as such, at least not until I am certain exactly what the moniker means and how it applies to today's standards and conditions that greatly affect the black male, or black folk in general. However, it was Malcolm X's assertion of Martin Luther King being a "twentieth century uncle tom," on the strength of diametrically opposed views that were mostly the result of King's primary non-violent weapon of choice being widely considered as the last remaining and perhaps the most effective means of subjugating and emasculating the black male, and oppressing black people as a whole.

It is mostly due to similar conditions, as well as others, that I will not completely relent on the notion that if a black male either shows supports or is in favor of another black male earning millions upon millions by wearing a dress in a society that is bifurcated by race and fueled by racism, racial stereotypes, and preconceived notions of the so-called minority class, then that individual with no uncertainty exhibits many of the symptoms of *Uncle Tomism*. Also, if you are a black male that willfully and unapologetically renounces an obligation that is critical in shaping young lives and preparing them for a world that has laid out the framework for either unimpeded exploitation or complete annihilation, then if you are not an Uncle Tom, you certainly fall short of fulfilling the definition of manhood or true manliness that has been defined throughout the course of this book; thus, ensuring a failure of the black male in successfully making this transition, as certainly the aforementioned are atrocities that continue to remain far too common in the day-to-day existence of himself, and of black people.

Seven

THE LOWDOWN ON THE "DOWN-LOW" PHENOMENON

I can recall as an undergraduate having a group conversation on the patio section of the Metro State athletic commissions building, appropriately called the "black hole," so named after the gathering of black students in the 1995 film *Higher Learning*. What made this particular group conversation interesting was that it was centered on a young black female's candid confession about her then boyfriend's experimental act of oral copulation with another male. Yet despite her candor, she also put up a vehement defense of, as she claimed," he is not gay though," spurred by the fact that the majority of those around her were just as vehemently asserting that her boyfriend's action, as described, was in fact a homosexual act. She also claimed that the boyfriend had explained to her that this act was sparked by something that he had been curious about doing and decided to assuage his curiosity once the opportunity presented itself. Since I did not know this young female that well, I decided to remain neutral—electing to listen to her defense—all the while musing how a male, whom his female partner claimed was not gay but in fact was straight (heterosexual), would by way of his own volition—driven by "curiosity"—engage in a sex act with another male.

In western society and culture, there have been all kinds of terms and designations that have been crafted to explain sexual acts and behaviors that fall outside of the realm of both heterosexuality and homosexuality. *Bisexual* and *Bi-curious* and *metro sexual* (the last however being identified more as a heterosexual categorization) are a few that immediately come to mind. Then in the mid-2000s, the world (or at least black America) was introduced to what would infamously become known as sexual behaviors that are conducted on the "down low" by black males (the expression was more accurately introduced in the mid '90s by R&B singer R. Kelly's single of the same title). Nevertheless, whatever one chooses to categorize or call this behavior, arguably it is a phenomenon that is widely perceived as one that is strictly and purely western. Additionally, I will make the claim that these are actions of black males that are the direct result of centuries of institutional racism, discrimination, and oppression that has inevitably succeeded in emasculating and effeminizing black males to a point where they no longer see selfworth, strength, and virility that is indicative of unmitigated manhood and manliness. Or better yet, allow me to pose this question: can a male sleep with another male and still be considered as a Man in this society?

The black male in America has had the essence and core of manhood lynched, burned, castrated, and beaten out of him by a system that, as Neely Fuller Jr. theorized, engenders only one MAN as truly functional and who reigns supreme. Basically, being bisexual, bi-curious, and on the down low for the black male is the result of dehumanization that has constantly and continuously beaten him over the head like a piston or mallet, for the sole purpose of stripping the black male of any semblance of TRUE masculinity, regardless of biological endowments. Consequently, over seventy percent of black children, many of whom are young boys, growing up in single-parent and fatherless homes are the result of conditions of institutional racism/white supremacy that has and continues its undertaking of completely eradicating the existence of the black male, or is steadfastly succeeding in completely stripping him of his dignity, self-worth, and manhood.

As people in a country that passes legislation, enacts laws, and gravitates towards a culture of complete and utter tolerance, particularly of those whose lifestyles seem to be on the fringes of traditional American and conservative values, for victims of institutional racism/white supremacy, disproportionate levels of single-parent homes and absentee fathers has played a critical role in the effeminizing and emasculating of the black male. This, of course, is in addition to the other conditions that hinder and obstruct the advancement of black people as a whole; conditions such as substandard living conditions, inadequate access to healthcare and education, weakened or nonexistent communal and political infrastructures, complete socioeconomic disenfranchisement, and, as Michelle Alexander points out in her book *The New Jim Crow*, systematic mass incarceration of black and brown males.[41] Furthermore, America's over seventy percent of black children being reared in single-parent and fatherless homes purports the highest figure of any other ethnic group than any nation on the planet, adding a solid argument as to why the down low phenomenon is not only uniquely American, but is widely perceived as a "black thang" and is inextricably linked to the black male, considering that at the time the trend (at the height of its popularity) was mostly cultivated and nurtured in black communities.

"Keep it on the down low, nobody has to know"[42] —R. Kelly, Down low

Surprisingly, J.L. King, author of *On the Down Low: A journey into the lives of Straight Black Men who sleep with Men*, and the black male who, as it relates to other than heterosexual sex, brought the term down low to the consciousness of America, has stated that being on the down low is not a black thing; nor has he identified its practices as being brought on by conditions of race and racism in a society that has both physically and psychologically decimated the black male. However, his evidence and his own lifestyle, and the lifestyles that he has purported of other black males in his book, belies this claim. In reading Mr. King's book, as well as seeing him on interviews such as his appearance on the Oprah Winfrey show, I both applauded and admired his courage and conscientiousness to extrapolate the dynamics involved in his own life and attempt to bring the down low debacle to the forefront. Yet even in his attempts to expose the deceptions and dangers (i.e., the exponential increase of black women acquiring HIV/AIDS because of sex with males on the down low), his illustration and premise of what the down low is all about is mired in paradoxes, loopholes, and inaccuracies; observations that you don't have to be gay or live that particular lifestyle to notice is painfully obvious.

Even more revealing is how Mr. King fails to get to the true root and crux of what it is that essentially causes black males to lead such depraved and hedonistic lifestyles—all under the guise of feigning a sense of moral values and human sensibilities, as well as proclaiming and disseminating the importance of manhood. And though it can be argued that people in general—regardless of color or ethnic background—lead depraved and immoral lifestyles, resultantly nullifying any claim that this is an issue that deserves extra vigilance and focus, the down low crisis stands out because it crosses the boundaries and threshold of actions that are solely based on individual preferences and incidentally should be addressed as such. What is also inaccurate is the assessment that it is an issue that has aided in disrupting the equilibrium of the black experience and the tumult that ensues due to a climate of racism that is highly toxic in many respects.

It is therefore my assessment that J.L. King has done an additional disservice because of his attempt to offer the down low experience as one that is based on individual preferences and unique life experiences, rather than an issue that is aiding in eradicating both the integrity and existence of the black male because of the practices of institutional racism, genocide, and the endeavor to destroy the black male, leaving the black female as a wanton and dispensable casualty in this attempt.

Thus, Mr. King's omission of the real problem with being on the down low leaves it simply to be deemed as a catchphrase—engineered by the black male's attempt to discredit his own manhood and manliness—confirming the base and meaningless existence of the black male that the system of institutional racism/white supremacy predicates.

The origins of the down low and same-sex practices

"There is something powerful about the penis and sex with men"
—J. L. KING

Prior to his admission of being gay, J.L. King's implication of the mystique of being on the down low was that both he and the other black males he illustrated as being on the down low were not gay. But here's a question: does the above confession (or passage) sound like that of a man who is straight? Nevertheless, despite the obvious illogicalities, the success of J.L. King's *On the down Low* was difficult to not take notice, as the success of the book arguably was the catalyst for a burgeoning trend that was taking place in American society. For thirty weeks his lurid tales of black males leading doubled-lives—breeding deception and discontent in the process—was atop the New York Times best sellers list. And when his documentary purporting down low behavior aired on black entertainment television, it was the top viewed program for the year that it made its debut. Perhaps all of the sensationalism and, even acclaim, was for good reason; because, when considering that homosexuality—and its various sexual practices and behaviors—in western society and culture is far from new in terms of social activity, the down low phenomenon arguably set an unprecedented standard as well as changed the game for the psychopathology of homosexuality and all of its subsequent variances.

Homosexuality and the practice of same-sex copulation date back to both ancient Greece and Rome, illumining the fact that although same sex preferences and coitus relations have a primordial legacy, such practices are deeply rooted in European traditions and customs. Western society and culture (according to Neely fuller there is no such thing as western civilization, the obvious implication being that this society is civilized), which primarily consists of countries and states that are predominately European, hence are steeped in European values, mores, and ideologies, has become a haven for homosexual practices. And although these practices are common, they have also continually been denounced as being vile, licentious, and sacrilegious. Even the religious tenets of Christianity have historically and contemporarily become infused and enshrouded in contradiction, as western culture, which is predominantly Christian, has embraced homosexuality despite its religious canons and provisos that have steadfastly demonized and condemned the behavior. In Abrahamic theology, Sodom and Gomorrah was an allegory for the vile and contemptible practices of same-sex copulation among human beings; so much so that the term sodomy, which derives from the name of the wicked populous, is historically defined as anal and oral sex between persons and animals.

Interestingly, J.L. King's exposé of homosexual behaviors (or being on the down low) encapsulates many if not all of the dubious negative behaviors that are associated with every theory, medical and scientific evidence, and literary proclamation of the aberrant and abnormal, as well as psychopathological proclivities of engaging in same-sex practices and behaviors. Thus, the book is a hard read because of the irresponsible and voracious tendencies towards male on male sex at all cost and by any means necessary—even at the expense of deceiving close family, friends, and loved ones. Moreover, putting the health and lives of many at risks, as well as despite a myriad of other potentially harmful ramifications—hence justifying the behavior being done under the guise of normalcy and claims of undeniable virility, strength, and manhood. Also, and perhaps most telling, is that its practices are a profound and frightening symptom of cultural depravity that is a direct result of the potent and powerful effects of institutional racism/white supremacy and conditioning that effeminizes and emasculates black males in a number of ways, yet deludes those who live a down low lifestyle, as well as readers of his book, into a false sense and claim of masculinity.

It is because of this rationale that there is a glaring distinction that needs to be illustrated. That distinction is that homosexuality and being on the down low is not the same thing; in fact, they are two different species of animal, altogether. However, what can become confusing is that the cohabitation of these two distinct species are close enough to where paths can cross and the differences, if any, can become infused and even enmeshed. What follows is the creating of a new kind of pathology that has never before been seen and that stems from a human behavior that is argued to be as old and as primitive as civilization itself. For instance, years prior to 1973, when same-sex sexual practices were removed from the Diagnostic and Statistical Manual of Mental Disorders, homosexuality was diagnosed as a psychiatric illness. Moreover, the practice, or lifestyle—whatever one considers it as being—was considered abnormal behavior and an abomination, a claim that is underscored in Judeo-Christian theology. Contemporarily speaking, however, there is both a national and global push for the acceptance of homosexual practices and lifestyles, despite the fact that the historical doctrines or religious tenets that vilified and demonized homosexuality have not at all changed and remain indelibly enmeshed in Christian Science and philosophy.

Where am I going with all of this? Or, an even better question, one that I have often been asked while writing this book: Why is a color being placed on homosexual and same-sex unions, considering that both black males and white men engage in this behavior or live this type of lifestyle? Additionally, and perhaps an even more important question, what does racism have to do with any of this? Hence, if asked directly, my reply would be that institutional racism/white supremacy has a lot to do with not only homosexual practices between males of color, but that the conditions that black people in general have to endure throughout the course of their lives in a racist society is perhaps the most salient factor in analyzing homosexual practices among the black male, as well as lesbianism in regards to black females. Lastly, it aids in answering the question as to how and why the down low crisis came to fruition in the first place. In other words, all of the aforementioned factors are relevant.

So, when addressing the issue of color for behaviors and lifestyle practices that on the surface (arguably) are colorless and genderless, it has to be understood that the dynamics that influence (or cause) homosexual behavior in white men has very little if anything to do with black male homosexuality, or being on the down low. Since being removed from the diagnostic statistical manual of mental disorders, and now being deemed medically and scientifically as one of the three primary classifications of sexual orientation among social groups, homosexual behavior, or whatever pathologies or psychiatric deficiencies that it is still associated, remains uniquely distinct from the pathological behaviors that black males who are on the down low seem to exhibit. In fact, the down low phenomenon is in itself uniquely distinct from the lifestyle practices of openly gay black males, as well as transgendered and transsexual black males.

White Man's perversion...?

Because of some of the earlier claims and analyses offered, it should not be dismissed that among black males, being openly gay, having transgendered ideations (e.g., Tyler Perry), being transsexual, and living a double life that constitutes being on the down low, are all conditions of westernization and the indiscriminate practices of institutional racism/white supremacy that western society and culture has inflicted upon black people, especially black males. As I write this, a global debate wages on whether homosexuality was practiced on the continent of Africa prior to European encroachment and subsequent colonialism. Nonetheless, J.L. King's infamous book purports all of the hedonistic, depraved, and pathological nuances of black males who, although clearly psycho-logically and emotionally unhinged, are ideal mates for successful and enterprising black females.

Handsome, successful, virile, and intelligent are some of the attri-butes of the black male that King illustrates is on the down low and is leading a double, insidious lifestyle—including himself at one point. And without question, I doubt if anyone would deny that there are plenty of males—down low or otherwise—who fit these particular traits and char-acteristics. Even so, *On the Down Low* is a stark description of black males who purposely lie to their wives and deceive close loved ones and family members. King's book also describes these males' desire to engage in dangerous and high-risked sexual behaviors, almost by way of some fur-tive codification of other down low black males whom, similar to King, willingly engage in these acts and steadfastly embroil themselves in this lifestyle. Disturbing, however, is that such actions are done while claiming absolutely no responsibility to the potential consequences that inevitably ensues as a result. And, as previously mentioned, many of these males claim that they are not gay or homosexual. Indeed, this analysis is what makes being on the down low an altogether different situation than the oft-maligned, yet gradually growing trend of acceptance of homosexual-ity and same sex unions. Thus, being on the down low can be perceived as a byproduct of being gay, with the only difference being that down low actions are much more insidious and destructive based on its deceptive and depraved nature; somewhat similar to how crack cocaine, a substan-tive derivative of powder cocaine, is widely perceived—hence dealt with on a much larger punitive scale—by way of the criminal justice system.

Accordingly, J.L. King's descriptive candor of random and wanton anal and oral copulation between black males who repudiate the label of being homosexual is as compelling as it is unnerving. However, where King failed was his being remiss to delve into the origins and primary motivations behind these behaviors, which would have given the down low phenomenon credence if it had been aligned and juxtaposed with exter-nal forces and issues that on a day-to-day basis affects the lives of black males, rather than leaving being on the down low swinging and dangling on a precipice of individual preferences and decision-making that, perhaps, warranted more *don'ts* than *do's* in the final analysis. In order to fully understand not only the down low trend but homosexual and same-sex practices among black males in America, my theory of carefully evaluating the origins of certain actions in order to effectively analyze and address the aftermath becomes obligatory. In attempting to analyze the origins it first has to be understood the almost compulsory need of an oppressed and subservient people to live, act, emulate, and covet the ways and actions of the oppressor in order to effectively procure both liberation and acceptance. Therefore, when considering the global rallying cry for the acceptance of gay, lesbian, transgendered, and transsexual lifestyles, particularly in regions and areas of the world where the cultural histories and traditions are in stark conflict with these lifestyle practices, what should first become clear is the exuberant embrace of Judeo-Christian values. Especially if this is being done under the auspices that western society and culture is embracing homosexuality and same-sex unions with open arms. And from all appearances this may be true to certain degrees.

The world is obviously abreast to the mainstream and pop cultural successes of Tyler Perry, RuPaul, Lee Daniels, and the hordes of freaks and people whose lifestyles are a reflection of being on the fringes of political correctness and social decorum and/or acceptance. This appears to be the case regardless of whether these types are saturated in Hollywood, or on the streets of Mardi gras festivals, or take part in gay and lesbian pride and gay rights parades. Perhaps it is because of this claim that the question of whether homosexuality was prevalent on the continent of Africa prior to imperialism is the subject of intense debate. And perhaps there are many citizens of several respective countries in Africa as well as folks to the left who are intensely lobbying and fighting for gay rights. So, when attempting to analyze and answer the gay question as well as the down low crisis concerning black males in America, it is equally important to assess the issue in order to acquire some understanding of whether homosexuality is an integral part of Africa's glorious past and traditions; particularly since their seems to be dissension as to whether or not this is actually the case.

The fact that forty of the fifty-four countries in Africa have very rigid anti-gay legislation propels any claim that Africa is not so gay friendly as a great majority of the western world appears to be. For instance, Zimbabwe's Robert Mugabe and the (brutal) anti-gay policies of Uganda's Yoweri Museveni are significant examples of the vocal and extreme methods of denouncing homosexuality and of castigating its practices with brute measures and severe penalties. These measures are the result of the proclamation that homosexuality contradicts and sullies Africa's historic cultural traditions, and is a western behavioral trait that needs to remain restricted to western standards of living and customs.

How homosexuality and being on the down low can be problematic for black males in a racist society

To summarize my previous point, I would favor the argument that homosexuality is based on practices and behaviors that are encouraged by western standards. Moreover, any claim that expunges Africa and several of its respective nations from embracing any western standards and behavioral practices that are deemed immoral and antithetical to African roots and cultural traditions, possess strong merit and should be taken into consideration when attempting to assess whether homosexuality is a human condition that is colorless, or if it is indeed a white man's perversion that has ensnared countless other non-white cultures, ostensibly due to westernized indoctrination and hegemony vis-à-vis —racism (white supremacy).

As a direct consequence of being subjected to centuries of imperialism, I would also make the argument (and evidence confirms) that many African nations can no more afford to be emasculated due to white racism and its superiority framework than the black male can afford to be emasculated here in America. As a mentor raised an important question to me as to the relevance of the past history of homosexuality in Africa to present conditions that are going on and that grossly affect the black male in American society, my response was that the answer is simple: Important distinctions need to be made regarding the African's response to institutional racism/white supremacy and the black male in America's response to institutional racism/white supremacy.

It is statements such as comedian and author, Steve Harvey's claim that despite the obvious negatives, America is still "the best thing going" that warrants a "how so?" inquiry, as well as engenders further analysis of such an audacious yet erroneous claim. While it is debatable whether or not black citizens of the richest and most powerful nation in the world should be the prototype and modern example of how racism is an ugly, sordid relic of global society's debauched and degenerate past, the fact of the matter is that it is the black male in America who should look to his embattled brother in other countries and cultures (e.g., Africa) in order to effectively gaze at what real attempts at self, communal, ethnic, and cultural liberation looks like and what such attempts indeed entail; particularly for results in the long-run. Furthermore, it is equally obligatory for the black male in the western hemisphere to take notes on how to acquire full and complete liberation, either restore or maintain cultural ties, take back control of family and community, and map out the appropriate route to TRUE manhood and manliness—an endeavor and prospect that remains confounding as well as unachieved.

Without question, rich (and deluded) black entertainers such as Steve Harvey could be accused of seeing blackness in America from the vantage point of those who no longer have to endure the day-to-day drudgery of the majority of black people as a whole in this society, regardless of where it is that these rich, successful black people claim to come from. And considering that I don't know Steve Harvey personally, I can see how easy it is for someone in his position to make such a claim. Of course, I could be proven wrong if Steve Harvey took his success and poured his resources into ameliorating the conditions of young black girls and boys in the Cleveland ghettoes of which he claims he is a product. This should be the endeavor of every rich and successful black person in a society that is knee-deep in racist and genocidal practices, rather than mentally immersing oneself in the fallacious notion of "I made it, why can't they." Despite the fact that the African is rejecting homosexuality and same-sex unions, the black male in America is inundated and consumed by the conscious reality of white people—thus completely vulnerable and impotent to staving off perversions and immoral acts that, similar to the African, are antithetical to his very nature and being. Yet there are many black people in general in American society who dare to point the finger at the African and say that it is the inhabitants of the "dark continent" (a completely racially-charged description) that are primitive, uncivilized, destitute, homophobic, and in need of humanizing.

It is quite disturbing how this is the sentiment of foolish and neurotic black individuals who believe that they can break the shackles of their blackness by cloaking themselves in complete whiteness—white ways, actions, and mannerisms—as if white people are going to somehow forget who these black individuals truly are and where it is that they actually come from. Think on this for a moment: If America truly has improved in terms of race relations, as well as cultivated amorous ties to its black citizens and former slaves, then America would certainly have an equally palpable relationship with the inhabitants of the continent where its former slaves are aboriginal; rather than continue to be the forerunner of exploitation and mistreatment of Africa and Africans, same as it has been and continues to be to so-called "African Americans" in its own backyard. Nevertheless, and unsurprisingly, several African leaders are the subjects of close global scrutiny and upheaval for their antigay stance; however, J.L. King's book was widely lauded and acclaimed—despite that fact that it is a self-portrait of a black holocaust, meticulously crafted and wrapped into some sordid yet cerebral fairy tale. Moreover, King's attempt at piety over degradation and being stoic rather than iniquitous is as vexing as it is intriguing.

Despite King's admission of the most vile and licentious of human sexual behaviors, he invokes the benevolence of Judeo-Christian sanctity and brotherhood by reminding his reader of the malevolence of being judgmental. Yet this attempt at piety was bone chilling; primarily, because of how hackneyed, typical, and outright ignorant his approach at doing so, as well as his ignorance of assessing his own condition and those of other black males on the "DL." For example, In addition to King's proclamation that he was born attracted to other males, he attempted to compound the sensationalism with claims that his God demands his 10% tithes from his mortal, pious followers.[43] Under close examination this attempt was obviously geared towards debunking research studies that have failed to confirm that homosexuality is genetically determined, as well as reemphasizing the obligatory need for the separation of church and state. Evidently, according to King, God, "himself", is a capitalist who is just as equally concerned with generating monetary and tangible revenue and profit as "he" is with procuring souls to join "him" in "his" self-made kingdom of heaven.

Biological and genocidal warfare

The top four killers of black males in American society are (1) HIV/AIDS (which is actually the third leading cause of death), (2) homicide, (3) accidents, and (4) suicide. Additionally, there are over one million black people who are living with HIV/AIDS, which is nearly forty percent of all cases of those who are infected in this country. What these four elements add up to is the complete and total annihilation of the black male, as certainly these are conditions and circumstances that are conducive to an indiscriminate and efficacious system of institutional racism/white supremacy that has incapacitated the black male, as well as black people as a whole. Furthermore, the conditions of institutional racism and subjugation have engendered high-risks and self-destructive behaviors that are designed to make it appear as if the black male's inevitable and highly probable demise is the result of his own doing, as J.L. King would no doubt agree, based on his own unique and insightful analysis.

The real facts however are that, no, J.L. King was not born gay, nor was he born a heterosexual male with an inexplicable and aberrant urge to sleep with other males. Hence, the dreadfulness of King's expose' is that in addition to delineating the most bestial and repugnant aspects and characteristics of seemingly successful and accomplished black males, it also failed to truthfully and accurately analyze the real crisis that greatly affects and alter the lives of black males in a racist society. Unless it is true that black people as a whole are the subhuman, inferior, and insignificant mass of human waste and rubbish that institutional racism/white supremacy asserts, what else could explain why blacks constitute the highest transmission rate of HIV/AIDS infections, as well as other STDs, across many categories? Keep in mind that this epidemic includes gay, bisexual, heterosexual males, females, and infants. Therefore, if these factors are not the result of a massive genocidal effort conducted by a country with an indelible history of extreme racial animus and hatred towards blacks, what other explanation is there? Other factors such as immeasurable rates of annual homicidal deaths and fatalities, mass and disproportionate levels of imprisonment and incarceration, and disproportionate levels of poverty and denial of access to employment and health care, facilitate any argument that, if race is not the problem, then something is definitely wrong with the American infrastructure of wellbeing and unobtrusive opportunity in regards to how it relates to blacks.

Poverty, crime, homosexuality, disproportionate levels of substance abuse (greatly contributing to high rates of HIV infection), and unemployment and underemployment are all factors that are either destroying outright the existence of the black male or is greatly compromising the existence of black people as a whole in America. However, the liberal global society that ostensibly is taking cues from western standards is vilifying sovereign nations of Africa—the American black males once embattled brothers who have and continue to work to escape the clutches of European hegemony and imperialism—for both explicitly and implicitly proclaiming an emphatic "hell nah" to the genocidal politics and pseudo liberal prose that is destroying the black male in America; primarily because of the black male in America's powerlessness and ignorance.

What must be clear, however, is that the same deceptive and genocidal tactics that are in full throttle and paying dividends in America are also in full swing in several countries in Africa. The only difference evidently is that the folks in Africa who are in positions to make decisions can both see and smell the con and caper. Hence, it is numbing and perplexing that South Africa, which is considered to be the most "gay friendly" nation on the continent of Africa, also has the highest HIV/AIDS infection rate of any nation on the planet. Yet here is the concomitant in terms of its global ramifications: While J.L. King offers a disclaimer of not being judged for his and other "DL" males' behaviors, invoking his position as a Christian to assuage and normalize his behavior, as well as his lobbying for black males to be able to freely lead openly gay lives (since he now sees the evils of being on the down low), nations such as S. Africa, on the other hand, are lobbying for the unhampered and unimpeded practices of same-sex unions and living gay lifestyles amid an HIV/AIDS holocaust.

Clearly, this is a time when there is a need for conspiracy theories, especially in the face of disproportionate and cataclysmic death and destruction for those whom the purpose of this massive destruction was designed in the first place. Unsurprisingly, J.L. king denounced the issue of a conspiracy theory or that HIV/AIDS was the result of biological warfare to destroy black people.

Homophobes

"You know, I hate gay people, so I let it be known.
I don't like gay people and I don't like to
be around gay people. I am homophobic. I don't like it.
It shouldn't be in the world or in the United States."
—TIM HARDAWAY

Homosexuality supposedly is in direct conflict with the religious and theological tenets that American society prides itself, and elevates its moral compass above those of other nations and societies—thus not just making it the premiere and stand-alone superpower but the world's true moral leader. Because of this fact, this is not homophobic rhetoric that is being unilaterally spear-headed from my personal vantage point. Homophobia, like racism, has always been ubiquitous is this country. Consequently, homophobia also could be argued as being as uniquely American just as easily as it could be deemed strictly a by-product of predominate westernized cultures.

A vast consensus in Africa (and other colored nations) confirms that homosexual practices not only was not prevalent in Africa prior to European encroachment but that, if anything, what European colonizers succeeded in doing was bringing homophobia to Africa. And again, consequently, this hypothesis is plainly indicative of the continent's extreme anti-gay stance that exists to this day. In the imperialistic campaign of Christianizing and civilizing Africa as well as other predominately colored nations, Christian theology's lambasting of homosexual practices carry a tremendous degree of merit. In Leviticus 18:22, the proclamation of the foreboding of lying with mankind because of it being an abomination is pretty clear. Furthermore, it was the Apostle Paul's claim that same-sex relations are what he referred to as "shameful lust." Nonetheless, and despite these assertions and quotes, I will still make the claim that homosexuality in general is not the problem, or at least not in terms of how it applies to other races and cultures.

The fact of the matter is that I do not have the time, knowledge, nor do I have the inclination to attack human beings that are outside of my purview strictly on the basis of whom they choose to have coitus relations with. But on the other hand, what I am asserting is that homosexual behavior among black males in a racist society is highly problematic, particularly same-sex practices that are encouraged by deception and high-risk behaviors that equate to imminent cultural self-destruction because of the pathology that lies dormant in terms of the motivation behind these acts. As J.L. King's book was lauded and celebrated and became a cultural phenomenon for years after its subsequent release, I wonder how many took the time to consider how deeply disturbing it is for males to have sex with other males, yet claim that they are not homosexual or bisexual but, as many claimed in King's book, "I'm [being] just me."

Consider these simple questions: Is not pathological behavior premised on a lack of respect for honesty or loyalty? Furthermore, is pathological behavior the ability to exaggerate an act or incident that is directly disproportional to an event that is actually taking place? More profound, have excessive and constant exposure to institutional racism/white supremacy completely decimated the psyche and mental stability and well-being of its victims? Consequently, the popularity and sensationalism of King's *On the Down Low* is attributable to self-indulgent and moral lawlessness in a society that embraces and rewards freakish behavior and social dysfunction; just ask Nicki Minaj, Lady Gaga, Lil' Wayne, and Brittany Spears, just to name a few among many (actually, practically the entire entertainment industry).

America is a society that is firmly planted and deeply rooted in the idea of rampart-like global power—capital acquisition and control and European-dominated ethnocentrism—everything else is a cesspool and fortress of contradiction. The word sodomy pertains strictly to bestiality in European culture i.e., western society and culture; therefore, only a black male and other black males whose minds have been completely eviscerated by racism and European westernization could either normalize or make trendy the practice of wanton sodomy and debauchery, rather than completely denouncing and finding entirely contemptible this lifestyle and its subsequent behaviors. This is especially true in terms of how it relates to black victims of institutional racism/white supremacy. J.L. King wants to be an American, albeit in black face, who invokes the spirit of Christianity—a likeness to the oppressor that many blacks hold sacred—without an understanding that the system of institutional racism/white supremacy feeds off any notion or practices that confirm the effeminizing of black males or behaviors that lead to their self-destruction. Strangely, this is despite the fact that there are many gay black males in their ranks, as well as white men who lead the same double lives that King's book purports. However, the contradiction is that being on the down low was not advertised or sensationalized to be a color-neutral trend, and it certainly was not drawn up to confirm homosexuality as a white man's perversion. While it may be true that both black males and white men engage in dual-coitus relationships with males and females, the down low designation, however, became strictly synonymous with black males in popular and mainstream culture, as did the fallacious claim of copulating with other males while maintaining heterosexual status.

Certainly, being on the down low has nothing to do with one's God, one's religious views, or one's spiritual connection; therefore, its practices cannot be assuaged or accounted for by appealing to Christian theology as a means of evoking sameness to white people rather than fostering and promoting glaring distinctions and differences among the two. In the bible that Mr. King and others clamor to for psychological and spiritual refuge and solace, there is a term called *arsenokeitai* that encompasses the actions of males abusing themselves and their wives by way of actions and behaviors that are driven by male weakness and effeminacy—all of which are behaviors that being on the down low actually describes and underscores in the grand scheme of things. According to author/educator Jack David Eller, in his book *Cruel Creeds, Virtuous Violence*, social reality is the only kind of reality that exists.[44] In agreement, I will go a step further and state that because of the present reality there is something terribly wrong about the burgeoning trend of black males in a harsh, racist, and oppressive society, dressing up as females and engaging in effeminate behaviors. Equally problematic (or perhaps more so) is indulging in high-risks and self-destructive sexual behaviors and practices e.g., the down low. Also, succumbing to homosexuality and cross-dressing because of transgendered fetishes, as well as becoming transsexuals because of a belief that is easier to deal with the problems that confront the black male as a black female as opposed to dealing with life's challenges and injustices (i.e., institutional racism/white supremacy) as a black Man.

The bottom line is that it takes warriors to rebuild a nation and restore its cultural pride and traditions. Therefore, when speaking on the African, on the continent of his origin, my final assessment is that the African, although still in psychological bondage of global European hegemony, is no fool; as he, along with the rest of the world, has to see the burgeoning movement of clowns and sissies who control the spotlight and take center stage in America. It takes MEN to raise a family and strengthen their communities—cultivating and molding their sons into warriors. In America, the age of Tyler Perry, J.L. King, RuPaul, and Oprah Winfrey prevail, and totally upends the previously mentioned option, as homosexuality, bisexuality, and suspicions of sexual orientation predominates.

The black male is an endangered species in America, and has been since the reconstruction and abolishment of slavery. In order to escape the prospect of annihilation, the black male has learned to either conceal his masculinity in order to be perceived as less-threatening or flaunt and celebritize his homosexual and/or effeminate status. As a graduate student at New York University, I had to come to terms with the possibility that there was a veiled consensus that the safe black male was either a gay one, or one who was extremely white-identified. I was neither, so imagine what I went through.

Yet homosexuality appears less-threatening and innocuous in its own right when compared to some of the other dissolute sexual practices and lifestyle choices that are associated with it. J.L. King's *On the Down Low: A Journey into the lives of "straight" Black Men who sleep with other Men,* and the down low phenomenon, regardless of whether it started with Mr. King's analysis or preceded the notoriety of his book, is not only a stark contradiction based on the title alone, but also is irrefutable evidence of how institutional racism/white supremacy is either outright physically destroying the black male in America or is gradually taking a pernicious toll on his psyche and mental stability. Furthermore, this feat renders the black male completely devoid and destitute of Manhood and Manliness in a society that has seemingly perfected its endeavor of unmanning and emasculating its sworn and natural enemy.

Eight

BLAXPLOITATION: THE TRUTH OF THE BLACK EXISTENCE IN SPORTS AND ENTERTAINMENT

"A well paid slave is nonetheless a slave"
—CURT FLOOD

Back when I was a fan of major sports (particularly football, basketball, and boxing) and an active participant in sports chat with other avid sports fan, I can vividly recall conversations with white men, who invariably set out to demonstrate their advanced and superior knowledge of *the game*—which consists of all major sports—despite the fact that, on average, blacks both numerically and physically dominate nearly every major franchise sport in America. It would take years before I realized the reason for this is that white racists understand that despite the numbers and physical dexterity of the participants, they are the *ringmasters* and sole proprietors of these events; same as it was the masters and slave owners who determined the productivity and worth of the slave, despite the fact that they were vastly outnumbered by them.

Nonetheless, and despite either the perceived validity or absurdity of the previously mentioned assessment, a practical question would be whether or not sports and entertainment can truly be viable mechanisms for the black male in a country with a sordid and deplorable history of its treatment of him and black people as a whole? Or, Can former sons and daughters of slaves and burden-bearers utilize the entertainment industry and sports and athletic associations to break the barriers of age-old racial stereotypes? Lastly, is it possible for such edifices to be used as plausible platforms to humanize and bolster the cultural worthiness, virtuosity, and dexterity of the black male? On the surface, the answer would appear to be a no-brainer, yes response. As certainly the black male in sports and entertainment appears to represent the pinnacle of American success, even surpassing that of the average white person, or so one would think.

The black male in sports and entertainment is highly visible in the public eye and is considerably compensated for his services and/or dis-services. And in a country of a diverse population that uniformly invests countless hours into television, various online and internet-based social media outlets, and spends an exorbitant amount on movies, films, sporting events, and sports paraphernalia; unsurprisingly, celebrity entertainers and sports figures are imbued and endowed with the highest of qualities, honors, and character traits. How often is it that in barbershops, bars, and backyard barbeques at family gatherings, many refer to celebrities as the quintessential prototypes and barometers of what ideal mates are to look like and how certain standards are to be based in the prospect of choosing potential mates (e.g., who's sexier, Beyonce or Rhianna, or whose butt is bigger, Beyonce's or J-Lo's)?

While America claims to be a pious, Judeo-Christian society, it appears that the true heroes of this culture are those who have successfully accrued excessive wealth, prestige, and social and cultural validation and acceptance. So much so, that many people in general perceive these celebrities as either suitable archetypes or conduits for improvements in personal and individual success and spiritual and pious personal developments. This is indeed the perception despite the affront of fostering a certain posture or image that many of these celebs exude purely for the purposes of maintaining their social and mainstream standing, while continuing to accrue vast wealth. Take your pick when deciphering how many celebrities in general speak of God and espouse high-wrought spiritual beliefs, yet appear to lead lifestyles that appear to be completely ungodly and immoral, and make certain contributions to the mechanisms of mainstream media and popular culture that are highly discriminatory and stereotypical in their depictions of race, class, and gender—actions and facts that couldn't be any further from being in concert with behaviors that would be considered as Godly.

The truth is that there are many people in America— both black and white—who worship success and monetary acquisition, and often call on God during the coveting process of these things or give credit to a higher power and/or authority when these things have been acquired. So, when the question is posed as to whether the industries of sports and entertainment serve well the former slaves and burden-bearers and supposed contemporary beneficiaries of prestige, wealth, and privilege in a so called color-blind society, I appeal to the exorbitant number of black individuals—both male and female—who represent these industries that invariably appear to have sold their souls for proverbial "fame," and would thus apply an emphatic, NO. The reason being is that it is my claim that the institution of racism/white supremacy not only does not work that way but is much more complex and far less forgiving.

Hollywood is perhaps the most visibly racist and exploitative institution in America, besides the institution of American racism in and of itself, or is it all the same? This is particularly the case being that the real insidious roots and nature of Hollywood lies in the fact that it overly compensates and makes excessively wealthy its present-day black victims for their part in continuing to cultivate age-old racial stereotypes and reinforce any notions of white superiority and black weakness and subservience. Moreover, it creates a slew of black individuals who are merely black in appearance but have absolutely no stake in the advancement and preservation of the black male (America's most assiduous target) or black people as a whole, and instead immerse themselves in a pool of whiteness and contribute to belief systems that accommodate white people's belief of their superiority and the inferiority, objectification (particularly sexual objectification), dependence, and lower functioning of blacks. Similarly, the sporting industry's courts, fields, and diamonds are nothing short of modern day plantations that accommodate American society's need for entertainment and cultivate exorbitant and exponential industry wealth on the backs of strong-bodied yet corporate and socioeconomically powerless black males.

The merciless Sports and Entertainment Machine

Where is the proof of such harsh rhetoric? This is no doubt the question that one, if not many, might ask; especially references that could easily be perceived as diatribes directed towards people who are throughout this reading being identified as victims rather than as perpetrators or, better yet, perpetuators of the problem that's being identified. Well, truthfully speaking, opinions and assessments offered throughout the course of the book are comprised of a little of both—harsh condemnation towards the system of institutional racism/white supremacy, as well as criticisms of those black individuals who, by all appearances, seem to support its causes. But for clear-cut evidence, or proof, consider the following.

The Miniseries *Scandal* is a televised drama that purports the life of a high-powered, highly successful black female played by black actress Kerry Washington, who is a crisis management official that specializes in employing damage control in the dealings of high-powered and high-profile white house officials. The show is inspired by the real life exploits of Judy Smith, who is the former press aide of former president George H.W. Bush. The series, crafted and conceptualized by Shonda Rhimes, who is the brainchild of other prominent television dramas such as *Grey's*

Anatomy, completely decimates the notion of art imitating life by way of blatant disregard of the achievements and accomplishments of black females such as Smith, and former national security advisor and secretary of state, Condoleeza Rice. Hence, the irony to all of this is that despite the black existence and experience in a highly racist and toxic society, it takes a black individual (whom is also a woman, hence the irony) such as Rhimes to disparage the integrity and virtuosity of the black female, particularly those whom, as mentioned, have found success and prominence in the white house by way of their talent and hard work. What is instead demonstrated, as well as depicted, is a willingness to engage in the effacing of these achievements by portraying Washington's character as having an illicit affair with the president, as well as lascivious predilections toward others (typical of the image of the modern-day black whore, despite how intelligent or successful). Furthermore, while Washington's character is black, the president is white; a fact in and of itself should be worthy of notice amid the era of the country's first black president.

Such observations and analyses obviously do not make the show *Scandal* unique or authentic. In fact, it is the beast of Hollywood and its depictions of the neo black/white duality that has become so pervasive that it would not be at all surprising if many or anyone believed that this is the new, pervasive inextricable linkage of white men and black females in a so-called post-racist society. On the contrary, and similar to how the black male is utilized (exploited) in sports, it is nothing more than slavery revisited. For certain, Washington's character could just as easily be perceived as a modern day Sally Hemmings, rather than that of a successful black female who fortuitously got caught up in a "scandal" as the series attempts to purport. Incredulously, in an era where certain blacks are said to be making great individual strides and commendable personal and professional advances, Hollywood's portraying blacks in roles of detestable concubinage as opposed to being the *First Lady* (which would be a more accurate portrait of art imitating life) is still the order of the day in a society that is geared towards practicing institutional racism/white supremacy and the various forms of dehumanization and objectification that ensues. The only difference now as opposed to then is that black folk are compensated for their debauchery rather than the forcible coercion that the system of chattel slavery imposed.

The fact that Black people in general are actually making noticeable strides in terms of socioeconomic advancement is indeed true and leaves very little if any room for dispute. The problem, however, is Hollywood and mainstream media's objective of obfuscating these advances by telling stories via film and television that are designed to relive the days of unmitigated black conquest and servitude (e.g., *Twelve years a slave*), or creating images that juxtapose black progress with white benevolence or gratification—sexual or otherwise (e.g., take your pick).

Kerry Washington, despite her tremendous talents, is a prime example of how easy it is for individuals (especially black victims of institutional racism/white supremacy) to be bought out (modern day slavery), as the financial rewards and acclaim that she receives (she won an NAACP Image award for her portrayal) pales in comparison to the stigma and deleterious labeling that ensnares black people collectively. Even adding to the irony (or intrigue, depending on how one might see it) is that despite Judy Smith's admission that she never had an illicit affair with former president Bush—dismissing it as pure fiction—she nonetheless apparently found herself susceptible to the financial rewards of endorsing such a specious portrayal by acting as one of the show's producers.

What is highly contradictory and hypocritical in a supposed post-racial and colorblind society is that overwhelmingly white people determine how blacks are going to contribute to the genre of entertainment. And it is because of this fact that black actors and actresses' contributions are more than likely based on how it benefits white studio executives, screen writers, producers, filmmakers, and mostly white viewers and audiences. And even though a great majority of black people who are ensnared in this culture (good or bad) sit and watch all types of television shows daily and at a disproportionate rate, and contribute to box office ticket sales at an excessive amount annually, the cold hard facts are that blacks have absolutely NO power in Hollywood. And, subsequently, blacks have very little control as to how other blacks are to be portrayed, lest they are depicted and portrayed in manners that are suitable to white people and that encourage misconceptions of blacks; hence, the success of individuals such as Shonda Rhimes and Tyler Perry.

If close attention and scrutiny is paid to the burgeoning flow that is taking place in modern day movies, films and television dramas, it is hard to miss a persistent theme. While there may more than likely be a person of color amid a group of whites, as even Hollywood understands the benefits of procuring a diverse audience, often where/or when there is a black female there is virtually no black male. Likewise, where there is a black male there is no black female. Moreover, if there is a black female, she is more than likely the only black character, as is the case for the black male. And if there is a black male and a black female simultaneously cast, chances are that they are at odds in some way shape or form, discouraging or excoriating any measure of alliance between the two.

To understand this practice, it first has to be understood that during the times of slavery, when black slaves were placed on the auction block, there was a systematized modus operandi of separating the black male slave from the black female slave, being that the efficacy of slavery was contingent upon destroying any family bonds or interpersonal alliances. Consequently, the Tyler Perry's and Shonda Rhime's of the co-op of black Hollywood are in high-demand, and the Spike Lee's are now far and few between. Moreover, racist whites understand the legacy and enduring effects of institutional racism; evidently, much better than do their black victims. As a result, it is my belief that the decadence that is on constant display on television and in film, and the frivolous acts that by all appearances encapsulates the lifestyles of so many professional black athletes is sufficient and irrefutable evidence of the indiscriminate nature of the system of racism/white supremacy. Therefore, it is just as much a condition of the slave mind that would compel a black female to debunk and denigrate the accomplishments of black people than it is for whites to script such negative images that are fueled by deep-rooted racial enmity.

Blacks in Sports and Entertainment: A retrospective

Historically, black people as a whole have always used entertainment as a means to mollify and circumvent their condition as victims of systematic racism and oppression. During the times of slavery, following a grueling days' worth of toil and labor, slaves would gather by a nightly camp fire and entertain each other with music via the banjo or harmonica—dancing and singing to the rhythm in styles and mannerisms reminiscent of the their African roots and traditions. Old sages and elders would entertain with stories of life in the old country, and would infuse these folktales with the ardent spiritual zeal and devout fervor of the day when earthly slavery ends and eternal salvation and prosperity begins. Hence, combined with the rhythmic and soulful expression that encompasses song and dance—which descendants of African lineage and roots appeared to be culturally endowed—the story teller, comedian, and preacher seemed to have also stamped their indelible mark on the black experience in America; most of which would become manifested as oppressive, murderous, harsh, and vituperative during the times of slavery. Ironically, these cultural traits and attributes would come to be synonymous and symbolize cultural and rhetorical expressions of blacks even leading up to modern times. Thus, song and dance e.g., pop and rhythm and blues, storytelling—translated into musical forms of expression such as blues and jazz (other forms of musical and artistic expressions such as hip hop and spoken word poetry would come later)—and comedy, with the latter arguably being considered as a confluence of all of the aforementioned as well as the inclusion of social and political commentary, would come to practically encapsulate the black existence in America. Or, these forms of expression would come to be widely perceived as mechanisms that aided in paving the way for success for blacks who would otherwise remain consumed by poverty.

In contrast, when analyzing sports and black athletes, it would take years before the black male would successfully break into sports, with boxing being one of the first forms of physical competition that black males would not only successfully break into but immediately display near dominance. Heavyweight champion pugilist Jack Johnson dominated the sport of boxing with both and iron fist and an unapologetic and uncompromising stance against the status quo in the late nineteenth century. Such accomplishments and demeanor, however, lead to his inevitable downfall as champion, and also played a pivotal role in ensuring that it would be several decades before a black male would claim the coveted and esteemed honor of being called heavyweight champion.

Baseball, similar to boxing, found prominence from the vantage point of black males during the late nineteenth century; even though official Negro league organizations would not be formed until the early part of the twentieth century. Similar to the obstacles that the black male encountered in boxing, standout, highly acclaimed, and notable black baseball players were restricted from playing in both the minor and major leagues with white players. Instead, these talented black athletes were restricted to menial and underfunded black organizations that minimized salaries despite their abilities and obstructed exposure and notoriety. It would not be until 1945 that a black male would be the first to be allowed to play in the major leagues.

Jackie Robinson, although hardly the apotheosis and quintessence of pure talent, was lauded for the talent that he was not only endowed but also because of the virtues that he embraced—many of which were mostly construed as virtues that were on par with those of whites. And although Robinson demonstrated a temperament of intolerance in the face of discrimination and could be combative when confronted by racism, he was also a decorated serviceman who was a proponent of Lyndon Johnson's Vietnam campaign, which was in direct opposition to the tumult of an overwhelming movement of black conscientious objection towards the war effort. Furthermore, he lambasted up and coming heavyweight champion Cassius Clay, who would later change his name to Muhammad Ali, for his refusal of induction into the armed services. It was Robinson's assertion that Clay had displayed complete ingratitude when summoned to serve a country that made his acquisition of fame, fortune, and notoriety possible.

Despite Robinson's attractiveness and agreeability to whites and the white establishment for reasons other than his talents, Robinson's accomplishment of being the first is striking because, unlike other major franchise sports—all of which had splinter and subsidiary leagues before merging into major organizations, similar to baseball—Robinson emerged into the most popular sport in America at a time when there was a uniformed and collective freeze of black players in other major sports franchises. Moreover, black players who participated in other sports either integrated in numbers or had sporadically played in some of these major organizations. Robinson, on the other hand, single-handedly integrated baseball and was arguably under much more pressure and scrutiny, as certainly the "credit to your race" creed was much more lively and effusive then as it is now. Nevertheless, Robinson was not your prototypical black, let alone your prototypical black athlete. In fact, Robinson, similar to Jack Johnson, imbued a demeanor that overshadowed mere athletic prowess and personal accomplishments, and was emblematic of manhood and masculinity that warranted if not admiration—respect. Years would follow after Robinson's accomplishments before both football and basketball began regularly recruiting black athletes, as successful mergers of the ABA/NBA and AFL/NFL would both open doors and preserve the need for black athleticism that would ultimately pave the way for black athletic dominance in these respective sports, particularly Basketball.

———

Conceived by Dr. James Naismith, a Canadian, the first organized basketball league did not appear until 1920; however, it would not be until 1950 that three black players—Earl Lloyd, Chuck Cooper, and Nat Clifton—would open the flood gates for the uncontested dominance of the Bill Russell's, Wilt Chamberlin's, Julius Irving's, Magic Johnson's, Michael Jordan's, Kobe Bryant's, Tim Duncan's, and Lebron James's. Similar to the other major franchise sports, before breaking into the big leagues by crossing the color barriers, black males have always thrived in basketball since its inception. Thus, many blacks made names for themselves in all-black organizations such as the Harlem Globetrotters and the New York Renaissance (Rens) during an era when the first basketball league was established.

Similarly, blacks have always both played and excelled in football, with Charles Follis being recognized as the first black on record to play the game back in the late 1800s to early 1900s. However, before the dissemination of splinter factions or more marginal organizations, as well as the subsequent lockout of black players, both Fritz Pollard and Bobby Marshall made a name for themselves as the first blacks to play in what was then the NFL in the 1920s. Desegregation of blacks in 1933, however, would be maintained until after the Second World War, and similar to the other major sports franchises would permit a wide array of black players following the successful merger of the two major factions into the one, big organization that is the National Football League that exist to this day.

How the Stage, the Court, and the Fields became the new Plantation

Perhaps even superseding all other forms of entertainment, and the various forms of physical sport and competition that the black male would come to dominate, comedy arguably served as the primary sedative for black suffering and oppression. Comedy, as one contemporary black comic put it, transforms the tears to laughter. Hence, at the slave quarters, a comedian or quarter's jester was just as omnipresent as the banjo player or the sage storyteller. The comedic entertainment that was oft-well-received and therapeutic or, in some cases, would whip the slaves into a nostalgic frenzy, would later be duplicated in minstrel shows by racist whites who dressed in black face for the purpose of caricaturing and impugning the celebratory mental escape from the harsh conditions that slavery imposed. Nonetheless, comedic relief persevered in oppressed black communities even following reconstruction and Jim Crow. From Mantan Moreland to Dick Gregory to Redd Foxx, comedy would undergo a metamorphosis of conceptual buffoonery to incisive profaneness to socio-political awareness. Yet even with the advent of black comedians, who would take the art form to a whole new level and raise the level of consciousness to heights never previously attained, buffoonery never completely waned. In other words, for every Bill Cosby there was a Flip Wilson; similar to the state of today's contemporary duality that presupposes that for every Chris Rock there is a Mike Epps or a Kevin Hart.

Yet even when considering the legacy of Richard Pryor—perhaps the first black comedian who effectively combined knee-weakening humor and laughter with profound social commentary—the brazen and oft-profane yet aesthetically pleasing audacity of Redd Foxx, and the megastar status and crossover appeal of Eddie Murphy, black comedy would eventually hit a stalemate. And, presently, its trajectory now appears to be taking the same precipitous plunge that has sullied and practically made a mockery of Rhythm and Blues and Hip Hop music, at least in terms of the past glory and acclaim of each, respectively. Surely this can be attributed to the gradual weakening of black culture, as blacks as a whole no longer appear to embrace the unique qualities and cultural nuances that were the main impetus that caused blacks to excel and surpass other racial groups in all areas and forms of entertainment, including sports.

I will also make the argument that the popular and mainstream culture of America appears to be fully complicit in this endeavor. Take for instance that top black singers and artists no longer represent rhythm and blues and soul music; in fact, the dearth of black soul artists who remain are consigned to the now obscure and marginalized genre called *Neo Soul.* Contemporary top black artists such as Beyonce, Rhianna, Ciara, Chris Brown, Usher, and Bruno Mars (Mars being nonwhite, although not black) are relegated by consumer popularity to the same genre and, due to this fact, are forced to compete with artists such as Brittany Spears, Christina Aguilera, Sam Smith, Justin Timberlake, Justin Bieber, and British (soul) singer Adele—all of whom evoke and imbue the sound and qualities of black singers. Moreover, these white, "who-stole-the-soul" marauders are internationally lauded and receive rave reviews for mimicking a style and sound that today's black singers steadfastly reject for crossover appeal.

———

In the mainstay of sports entertainment the circumstances are strikingly different. That is why the conditions that black athletes have to endure are not so much a situation of choice but more so standings in which they are circumscribed that are strictly due to race. One might ask how this is at all possible, or how is any of what I have previously described possible; instead, surmising these factors as choices of career paths that have nothing at all to do with racism or subjugation. And depending on one's perception, there might be some truth to such objections or differences in terms of perspective. However, like anything else in society that is controlled and mostly dominated by white people (e.g., the economy, political infrastructure, and corporations), black people in general, who endeavor to have a place in these institutions and organizations are automatically circumvented in terms of their role, productivity, and potential for both growth and success. More astounding is that the conglomerates and edifices that are geared towards entertainment very seldom recruit and employ the type of blacks who are endowed with the levels of forethought and consciousness to take their resources, successes, and social standing, and utilize these endowments for the purposes of changing the conditions of people who are from the same communities and are confronted with the same life challenges that many of these athletes and entertainers have overcome and risen above.

Black scholar and social critic, Harry Edwards, observed that in the 1960s black athletes were united by the struggle to overcome oppression; now he states that they are divided by their success. Unfortunately, in a capitalistic society that is driven solely by individual success and self-worth which is invariably determined by what one has materially and monetarily acquired, black victims of institutional racism/white supremacy do not see the racial component at all when it comes to blacks in entertainment. What is instead observed is the belief that these blacks have both literally and figuratively escaped the confines of "the hood," and that fact alone encapsulates the pinnacle of black success in America. As a result, perhaps the primary reason why celebrities in general are revered in this society is the fact that they are widely perceived as being endowed with gifts, talents, and, in some cases, internal valor and fortitude that the great majority of people in this society are seemingly devoid.

For instance, in conducting random surveys for the purposes of research, I asked several black college students if they watched Tyler Perry movies (some even attended his plays), and an overwhelming majority stated that they in fact had done so. And when asked for what reason they watched his films, again, an overwhelming majority stated that they did so strictly for the entertainment value of his works. Some even revealed their attraction to the messages in his films—a matriarchal opus of faith-based family values and (supposed) black, southern aesthetics—that have become an all too familiar theme in Perry's films. Others pointed out the legitimacy of Perry because of his rise from poverty and personal tragedy to being a Hollywood success story, which in itself is probably perceived as the epitome of the American success story and the American Dream that is erroneously perceived as colorless and transcends race.

Perhaps the entertainment industry in America is mostly seen as being an American mechanism that instead of being separated by black and white is a permutation of both; thus, making it highly entertaining, exorbitantly lucrative, and uniquely American. This could not be further from the truth, however. In fact, what may on the surface appear to be symmetry among the two cultures and a microcosm of American diversity is instead an industry that is disproportionately overrun by white studio and music label executives and franchise CEOs and owners, who determine who will be the next big thing in popular music (whether its pop, R&B, hip hop, Rock, or country western). Or, who will be the next box-office cash cow in film or academy award winner; or, who will be the next multi-million dollar athlete, particularly one whose picture is on a box of Wheaties (cereal) or whose name is stenciled on a pair of Nike sneakers. In other words, the black male in America and black folk in general are not in the entertainment industry for the purposes of mitigating their historically perceived "otherness" for unquestionable American loyalties and common bonds. If that were the case, America would not be a society that is still separated by black and white; particularly being that the entertainment industry is the most viable and visible edifice that intrinsically infuses both cultures. Instead, the black male has and continues to be used as fodder for an industry that is primarily concerned with either maximizing profits or reinforcing racial stereotypes (actually, it effectively does both), with the latter prospect sadly being in direct conflict with black and white commonalities and sensibilities that are gradually taking place in the REAL world.

The Three Mikes

"I'm the best ever; there's never been anybody
as ruthless. I'm Sonny Liston, I'm Jack Dempsey;
I'm cut from their cloth, there's no one that can match me.
My style is impetuous, my defense is impregnable,
and I'm ferocious I want your heart. I want to eat his
[Lennox Lewis's] children. Praise be to Allah!"
—MIKE TYSON

Mike Tyson Not since the great Muhammad Ali had a heavyweight come onto the scene of championship boxing/prizefighting and generated the kind of fervor and excitement that Michael Gerald Tyson had done, singlehandedly. A Brooklyn born and raised miscreant, Tyson from the onset of his career, and as described by one boxing critic, "had the ferocity of Sonny Liston and could punch like Jack Dempsey." Because of this, Tyson quite possibly generated even more excitement than Ali because, unlike Ali's out-fighting, safety-danced mastery of the so-called "sweet science," Tyson was an urban behemoth whose murderous punch, as another pundit put it, appeared to be "drawn from the primordial ooze of civilization as we know it."

Winning the heavyweight title at the tender age of twenty—making him the youngest to do so—secured Tyson's status as a bona fide modern day sports hero and cultural celebrity. Yet even with Tyson's physical gifts, what would become clear throughout the course of his perilous and tumultuous career was that Tyson was a product of external forces and circumstances that would both stymie his advances to iconic and global immortality, and reduce him to the ranks of drudgery and condemnation that affects a disproportionate number of black males; especially those who are by-products of the same urban decay and psychologically and physically eviscerating conditions that both made and compromised his life and career.

Typical of the plight of so many young black males in America, Tyson was a product of a single-parent, fatherless home amid crime, drugs, and violence. Also similar to so many other young urban dwellers, these circumstances and conditions would shape and mold the type of psyche in Tyson that would compel and exhort a trajectory to violent predilections, petty crime, and malfeasance that would peg him a label of urban menace—the kind that is widely and justifiably perceived as going in either one or two directions: a lifetime of incarceration or certain death at an early age. However, unlike many of his other young urban contemporaries, Tyson was fortunate enough to have been removed from the environment that often destroys its inhabitants, and instead was put into a comfortable middle-class domicile that would serve as a launching pad to ensure Tyson's path towards immeasurable wealth and prestige. This escape was accomplished by way of his being brought into the fold of famed and legendary boxing trainer Cus D'Amato who, to his credit, had aided in shaping and molding the careers of former light heavyweight champion Jose Torres and former heavyweight champion Floyd Patterson, who similar to Tyson once held the incontestable distinction of youngest ever heavyweight champion.

It would be in the mountains of Catskill, New York that D'Amato would remove Tyson from an environment that is typically conducive to creating the socially and culturally polymorphic "black boogeyman," to a much more comfortable setting that would create a champion prize fighter who would exceed all others before him. However, it would be the failure of D'Amato to rear an intrinsically disadvantaged black male in a racist society that would both prove Tyson's inevitable downfall and expose D'Amato as a man blinded by his own vicarious ambitions.

While young, strong, endowed with uncharacteristic punching power, cat-like reflexes, unflinching speed (similar to Ali was considered abnormal for a heavyweight), and at the time seemingly uncorrupted, even Tyson's collage of physical gifts that would catapult him to boxing supremacy and unmitigated cultural intrigue and fanfare could not override the inner turmoil and trauma of his being a poor, young ghetto misfit and hoodlum. This is especially true of a ghetto youth who was all of a sudden thrusts into a fraternity of an upper class of the world's most powerful nation, as well as becoming one of its most visible public personalities. Even Cus D'Amato's undertaking of saving a lost and indigent soul, putting him in an environment strictly conducive to his becoming a champion prize-fighter, and allowing his young charge to soak in all of the disciplinary and studious accoutrements along the way, could not ascertain an inextricable linkage of both the physical and mental necessities that D'Amato philosophized were essential to becoming the heavyweight champion of the world.

Cus D'Amato, a man just as notorious for his eccentricities as he was his brilliance of, what Tyson would later coin "the hurt business," spent a life-time instilling in his fighters the obligatory nature of acquiring the physical, emotional, and psychological traits that were essential in not only becoming a champion but also enabling one to carry the championship with pride and living the life of a champion, and not trading off or sacrificing one characteristic for another. Yet it was either D'Amato's failure or complete disregard to speak truthfully about the scrutiny and dubious honor of being both a black heavyweight champion and human being in a racist society that arguably caused Tyson, somewhere throughout his career and amid his personal trials and tribulations to discard those teachings and philosophy. Subsequently, a feasible question then would be, how much of a difference was there between the teenage Tyson that had an emotional, tear-drenched breakdown in the arms of then trainer Teddy Atlas, immediately preceding a match at the Olympic trials, than the Tyson who literally quit fighting and mentally convinced himself that he could not be competitive after receiving a Lennox Lewis uppercut in the first round of their much anticipated championship bout? After all, Lewis was the man whom Tyson claimed that he would not only destroy in the ring but would also "eat his children" (increasing the irony of such a statement being that at the time Lewis had no children).

Indeed, Mike Tyson's career could be summarized as either that of a flash-n-the pan, fly-by-night phenomenon that should have been but never completely amounted to, or as another example of the crippling effects of a black male in a racist society's failure to thrive and flourish despite the advantages that he was not only given but are deprived to a great many other young black males. Despite being estimated to be worth nearly half a billion dollars during the height of his popularity, Tyson could not avoid becoming a victim and statistic of institutionalization—a fate that is the inescapable reality for many black males in this country. Also, Tyson's publicity and notoriety was merely a stage for deeply embedded insecurities and uncouth qualities that lied dormant and, for a brief moment, well-hidden under the veneer and physicality of unquestionable manliness and virility. Yet even after Tyson's conversion to Islam and self-avowed redemption following a three-year prison stint for the alleged rape of a beauty pageant contestant, Tyson's ear-biting fiasco against heavyweight champion and long-time nemesis Evander Holyfield was irrefutable proof of an individual who was still fully engulfed and incapacitated by the same demons and insecurities that had haunted him all of his life. In addition to a display of actions that were anti-climactic of the principles that D'Amato had so feverishly and nobly tried to instill.

Tyson's legacy, that started off as a spectacle of perhaps the most dominant heavyweight champion the sport had ever seen has now often been legitimately argued as one of a high-profile bully who, once he himself was stared down by eyes that were devoid of fear and intimidation, reverted to being a caricature of the pummeling, pulverizing skills that he once displayed in the ring. Similar to most, if not all bullies and brutes, Tyson immediately sensed fear in his opponents, and it was the fear factor that was in hindsight the mystique of Tyson's ring dominance, even superseding his strength and skill level. However, Tyson, former heavyweight champion and self-professed "baddest man on the planet," was capsized by his own insecurities and fears; fears that in hindsight—similar to his opponent's fear of him and his own ring supremacy—were not due to any fault of his own. Thus, similar to the criminal assault on Evander Holyfield in the ring, the incident of Tyson crashing a car that was moving at thirty miles per hour into a tree was far from a suicide attempt. Instead, it was more of a cry and plea for help from a universally admired and culturally revered black athlete whom obviously was ill-equipped to deal with the rigors of being a poor black youth from the gutter and was subsequently under intense scrutiny and hyper vigilance in a racist society. According to the philosophy of former trainer and now christened boxing guru Teddy Atlas, Tyson, from a young age possessed the size, strength, and drive to be a potentially great heavyweight; however, it was the absence of character that would ultimately be Tyson's Achilles' heel. And that it is the character of the champion, compounded by his skill level that is the true calling of a heavyweight champion.

There are perhaps many who would argue that Tyson was besieged by personal problems and was beset by issues that were taking place outside of the ring that ultimately had an effect on his performance and mental state inside of the ring. Even if this is true, it confirms the philosophy of both Atlas and D'Amato in regards to the importance of maintaining professionalism, and how character and mental and psychological strengths are equally as important as physical strength in overcoming such barriers. Perhaps Tyson's subsequent humiliating defeats at the hands of other champion-caliber fighters who either completely demonstrated more "manliness" than himself or proved that Tyson was not the only person with problems, is testament to D'Amato's own contradictory approach to making Tyson the next great heavyweight champion. In hindsight, it was D'Amato's overzealous ambition of strictly socializing Tyson in a manner that sportswriter Robert Lipsyte described as "an American pit bull," and failure to socialize Tyson in a fashion appropriate to him being a high-profile black male athlete in a society that is still largely consumed by race and continues the practice of adverse and sordid race relations.

It is because of this approach at socializing and subsequent failures that what Tyson was predestined to become was largely based on his not being encouraged to do well in school, failures to effectively address and correct distasteful and aggressive behaviors enacted towards other people (particularly young girls), and failure to instill that there are certain expectations and responsibilities to be considered when you are both a black male and the heavyweight champion of the world. As D'Amato's sister-in-law, Camille Ewald so aptly stated, "Cus taught Mike how to be a fighter, but he didn't teach Mike how to live." (The author does acknowledge however that over the past few years, Tyson has successfully reemerged as an adored national celebrity and entertainer, making appearances in several successful box office films, as well as starring in a series of successful on-stage plays based on his life).

Michael Jordan- The black male without question has been the most prolific and proficient athlete in America both before and throughout the popularity and marketability of franchise sports. Even white racists have grudgingly had to accept this simple truth, despite current efforts to either neutralize or neuter the dominance of black athletes. For what other reason would Tom Brokaw asks the machismo-reducing and debilitating question to white men and the white world, "are black athletes better than white athletes?" in an NBC news special in April of 1989. However, the subjective nature of the question and the affirmation of my claim does little to negate the fact that even incomparably great black athletes have and continue to succumb to the white supremacist system and mindset that overwhelms black people, especially the black male, regardless of how physically dexterous and recreationally skillful.

Mike Tyson, previously discussed, and similar to Michael Jordan, was enveloped in a state of white racism and conscious and unconscious racial nuances, from both those who outwardly debased and scorned him, as well as those who sought to displace him from the dudgeon of ghetto life and make him a great champion prize fighter. Even Teddy Atlas's intelligent analysis of Tyson's lack of inner fortitude as being the main culprit of thwarting his reaching the apogee of his potential does not overshadow Atlas's recounting of the incident in which he put a gun in Tyson's face after Tyson allegedly sexually assaulted a young female acquaintance, stating his reason for doing so was to protect "his people" and those closest to him. But unlike Tyson, and even Michael Jackson (whom I will discuss shortly), Michael Jordan was not a precocious basketball prodigy, or one of any sort for that matter. In fact, at best, and contrary to how Jackson showed the innate gifts of the next great fleet-footed, soul-singing *phenom* by the time he could walk; and Tyson who demonstrated the physical gifts and unpredictable, uncouth characteristics of the next "eat lightning and crap thunder" heavyweight champion; Jordan's trajectory and impending legacy appeared to be more on par with a desire of being the next Willie Mayes rather than Oscar Robinson or Earl Monroe. Incredulously, Jordan, as he coincidentally gravitated towards the sport that beckoned his burgeoning gifts and trumpeted the "hoop dreams" that would make him both a sports hero and cultural icon, was actually cut from his varsity basketball team as a sophomore in high school.

Yet despite this, the Brooklyn born, North Carolina raised Jordan would become perhaps the greatest offensive player and most feared competitor the sport has even seen. Listed at 6'6 inches tall, Jordan did not possess the goliath-like stature of Kareem Abdul-Jabbar, the league's all-time leading scorer, or the bull-dozing Adonis-like physique of Karl Malone, the league's second all-time leading scorer. Jordan didn't need the bulk or the height, as his perfectly symmetrical frame that was a flesh and blood launching pad for mongoose-like reflexes, cat-like speed, deceptive leaping ability, and an IQ for the game that made Jordan a cerebral giant and scoring juggernaut in a game that was afflicted with just a dearth of one or the other, but practically extinct in endowments of both. Arguably, however, it was Michael Jordan's reluctant blackness or questionable loyalties or allegiances to his black identity (even presently, Jordan is married to a white woman) that took several manifestations and that evoked the profundity of actor Morgan Freeman's swipe on Black History Month, proclaiming the ridiculous and erroneous endeavor of "relegating" the extensive history and experiences of blacks in America to the shortest month of the calendar year.

On the surface, and in addition to his unparalleled talents, Jordan appeared to be the embodiment or paragon of the American black athlete. He was raised in a traditional, nuclear southern black family that emanated southern black values. He was the first to wear baggy shorts on the court, a manner of self-expression within the rigid confines of professional and franchise decorum that was deeply rooted in the couture of ghetto youth in urban playgrounds across the country. And, his trademark Nike sneakers by all appearances, initially, seemed to have been designed and marketed to integrate black youth into a mainstay of corporate enterprise that went beyond just simple consumerism. But similar to Morgan Freeman's assertion that the precipice of race-relations hinges on America's desire to be consumed by color, Jordan refused to hang himself in effigy of black athlete; choosing instead to package himself as an American athlete who represented and spoke for all Americans in regards to his success.

Social critic, educator, and author, Michael Eric Dyson in his book *Between God and Gangsta Rap*, illustrated Jordan's desire to shake the shackles and stigma of color, disavowing himself from both a black and white existence and espousing his being contented with just being Michael Jordan.[45] And similar to the plight of Tiger Woods, the sport's worlds other endorsement giant and media phenomenon (and who also has a voracious fetish and jones for white women), both succumbed to the delusion and fallacy of being colorless deities, premature to even Freeman's analysis that America had yet to reach that threshold. Furthermore, the delusion seemed to presuppose that blackness could be bought, sold, or, in Wood's case, negotiated based on degrees of hue and color and hodgepodge of cultural heritage and ethnicities.

During the twilight of Jordan's basketball dominance, and even prior to his first retirement and subsequent return, what would become widely publicized were some of the demons and vices that were hidden beneath the veneer of basketball immortality and well-guarded public persona. In the tell-all biography *The Jordan Rules*, a kid-friendly, iconic sport's giant that was never bested by an image or photo that depicted anything other than a smile was supplanted by that of a quick-tempered and, sometimes violent, voracious competitor who was more preoccupied with winning than preserving a PR campaign. Furthermore, an intense gambling habit had come to the forefront; one that was allegedly so severe that it was briefly rumored that his father's tragic and violent death was related to Jordan's adverse gambling habits and debts that he (supposedly) owed. Indeed, a prospect even more engrossing being that delving into Jordan's true character also revealed that the only things that were loose when it came to his money were his baggy shorts and garb, in which he was perhaps the first to make both trendy and a trademark.

Despite this analysis, however, what is important is that it is first understood that this is not an attempt at a malignant character assault. Clearly, Jordan, and Tyson, despite their physical gifts are no different than any of us. What is equally important in terms of clarity is that their statuses as sports heroes do not exempt them from being susceptible to vices that humanize and strips the abnormality of those who physically excel the great majority of other human beings across the globe. It is therefore my argument that the Jordan's and Tyson's of black America are victims of the same social order that has ensnared and psychologically decimated nearly all black people—male and female—in a white supremacist-minded culture and society; regardless of whether they are athletic, non-athletic, fighters, or pacifists. Also, that the actions of these high-profiled black persons are a conflation of inherent personality traits and external racial dogma that are equally as responsible in choices and decision-making than are those that are based on their own volition and merit. There is a saying, "keep it real," in Hip Hop culture that posits the importance of staying true to self despite the odds and fringe temptations. Unquestionably, an aphorism that is invaluable; hence, its appeal to socially-disadvantaged youth who not only crafted Hip Hop music/culture but also aided in making Jordan both a cultural icon and a multimillion dollar athlete.

Even so, just maybe it was Jordan's accidental blackness and reluctance to identify himself with poor, urban black kids that caused Jordan to miss this point, and that also rendered him morally incapable of intervening—be it by public appeal or reneging of contractual obligations—when it became apparent that urban youngsters were slaughtering each other on the streets and in droves over his excessively priced Nike sneakers and other Chicago Bull's regalia. The problem then, at least in terms of my analysis, as well as in regards to Michael Jordan's subtle renunciation of racial classification is that during his time as a star athlete, it was contradictorily masqueraded as an obvious bartering tool in regards to the poor and disadvantaged who lionized and deified him. Also, this deception was concocted and thus carried out, all for the assurance of wealth and guarantee of neutrality to the powers-that-be who both envied his physical attributes and sought to financially gain from them. Yet, at the same time, those same powers seek to vilify and destroy young urban males who potentially possess those same gifts and talents.

Michael Jordan is perhaps the greatest basketball player that has ever lived. However, along with that esteemed honor is the fact that he is also symptomatic of the black male in a racist society who caters to prestige and riches over issues of race, racism, and social justice. Moreover, Jordan is without question symptomatic of those who delude themselves to a misleading claim of human beings being endowed with free will and an unobstructed path to whatever it is that they choose or aspire to be in life. Perhaps Jordan should take a page from other notable athletes who believed that they were above the social construction of self-worth and personal legitimacy based on color, such as O. J. Simpson and Tiger Woods. Perhaps only then will Jordan, and other athletes and celebrities who possess a similar mentality, understand the importance of keeping it real; especially in a society that is driven by a racist and white-supremacist mentality, and spurred by a bloodlust to destroy black males and boys.

Michael Jackson-There has quite possibly never been a more tragic, high-profile victim of the racial caste of the American social order than Michael Joseph Jackson, a black male whose universally-recognized talents were shrouded by a cyclonic cloud of personal tumult and deeply-embedded self-hatred. There also has never been a black entertainer who succeeded in achieving unprecedented massive appeal and a globally deified stature by way of the burgeoning popularity and appeal of rhythmic song and dance, despite the inevitable yet serendipitous transformation that would take place due to extreme oddity and eccentricity.

Michael Jackson was a black male whose child-like innocence, though a rarity in a genre of flamboyance and effusive sexual virility, seems to have engineered vacuum-like intrigue. Latent, however, was the fact that this disposition was the result of the undertaking of the emasculation and effacing of manliness in the black male as result of the conditioning of institutional racism in a society that imperceptibly boast yet brazenly practices white supremacy. A process that has in the past and continues to be employed, regardless of innate vocal qualities and physical gifts and incomparable talent endowed in individuals such as Jackson that white people had never possessed prior to Jackson's popularity and have since failed to surpass or even duplicate. Despite what the sentiments of racists and racism posits or dictates, Elvis was no Michael Jackson, and the contemporary "who stole the soul" marauders (similar to Elvis), such as Justin Timberlake, are but a mere joke and visage of modern-day musical minstrelsy turned *blackwards*.

Cut from the same cloth as Jackie Wilson and James Brown, yet bequeathed with a combination of the sweet soul of Motown and the rapidly evolving nuances of popular music, Jackson appeared to be the perfect musical culmination of both past and future vocal greatness and on-stage artistry and creativity. Born the third to the youngest of ten siblings (officially there are nine after the death at birth of one sibling) in a working class home in blue-collar Gary, In., the Jackson family would go on to procure the distinct title of the First Family of Soul music. And it was Michael who both established and raised the bar of a megastar, as well as universal iconic status.

At a young age, Michael stood out from his other brothers and sisters as a result of his precocious vocalizations and his mastery of artistic mimicry—particularly artists who mastered as well as redefined the skill of song and dance—as he eventually would as well. If there is any proof to the notion that some individuals are unabatedly predestined to become whatever it is that they had become, from all appearances Jackson was born to be the ultimate entertainer, colossal celebrity, and global *phenom*. In addition to his immense talents, which would become practically incomparable at the nascent stages of his career (*Off the Wall*, a colossal success, and considered as Michael's fifth studio album is actually his first solo album, as previous albums were part of the Jackson 5 franchise), Jackson also pioneered trends in fashion (e.g., high-watered and parachute pants, beat-it bags, and glittered gloves which were popular around the success of his *Thriller* album). Furthermore, he, along with burgeoning sports Icon Michael Jordan, was the first of a fraternity of black celebrity mega-endorsers of corporate conglomerates (e.g., Jackson Pepsi and

Jordan Nike). Jackson also is perhaps the most influential musical artist that has ever lived, creating an ever-increasing cadre of songsters and entertainers whose gimmicks and stage performances and routines are visibly (and explicitly) influenced by Jackson's sound and style.

Now, in order to analyze and dissect the travails and ultimate destruction of Michael Jackson with thoroughness and verity, it has to first be understood that in a society where the dominant function is by way of a white supremacist model and racist doctrine, blacks who straddle out of white people's safety net or attempt to cruise into their no-fly zone are the ones who get the worst of white racist reprisal and the brunt of their wrath for not knowing their place. Civil rights leaders and social activists such as Martin Luther King Jr., Jesse Jackson, and Al Sharpton have always been and will continue to be either full beneficiaries of white condemnation (including death) or be viewed with an air of suspicion and are scrutinized very carefully.

Black entertainers, however, have never posed a threat to the white establishment or ruffled the feathers of whites, lest they made socially conscious music that heightened awareness, inculcated racial pride and self-respect, or directly challenged the status quo. Some of the artists that come to mind and who dared to traverse this path are James Brown, Sly and the Family Stone, Edwin Starr, Marvin Gaye, and Curtis Mayfield. But maybe with the exception of songs such as "they don't care about us," never was there an artist who chose the least path of resistance in addressing the oppressive social order and cataclysm of black injustice than Michael Jackson. If anything, his supposed and alleged criminal predilections may have only contributed to what many perceive are issues that have an exorbitantly negative affect on society as opposed to those things that are greatly in need of fixing.

Similar to most black entertainers, both past and present, Jackson sought comfort in just being considered as an entertainer. Even Bill Cosby, long before his uncharacteristic and derisive crusade of lambasting the black poor, nestled comfortably in his role as a simple entertainer and not a champion for the causes of black people. Michael Eric

Dyson in his provocative expose, *Is Bill Cosby right? Or has the Black Middle Class lost its mind,* illustrates Cosby's assertion of "I don't think entertainers can win converts."[46] Accordingly, what separated Jackson from other black entertainers wasn't just his reluctance to embroil himself in social injustices that affected the black poor and downtrodden, but also his soon-to-be-revealed identification with black people—not just culturally and aesthetically, but biologically. As one music historian and Jackson observer pointed out, "Michael just didn't know how to be a black guy who could be loved by the white world." Thus, Jackson saw all of the cultural, physical, and biological gifts that made him such a mesmerizing entertainer and global megastar as vices in the confines of whiteness and white supremacy. More tragic is how he would go about remedying the one flaw and defect that seemed to haunt him and that would ultimately destroy him: being black in a white/racist world.

Michael Jackson was undeniably a marvel on stage, combined with a supple yet rangy chocolate-velvet falsetto voice that took him onto an entirely different level than his peers. Yet at the height of his musical supremacy, Jackson started to undergo personality and physical transformations that would ultimately trump his indisputable talents; changes that initially appeared to have been the escaped skeletons out of the closet of an enigmatic individual who had begun to display all of the manifestations of his deeply-rooted eccentricities. And what would later become apparent is that these transmutations were the result of a black male who was completely decimated by his upbringing (or lack thereof) that, consequently, permeated extreme self-loathing and profound enmity towards his racial identity. Thus, what started off as sleeping with monkeys and in oxygen tanks, manifested into charges of pedophilia—allegations that both led to out of court settlements for substantial amounts of money and his exoneration in a court of law.

Many have argued, including myself at one point, that Jackson's troubled life was an obvious manifestation of both a troubled and deprived childhood. Also, combined with the physical abuse that Jackson and his other siblings were purported to have suffered in depictions such as the made for television miniseries *The Jacksons: An American Dream*, it had been revealed that Jackson suffered equally devastating emotional abuse; a factor that many surmise as the primary determinant that lead to his hatred of his physical appearance. In addition to an adolescent affliction of chronic acne, Jackson, as has been reported, was also often referred to as "big nose" from his father, Joseph Jackson. Yet despite the irony and cruelty of these acts, I will argue that these abuses were not restricted to the Jackson home. In fact, they are probably more accurately indicative of being staples in the black community when enacting and exuding expressions of self-hate in a nation that from its inception, boldly proclaimed and postulated the repugnance and un-American qualities of black skin and features. I, for instance, was constantly teased and made fun of for having full (or big) lips, as were other blacks who had non-European features, e.g., kinky hair, wide noses, thick lips, etc.

This is certainly not an attempt to give Joe Jackson—the patriarch of the Jackson family—a pass for this behavior if there is indeed any truth to these claims. Not for nothing, however, the idea that these acts were the primary factors that resulted in several facial reconstructive surgeries (at least 10 confirmed even though there was believed to have been many more) to minimize (or completely eliminate) African features, as well as Jackson allegedly immersing himself in the use of carcinogenic skin whitening creams such as porcelana—a mollifying ointment reported as being described by Jackson and sister Latoya as the most valuable beauty product on earth—are beyond incredulous.

Also, Jackson's collaborative creation of the USA for Africa campaign, driven by the multi-platinum selling and numerous award-winning single *We are the World* was not only rightfully panned by critics for the song's failure to address the root of famine and poverty in Africa—deemed more "self-aggrandizing" than genuinely humanitarian—the effort by Jackson should also in hindsight be considered as highly questionable because of Jackson's perceptions of blackness and black people. For this reason, it should be of little or no surprise that Jackson reportedly told one of his domestics that he did not like being black because of his belief that blacks were not liked as much as people of other races. And although it may be true that the previously mentioned statement can be written off as nothing more than mere speculation, what is undeniably true, however, is that Jackson's racial and cultural alterations were tragically to no avail; as his specter-like, grayish coloration that put him somewhere in the abyss of black and white, garnered him more scorn and derision than acceptance—particularly from the dominant culture he so longed to be a part of.

In some respects, his physical appearance was identical to his mental state, which was that of an individual who was neither black nor white but who existed somewhere between a black and white world. A tragic alternative for a human being endowed with so many gifts, yet despite those gifts was incapable of deciphering who it is he truly was, as well as being able to measure his true value and self-worth and finding solace in his black identity. Nevertheless, and despite his talents and mainstream status, Michael Jackson was a black male who ultimately caved in a hodge-podge of institutional racism, family dysfunction, and social and cultural emasculation. And it is because of this assessment that what I would implore of black folk, who continue to exists under a penumbra of white supremacy, that instead of dismissing him, or snapping our fingers and shuffling our feet the next time we hear a Jackson tune, Perhaps it would behoove all of US to take the time and learn from his tragic life and untimely death.

Sport and Play: How Worthless or Invaluable?

"You are African American, and myself and my friends, for the most part, don't care for the company of African Americans. Quite frankly, we're entertained by you; we're thrilled by your high-flying acrobatics on

Khalil Baaqi

*the basketball court, that wonderful sense
of rhythm you have, your animal athleticism.
But, apart from that, we have no use for you!*"[17]
—FRANKLIN, *BLOOD AND BONE*

Despite the fact there is a black male and a first black family sitting at the helm of the most powerful nation on the planet, black people as a whole, who remain powerless, find safety and solace in retreating to the manners of expression that have always assuaged their suffering and has always put them one step ahead of white people: singing, dancing, and entertaining. Check the commercials and advertising of networks that cater to blacks such as Black Entertainment Television (BET), Centric, and TV One, and it will be hard not to notice the synchronized dance and gyrations in unison as the networks navigate through the black shows and sitcoms that comprise their channel line ups (which are miniscule in quality and number, as the shows *Martin*, *The Jeffersons*, or *Moesha* can run throughout the entirety of the day or evening).

Major advertisements of big corporations also cash in on black culturally-oriented rituals and practices, such as a recent Chrysler's commercial showcasing a black gospel choir, engendering and evoking "good old-fashioned religion," negro-style, to increase the quality of their merchandise by way of depicting images of blacks that historically have been acceptable and deemed inoffensive (yet repugnant, nonetheless) to whites. Yet black people as a whole are not only comfortable with these images and depictions but find them encouraging, primarily because they are culturally conducive to the subtle nuances between black and white, and define who black folk are in a country that is bipolar in its acceptance of blacks. The problem, however, is the false belief that black folk's roots and aesthetics are culturally empowering and admirable to white people, when that notion could not be further from the truth. If anything, those differences are that much more magnetized—bolstering the racist ideology of Americanism and un-Americanism, being European as opposed to being African, and providing whites extra incentive to both resent and exploit those differences.

The real truth is that in America—again, the most powerful nation on the planet and, indisputably, the most racist—blacks and whites are put together to deceive, bamboozle, and disseminate the illusion of a colorblind and ethnically-diverse and tolerant society for the purpose of selling out sports arenas, increasing Nielsen ratings, and to boost box office ticket sells. In a society that has always practiced racism, fueled by a white supremacist mindset, and continues to believe that black/ness sullies white purity and has been dead weight in endeavors that are geared towards national advancement, it should be easy then to consider the claim that if there was no Hollywood—combined with the molasses-like growth of the so-called black middle-class—America would be nearly as separated by race now than it had been during the Jim Crow era.

According to Dr. Joy Degruy, author of *Post Traumatic Slave Syndrome*, America's denial of racism has kept it sick.[48] And it is this sickness that has caused black athletes and celebrities and those (few) blacks who have money and fame (considering that there are no real class divisions between black people) to invoke the falsehood of the Horatio Algiers theory, and levitate on a floating bed of nostalgia and false belief that they have made it in a racist society despite color and race. This is especially true depending on what it is that certain blacks do to live prosperously and comfortably, as certainly singing and dancing, telling jokes, and slam-dunking a basketball have always been viable alternatives. Consequently, many of these blacks drape themselves in a blanket of whiteness—live white, act white, talk white, embrace white values, date white people, copulate with white people and, occasionally, marry white people. All the while pretending to appeal to black sensibilities by virtue of where it is that they are from, the obstacles that they themselves had to overcome, the roles they play, the jokes they tell, and the awards they accept; thus, making them beacons of hope and shining examples of supposed black success in a racist society (but has winning Oscars and NAACP Image

Awards for playing maids and having illicit affairs with white people really changed the perception of blacks from the viewpoint of whites?).

Presently, what you have is a collage of performers, athletes, and entertainers who ply their respective trades for personal and monetary gain, prestige, and privileges, and who just so happen to be black. Subsequently, these individuals do not explicitly represent black culture or use their status to speak on issues that affect black people as a whole. Some even make mockery of themselves by way of their boast and coveting of personal excesses (e.g., Deon Sander's "must be the money," a remake of Secret Weapon's "must be the music"), or Steve Harvey's claim that despite his own admission of the trials and tribulations that black people in general are forced to endure by virtue of the iniquitous actions of racist whites, "America is still the best thing going." When thoroughly analyzing and/or witnessing the rest of the colored world's basking in their new-found freedoms, and gradual ascent to the amelioration and rebuilding of economic infrastructures and recoupment of resources that were pillaged and taken during European colonialism, Harvey's statement can only be interpreted as meaning that despite the (albeit slow) advances of people of color globally, things are still much better in "Massa's" house. Putting aside his own success and expensive suits, the latter perhaps being what his most famous for, Harvey should closely examine what it is that black people in America actually have, own, and are proprietors of that makes them better off than people of color elsewhere if he is going to legitimately boast such a claim.

More surprising is that there are many black folk who act as if their blackness can be reduced, marginalized, or even compromised once they have achieved a certain level of fame and notoriety. Thus, black-on-black marriages and other manners of inter-cultural alliances are almost a stark no-no if one wants to soar to the highest rungs of mainstream success, considering that being a high-profile black who successfully ingratiates into white folds on all levels is the ultimate level of achievement and highest form of validation. Furthermore, surgical and cosmetic procedures to obfuscate blackness—skin tone and features—are more prevalent now than at any time during the nation's past history, which is highly profound considering the ubiquitous national claim of racial tolerance and colorblindness.

Tyler Perry: Cultural Icon or Transgendered/ Emasculated Opportunist?

"You have no sense of shame, so you're no longer human beings; you've become a race of animals!"
—Louis Farrakhan

In one of my upcoming chapters entitled "Hyenas & Lions/Us vs. Them" I metaphorically attempt to dissect the ongoing racial conditions that continue to widen the gap between black and white existences in America. Most of us are familiar with the slogan that posits the Lion as "king of the jungle"; however, many of us may not be aware that Hyenas, similar to Lions, are sociable, clan-based animals that, unlike the Lion, are run by a matriarchal hierarchy.

An observation that I have often mulled over and a truism that I have come to conclude is often grossly overlooked in assessing the creative ambitions of Tyler Perry, is that he symbolically castrates himself whenever he dons a dress and engrosses himself in the visage of a gun-toting, boisterous, yet reverent matriarch that, as I have often heard it stated, every black family not only has but also can relate to. This observation is critical being that Perry is a six-foot-five inch black male who has become the wealthiest black entertainer in Hollywood by way of his propensity of delineating the lives of black people as a culture that is stabilized by a female-dominated family structure, as well as a culture whose survival hinges on the maternal trappings of the female and her influence as opposed to the contributions (or lack thereof) of the male (it should also be noted that not only are female Hyenas larger than the males but are more dominant and revered in terms of rank).

Fans or frequent patrons of Tyler Perry's films are privy to the fact that in most of his films, it is the female character that imbues all of the emotional and self-righteous sensibilities that the males seem to lack. Also, the females in Perry's depictions are crafted as being the *yang* to the *yin* of righteousness vs. indignation, an observation that speaks volumes and clearly underlines his base of mostly black female viewers, as well as his own compulsion for the melodramatic when he decides to put his buffoonish, transgendered convictions on hold (e.g., *Why did I get married* films and *For Colored Girls*). Therefore, when analyzing this claim it is interesting to note that in Perry's rare attempt to depict the black male in a positive light, as in the case with his film *Daddy's Little Girls*, which attempted to debunk the myth of the deadbeat black father, marked the first of a dip in Perry's opening weekend box office sells—proving two things: First, that Perry's mostly female base may not be so noble or at least race conscious as their unwavering support of his mostly black-everything films might appear to be on the surface; preferring instead to see either melodrama delineated from the female perspective or social issues and familial crises that are more female-specific.

Second of all, perhaps his large female constituency succeeds in finding more humor and entertainment value in the frivolous, buffoonish exploits of the behemoth Madea, as opposed to appreciating the value and worthiness of an attempt to address a serious issue in the black community. A crisis so severe that it clearly continues to contribute not only to the widening gap between black male and black female relations but also continues to swathe a path of uncertainty for black children. And unlike Perry's other contemporary black story tellers and film directors (none of whom Perry has ever acknowledge other than his sentiment that Spike Lee can "go to hell"), Perry, himself, has no film background or pedigree—academic or otherwise—that would justify his tumultuous standing. Moreover, Perry's works are the farthest thing from cinematic brilliance, which underscores his lack of formal training, combined with his failure to even complete high school. I mean, honestly, are those who are opposed to Perry's craft or question his legitimacy arguing against storytelling genius or failing to recognize an inherent gift and honest zeal of humanizing and civilizing black folk and portraying them in a positive light? Hardly!

In contrast, what Perry has succeeded in doing is catering to the weakest link in black culture, and currying favor from the dominant caste by exploiting the weaknesses and vulnerabilities of the dominant caste's weaker sub-sect and perpetual victims. Also, Perry has demonstrated a talent in showcasing black folk as a subculture that is purposefully cloaked and enveloped in theological subservience, as well as one that continues to blindly wander the path of least resistance in a society that is still pedagogically and theologically enveloped by the notion of cultural superiority and inferiority, by virtue of the same religious tenets that Perry depicts black folk as so precipitously and whole-heartedly encumbered. When Lion's Gates films gave Perry an unprecedented multi-movie deal to a black filmmaker that guaranteed him millions upon millions under the conditions that he tone down his religious zeal and pious rhetoric, a calling that was the sole result of the success of his plays before his ascent into film, the capitalist as well as pacifist in Perry saw no conflict in this compromise. Interesting enough, this is all justified or overlooked given Perry's commitment to providing to black actors what they would otherwise be denied in an industry that is by far the most visibly and ostentatiously racist and discriminatory in its portrayal and depictions of blacks, particularly black males. Thus, what subsequently follows is a concomitant of the proverbial "lesser of two evils," unsurprising given Perry's pious soliloquy that when he became unsure of the success of some of his earlier plays and was willing to throw in the towel, he heard the voice of God forewarning him of the consequences of quitting unless his God had ordained such a pronouncement.

Similar to former president George W. Bush's claim that explicit instructions by God were the root of his policy and administrative decision-making, it is interesting how those who have acquired an excessive amount of capital or who sit in positions of power are the only ones who can (literally) hear God's voice. As a poor black male, I cannot say that I have had the pleasure. On the contrary, I have endured a whole life spent believing that God speaks to me by way of conscious, rational decisions, thoughts, and actions. However, Perry's connection and rapport with God conceives that it is Godly and virtuous to reinforce negative racial stereotypes—most of which are done while in drag—and place destructive images and social dysfunctions of black people as a whole on the silver screen. While the religion of Perry's black constituency should be the religion of liberation and denouncement of black exploitation, as well its gravitation towards decency and progression and not regression, Perry's illustration of the state of black America is one that is copacetic as long as there is enough chaos, drama, volatility, chitterlings (or chit'lins), barbeque, guns, and bibles. Hence, the message that is sent is that the grown folks and chil'rens should be "otay," followed by a big thumb up to white America—most of whom do not watch his films nor do they think very highly of his films when they do take the time to watch them (according to my surveys and research a great many whites do not even know who Tyler Perry is, in addition to the fact that most if not all of his films receive subpar to negative reviews from critics)—but will generously financially support and accommodate his taste for black debauchery and buffoonery.

Nonetheless, what is difficult to dispute is that Perry has the intelligence of knowing that whatever hackneyed, trite, and erroneous garbage that he puts out on the big screen, black folk will endorse and offer strong support for it on the strength that this time the usual suspect just happens to be one of their own. And it is because of this that all is fair in the proverbial "love and war"; as very few, if any, boundaries or restrictions are placed on content, subject matter, intelligible discourse, and accuracy of images and depictions. Also, very little if any inquiry or scrutiny is conducted on who it is that has been christened to put forth such false imagery and reprehensible representation of black people, particularly black males. Thus, the question that remains is how is it that a male in his forties who has no children (currently however there is a rumor that is disseminating on viral that he is fathering a child from a so-called Ethiopian model whom I had never heard of prior, nor has anyone else I'm sure), who has never been married, and who is consumed by his own transgendered ideations, seems to fly under the radar in a society that is just as homophobic and gay-conscious as it is racist?

The answer is that white people are indifferent either way, as long as Perry continues to support their theory of black male effeminacy and collective inferiority. Moreover, black folk as a whole don't care either as long as Perry continues to personify the "little engine that could, "rags to riches" tale that is very seldom heard of and comes a dime-a-dozen in the true reality of black America.

"A hero ain't nothin' but a sandwich"

The bottom line is this: Tyler Perry is no icon; he's no hero; he's not funny, nor are his films funny or any good; he should not in any way be looked upon as an inspirational figure; and given his track record thus far, he certainly should not speak for black males or in any way take lead in putting on display to the world the specious images and illustrations of the black male and black people by way of his bogus films, subpar creative talents, and "tell it like it ain't" tendencies. Nor should Perry, or others who endorse his program, act as delegates for black representation or be considered as conduits for causes that work to the advantage of the black male (or in Perry's case, the black female) and the vast majority of black people in this society; especially considering that not many (if any) of these celebrities and black entertainers have ever aligned themselves with the masses of blacks—poor or otherwise—or seek to address real problems and issues that have serious and profound impact on the lives of black people.

Quite frankly, too many of his ilk and type choose to straddle the middle-grounds of neutrality and align themselves with those who aspire to achieve regardless of color. Hence, the real truth is that most black entertainers and black athletes are either deeply embroiled in their own agenda or they are discouraged—financially and creatively—to politicize themselves and work to ameliorate social dynamics and conditions that continue to marginalize and suppress people of color. As a result, the alternative for most is to present a façade that would lead you or me to believe that our agenda is their agenda, our problem is their problem, if the end result is the continued support in maximizing their financial status and indelibly preserving their brand, regardless of how efficacious or mediocre their presentation or product. Michael Eric Dyson identified this phenomenon as "social forces that put individuals of predictable pedigree in the right place and at the right time to enhance their innate gifts or to have their mediocre skills overlooked in a social order that favors them despite their deficits."[49]

Tragically, the goals and ambitions of many blacks—male and female—have very little if anything to do with the dream that Martin Luther King Jr. envisioned. Disproportionate rates of imprisonment, overrepresentation of blacks in the criminal justice system, disproportionate levels of black infant mortality, increases in substance abuse among blacks, exponential increases in deficits of black mental health, epidemic influxes of HIV/AIDS infections among blacks, increases in school dropout rates, and increases in numbers of black gays and lesbians has been offset by the dearth of black actors, athletes, and entertainers, under the guise or delusion that America is a multi-racial and diverse bastion of tolerance and acceptance. And even amid abstract poverty and despondence, there is a glimmer of hope—depending on how fast one can run, how high one can jump, how funny one is, how well one can sing (well, thanks to sound equipment and voice-over modules people don't have to know how to sing anymore), or one's willingness to play self and culturally-debasing roles on film and television.

The same people whom we view as colored champions, heroes, and beacons of our potential salvation and forerunners in opening up the doors of immeasurable wealth, financial success, fame, and notoriety, are the ones who either don't seem to get the racial and cultural divisions that America has always and continues to impose—even by way of sport and play—or they simply do not identify with the suffering that is the invariable byproduct of those conditions. Therefore, they do not nor can they speak for those black folk who are cognizant and mindful of institutional racism/white supremacy and, because of the obvious results of such a condition, seek freedom, equality, and social and cultural justice.

Finally, consider that Samuel L. Jackson, Jamie Fox, and Kerry Washington are black people with certain levels and degrees of talent, yet the promise of continual fame and financial rewards superseded the level of consciousness and cultural sensibilities and awareness that should have rendered any depiction of the black holocaust in America sacrosanct, unless the truth was being told. And, certainly, the film *Django Unchained* is far from an accurate portrayal of the black holocaust (even though many considered it as highly entertaining). Regardless, Quentin Tarantino, the film's writer and director, not only believed that it was a viable depiction but so did the rest of Hollywood and the white world. So much so that he was awarded an Oscar, although none of his black actors received such acknowledgment. Nonetheless, what should be certain and free of all doubt is that in Hollywood, when "massa" calls, the foolish and misinformed come "a runnin'."

Nine

URBACISM, THE RISE OF HIP HOP, AND
EXPOSING THE MYTH OF THE
URBAN ALPHA MALE

*"I sympathize/ with the brotha's on the street/
'cause it's genocide/ and we all gotta eat/ but,
do the right thing and you'll never be hungry/
I kept the faith and God made me funke"*[50]
—KOOL MOE DEE, GOD MADE ME FUNKE

In the realm of the American entertainment edifice, this is how the pseudo amicable duality of the black and white partnership or camaraderie is portrayed in the neo-colorblind, post-racial western world. There is a white detective and black detective who are either on the trail of a vicious killer or are trying to apprehend a drug kingpin. The characteristics of the two are for the most part, invariably as follows: The white detective is stoic, of few words, intrepid, reticent, yet calculating; and when he does speak, it is something that is either strikingly profound or tastefully yet acerbically witty. On the other hand, the black detective is more than likely frivolously talkative, obsequious, dull-witted, timorous, and whatever instincts that he has are conspicuously restricted to the banalities of the streets. And when confronted with a crisis he unravels emotionally, and in an attempt to tap into whatever limited undaunted chutzpah that he can muster, he ultimately acts in a more self-destructive rather than in a proficient and indiscriminate manner.

Given the entertainment world's illustrious tract record of illustrating the differences of manhood and manliness between black males and white men, we can intelligently hypothesize the fate of the two; particularly, the black male detective. However, the problem with these monotonous portrayals and characterizations are that they completely contradict the black male's true history and designation of global primogenitor; thus, the first adept and adroit hunter and gatherer; the first skilled master of mathematics, and forensics; the first skilled in the uses of herbs, medicines, and holistic knowledge and methods; the first to circumnavigate the globe and plant his indelible seed and expertise of culture, arts, and sciences; and, perhaps the most telling problem is the attempt to downplay the fact that he is a victim of an indiscriminate system of white racism that is by design meant to denigrate and destroy him.

Yet whenever Clint Eastwood, Charles Bronson, Sylvester Stallone, Steven Seagal, Arnold Schwarzenegger, and Matt Damon, had at any point—past or present—taken roles in films that purport the dominance and omniscience of white men, the message that is sent and intended to resonate is the total superiority of the white man over the black male—not just structurally but biologically, and not just institutionally but culturally. Often the movies of these cultural alpha males depict them displaying their physical dominance and superior perspicacious killer instincts and dexterity over black males in the urban landscape of America's gritty and grimy streets, confirming the prevalence of racial dominance and superiority directed towards America's most storied and invariable foe in what I have coined as *urbacism,* or urban racism.

This is not to imply that America's racist tendencies are restricted to American ghettoes and downtown and uptown slums; indeed they are not. The point, however, is to inculcate the persistence of America's well-oiled entertainment and media machine crafting tales that, for instance, describe how an unassuming, cumbersome, journeyman white pugilist can rise to the apogee of the heavyweight boxing rankings on sheer will and desire over his bigger, stronger, and better skilled black opposition; particularly during a time when black males dominated the sport of boxing, uncontested. Also, and much more disturbing, I would like to emphasize how a psychotic, criminal-minded thug with a hero complex can in a so-called post-racist society, stalk and murder a black youth and subsequently be found innocent of any wrong-doing in a court of law. Arguably, a degenerate and murderer such as George Zimmerman would have on any given day been held accountable for a hit-and-run fatality, hitting an old woman over the head to snatch her purse, tax fraud, or robbing his local convenience store. However, his killing of a black child was legitimized by those who both subscribe to and practice racism, or *urbacism*, confirming that such an act can be done with absolute impunity because, clearly, black children who are from urban communities, as well as black males of all age brackets and who are also from urban communities, are dispensable in a society driven by racists/white supremacists' bloodlust.

Nonetheless, and getting back to my original point, an iconic celebrity such as Clint Eastwood, who in his cult classic *Sudden Impact,* received raves for his stylistic and expert predilections for killing black criminals—and while doing so uttering a phrase that is forever rooted in the pantheon of favorite film and cultural catchphrases—"go ahead, make my day"; thus, when translated in racist lay terms can be interpreted as, "there are very few pleasures that are commensurate to a white man killing a nigger." The caper however is Eastwood's forever immortalized character of police inspector "dirty" Harry Callahan's cleansing America of the scourge of black criminals—the most reviled and feared living organism and disruption and threat to the American social order. In other words, black + criminal = nigger and nigger = black + criminal in American society; particularly as purported in these films. Even famed black comedian Chris Rock, in his fifth standup comedy special *Kill the Messenger,* explicitly proposed his stamp of approval of white people referring to a black person as a nigger only under the conditions of being robbed or falling prey to some other form of criminality perpetrated by a black person, especially if that person is a black male.

From Blaxploitation to Hip Hop Nation

"Let us begin/what, where, why, or when..."[51]
—BOOGIE DOWN PRODUCTIONS *MY PHILOSOPHY*

America is a nation of immense power and privilege, despite its rapidly increasing under caste. America is also a nation that is overly sensitive about race, irrespective of its invariably destructive treatment of its underclass population and failure to implement race-neutral policies to address the needs of its citizens who are in most need of assistance. So, rather than put into action policies that address abstract poverty, disproportionate levels of unemployment, lack of access to healthcare insurance, and criminalization policies designed to create overrepresentation of black males in the criminal justice system; America alternatively chooses to practice discrimination, oppression, and cultural subjugation based on differences in race, color, and ethnicity more so than any other nation, culture, and society on the planet. Yet when it comes to matters of race, because of this nationwide sensitivity and hush-hush campaign that ensues as a direct result, these same issues that overwhelmingly affect those that represent black America are scarcely mentioned in Obama's state of the union addresses. And, these societal ills are not discussed among blacks and whites who work at the same places of business, and are probably seldom discussed across the dinner table at both black and white households.

Capitalism and democracy are driven on the distinctions of caste, based on racial and cultural differences that ostensibly create distinctions in class, socioeconomic status, and draws and ever-widening and increasing gap between those who have political power and clout, and those who are disproportionately disenfranchised. Yet in order to maintain and expand those barriers with a clear conscience and be free of any moral constraints, anything that pertains to divisions that are based on structural impediments are dismissed as moot or as cop outs for those who lack what it takes to get ahead in a highly-competitive, technologically advanced society that is rapidly progressing and moving forward. It is because of this egregious supposition to race relations that Clint Eastwood, who although has directed and cast black actors in biographical dramas detailing the lives of historic and prominent black figures (e.g., Charlie "byrd" Parker and Nelson Mandella), gives very little forethought to racial animus and divisiveness that is both insinuated and provoked when he callously slaughters young black males on film.

Hollywood-made action films such as *Sudden Impact* and *Death Wish*—movies that depict the indiscriminate slaughter of fictionalized black criminals at the hands of noble, white, heroic figures—interestingly enough, came immediately following the civil rights era and the passing of legislation that guaranteed blacks civil rights as well as voting rights. Even more interesting is how during this era that followed the civil rights movement, black males, historically perceived as being inherently docile and submissive—a belief that exhorted the endeavor of enslaving black people as a whole—were now labeled as being inherently violent and criminal-minded. The problem with this theory, however, is that it is remiss of factors such as deindustrialization and blatantly discriminatory hiring practices and policies that lead to increased levels of crime, particularly violent crime in urban communities. Ironically, it is because of the perceived failures of civil rights and the rampant acts of institutional racism/white supremacy and discrimination that the hard-fought, newly acquired liberties that were supposed to have prohibited racism, discrimination, and oppression, yet failed, is primarily the reason why the underground economy and black-market were born in urban ghettoes. It is also due to the fact that civil rights activists and Black Nationalist's revolutionaries had met either violent deaths or were being thrown in prison in droves that the romanticism with the urban renegade, male and female, was born in burgeoning, mostly black-made films such as *Superfly, Dolemite, The Mack, Willie Dynamite, Coffey, Foxie Brown, Sugarhill, Cleopatra Jones,* and *Black Caesar.*

These films, although more anti-establishment than outright criminal, would precipitate a cultural movement known as "blaxploitation," aptly titled because of the creative and artistic cultural embracing of the anger, vileness, and unhinged nature that had become associated with black America. Because of the massive rioting that would take place in major cities following the assassination, political imprisonment, and exile of renowned and beloved black leaders and political activists, along with a myriad of other harsh and oppressive governmental campaigns, black rebellion and a gravitation towards violent uprisings supplanted acquiescence and peaceful protest. Hence, slogans such as "kill whitey" that resounded the marginal suffering of blacks, uprooted prescriptions to the universality of "brotherly love" as well as the egregious nationally-inclusive banter of "make love not war."

Despite some of the apparent flaws and criticisms of blaxploitation films (e.g., misogyny and criminality), these films, however, were crafted to bolster a sense of artistic independence, expression, and black male masculinity that were grossly denied or absent in white Hollywood's (emphasis white) portrayal of blacks, particularly black males. Quite frankly, It has always been the threat and fear of black male masculinity that prompted the images of the rampant slaughter of the urban black male and his being bested in the ring at the hands of America's white cinematic heroes; images and depictions of the black male that still persists in Hollywood films and television shows and dramas to this day. Subsequently, it was only natural that black filmmakers set about imbuing the black male with qualities that made him physically and sexually appealing and, if he was going to be circumscribed to the urban jungle, irrefutably lionized as its indisputable king.

Similarly, while cinema provided the reconstruction and visual appeal of the oft-maligned black male, Hip Hop culture would be the acoustic platform that would emblazon and magnify his urban adroitness and dexterity. But unlike the ephemeral movement of blaxploitation films, Hip Hop culture would prove to be much more vital and a have a much stronger cultural pulse; despite essentially being a mere auditory rather than visual replica of the same aspects, cultural analysis, and pros and cons that defined blaxploitation. Hence, analogous to blaxploitation films, Hip Hop music and culture has been pelted with the same misogynistic tag and accused of having ambitions of being enamored with and driven towards criminality. In other words, as the monopoly of the underground economy is depicted in *Superfly* (usually by violent means), or the misogynistic theme that is inculcated in *The Mack*; so too are these characteristics deeply embedded in the psyche of Hip Hop artists or haughtily and boisterously reverberated in many rap song lyrics. However, similar to how for every *Superfly* there was the socially and politically-driven *The Spook who sat by the Door,* for every Notorious B.I.G. there is a Nas. Moreover, for every N.W.A. there is a Public Enemy, driving home the argument that similar to how the blaxploitation era was a confluence of misogyny, violence, and political rhetoric, so too is Hip Hop music and culture.

The origins or, should I say, initial stages of Hip Hop can be called anything but avant-garde; in fact, it started off as a syncopated battle of wits made acoustically pleasing by way of improvised rhyme schemes, which would ultimately become rhythmically amplified by way of the infusion of turntables that provided the beats and breaks and scratches that complimented the rhymes and lyrical content. Long before local venues and gigs were booked, lucrative contracts were signed, and music videos were budgeted, young street kids endowed with the gift of rhyme engaged in park, rooftop, and sidewalk battles for supremacy of the mastery of urban slang and cultural colloquialisms, combined into the poetic art of confrontation and the spoken word of urban verbal warfare. And although this confrontational and competitive spirit of Hip Hop would compromise and distort some of its illustrious shine, even throughout the course of its ascent of becoming a global phenomenon and multibillion dollar industry, part of the allure of the genre is that from its birth its brazen social commentary and, even clairvoyant cultural proscriptions, were immediately apparent.

Concrete Roses

Despite its cultural significance, Hip Hop music/culture hands down has been the most vilified form of musical artistry and acoustic expression on the North American shores since its inception. This is unfortunate being that the genre was not only fresh and green compared to all other forms of music but also bold and audacious enough to paint a portrait of black urban existence and the rampant suffering that takes place in these environments; issues that were not being discussed in the black church nor were they a part of the social and political discourse among black politicians. Certainly, prior to the boom of Hip Hop culture, R&B artists such as Curtis Mayfield, Isaac Hayes, Donny Hathaway, and Marvin Gaye parlayed their immense talents and artistic brilliance into social activism, raising and elevating the consciousness of the oppressed masses with their enduring balladry and rhythmic jingles. However, notwithstanding the thoroughness and legitimacy of these artists, Hip Hop, unquestionably, took it to another level. Where Marvin Gaye's "what's going on" was as enlightening as it was rhythmically and vocally pleasing, Melle Mel and the Furious Five's "The message" was as grim as it was poignant and poetic.

Yet the allure of fame began to offset the need for intrinsic virtuosity. Groundbreaking records such as "The Message" and Mel and the Furious Five's "White Lines," a record that spoke of the scourges of drugs and unprecedented drug use in black communities, began to give way to the genre's burgeoning *B-Boy* era, where the emphasis was more on party records and lyrical supremacy than that of cultural awareness and uplifting. It was during this era, one that marked the beginning of the Reagan administration and the Iran/Contra scandal that would inevitably ensue, and is primarily responsible for flooding urban communities with drugs that Reagan's iniquitous and egregious assault on the black poor by way of his "war on drugs" campaign, kick started. Consequently, as the drugs proliferated so did the influx of crime and unprecedented levels of imprisonment among black males. It is because of the turbulent times during the Reagan/Bush era for blacks that the landscape of Hip Hop music and culture would once again go through radical re-cultivating.

During this same time period, Hip Hop's *B-Boy* era began to flourish, as groundbreaking artists and groups put Hip Hop music at the forefront of American culture. While solo artists such as LL Cool J., Big Daddy Kane, and Rakim from the duo, Eric B. and Rakim, were etching an indelible mark of the art forms artistic legitimacy and preserving its street credibility; groups such as Run-Dmc, Beastie Boys, Salt-N-Pepa, and the Fat Boys were laying out the framework of the genre's immense potential marketability as a colossal cash cow for the corporate and capitalist-minded fat cats of popular and mainstream culture. Prior to the advent of the iconic pop status of black artists such as Prince, Lionel Richie, and Michael Jackson, MTV imposed proscriptions on showcasing any Hip Hop or rap videos, only to reconsider after the grudging realization of the economic potential of the art form. In fact, Hip Hop became such a mainstream and cultural staple, expanding its audience base across all color lines, that the music television network whose initial premise was to only showcase rock, heavy metal, and pop music, created a show dedicated entirely to the playing of Hip Hop music and spotlighting rap artists. Thus, *Yo MTV Raps* was born.

But regardless—even then as is the case now—the campaign to vilify and defile the culture of Hip Hop because of lyrical content widely considered as misogynistic and deeply immersed in the glorification of violence and material excesses, egregiously, concentrated only on one side of a flipped coin. Hip Hop culture was a movement that was started overwhelmingly by black and brown urban youth, and it was these perceived vices that could be elicited from the genre's entirety that was packaged as if those vices were the genre's sole calling.

Every genre of music obviously has its signature, either by way of its sound, content, or fashion. Certainly, the sounds of blues and jazz were distinct and unquestionable. Rock n Roll could be distinguished not only by its sound but its embracing of the aesthetic accoutrements that were indicative of the times, as could disco. Furthermore, Heavy metal artists and their followers evoked the long-haired spirit of the hippy movement but with a harder, leather-clad image and sound. And although these genres too had their detractors and social critics, none of them endured the magnitude of social and cultural rancor and was perceived as threatening to both the moral fabric and social order of the country than was the case with Hip Hop. Because of the cultural and political backlash, coupled with the innocuous and predictable endeavors of Hip Hop's *B-Boys*, the genre spawned its own sociopolitical groups and artists to offset not only the attack on the genre but also to put the plight of America's urban poor, oppressed, and downtrodden on a global platform. Thus, groups and artists such as Boogie Down Productions, Public Enemy, Paris, Poor Righteous Teachers, Brand Nubian, X-Clan, and NWA (short for Niggers With Attitude), and The Fugees, upended the fashion-conscious, party-oriented, quick-tongued bravado that was synonymous with the genre's sound throughout most of the early to mid-eighties. The ambitions of these artists and groups (or most of them) during the late eighties to early 1990s, invoked the vision of the direction that the genre was attempting to take with songs like "the Message," several years earlier. And during the cap on the content that this particular era seemed to have lock, stock, and barrel, this appeared to be the apotheosis of what the genre was steadfastly trying to reach and was exactly where it needed to be.

During this particular phase of the genre, the search for black male masculinity and the uplifting and strengthening of the culture seemed to be almost inevitable. The problem that remained however was the residual effects of drugs, rampant crime and violence, and excessive malfeasance and discontent that manifested in urban ghettoes and communities as a direct result of the destructively racist and inimical war on drugs, vis-à-vis the poor, launched by the Reagan/Bush administration. Consequently, the lyrical rhetoric of groups such as NWA and Houston's Geto Boys that appeared to both glamorize and excoriate street life and culture, began to resonate much stronger, louder, and bolder with urban youth than the lyrical ethnocentrism of groups such as Public Enemy. More telling, white kids, Hip Hops newest and magnanimous converts, appeared to be more interested in hearing staccato-flowed urban rebellion than the poeticism of afro-centricity.

The Urban Alpha Male and the early symptoms of the decadence of Hip Hop

Avarice, hyper-masculinity, and material excesses (or in street layman's terms—money, ho's, and clothes) gradually became the order of the day in Hip Hop, rather than cultural advancement, solidarity, and collective liberation. Additionally, crime, drugs, and tendencies towards violence at the slightest provocation were explicitly the driving forces behind this new order or image, as opposed to embracing and resting on the laurels of pure talent, intelligence, and self and cultural awareness as being the main ingredients for positivity and legitimacy for both the artists and genre. The reality of the plight of the black male in urban ghettoes and communities across America was instead, as Michael Eric Dyson reverberated in his novel *Between God and Gangsta Rap*, the ubiquitous analysis of black males gradually becoming an "endangered species."[52] However, despite statistics that purport that there are more black males in penal institutions than in academic institutions, and that black males are more than likely to meet a violent death rather than die by natural causes, the urban alpha male—the dr. Jekyll to the Mr. Hyde of the newly designated "gansta rapper"—is untouchable. Moreover, he is both feared and admired, has sole access to all of the amenities and accoutrements of the 'hood, and is a self-proclaimed urban menace who, in addition to posing a threat to the established social order, terrorizes and has sole mastery of communities of his own ilk along the way.

Initially, Hip Hop music/culture was derided and dismissed as legitimate because of its supposed lack of substance and originality (the first breakthrough hip hop tracks were nothing more than rhymes laid down over disco records (e.g., Sugar Hill Gang's "rapper's delight"); later on, with the advent of so-called gangsta rap, and because it was an art form that was predominated by black and brown urban youngsters, it was on the receiving end of an outright frontal attack because the young black and brown male participants were deemed to be a major threat to white suburban life, as well as to suburban white youth. Nevertheless, despite the back and forth banter of profundity and depravity, many of these young artists were and are as esoteric and prophetic as they are predictable.

Artists and groups such as Nas, Common, Scarface, Ice Cube, 2Pac, Ras Kas, and Wu Tang Clan, stylized in juxtaposing their ghetto grooming and the violence and moral decay that comes with it, along with an insatiable desire for spiritual and mental growth and development. Moreover, these particular artists were just as eager to share this passion with their audience and urban peers as they were to remind them of the safeguarding of the ghetto's version of the thousand-yard-stare. There are many artists, however, who were not so gifted in the past and are not as gifted presently. And, surprisingly, the less talented they are the more profane their lyrics appear to be. And for those who are among the most talented, artists such as the late Notorious B.I.G., Snoop Dogg, and Jay Z, the lyrical vernacular is more concentrated on self-grandiosity and bombastic endorsing and embracing of all that is wrong with life in the 'hood, rather than inverting such profound insights and powerful per-ceptions as prescriptions geared towards urban youth for the purposes of escaping such harsh and volatile conditions.

For this reason, the *urban alpha male* is both epitomized and glamor-ized in a genre that, although exorbitantly popular and profitable, is widely perceived by opponents of the genre and social critics as an art form that is comprised of mostly derelicts and degenerates, whose craft and creative nuances are a direct result of their inherent primal indul-gences. Thus, it is the allure of fame and wealth that invariably stokes the fires of a self-fulfilled prophecy, prompted by a divisive society that is stubborn to the idea of disencumbering race and ingenuity strictly because of its intrinsic instincts towards racial animus and vitriol. Also, the fact that white kids in the suburbs and who are of socioeconomic affluence are lining the pockets of many of these artists, as well as those of record label executives and owners via record sales, and patronize rap concerts in droves, is the result of the exponential increases of many of these young artists bank accounts. However, this possibility perhaps only succeeded in hastening the naysayer's assault on the genre.

While arguably synonymous with Hip Hop music/culture, the urban alpha male did not, however, encapsulate all that was Hip Hop or all that was relevant in Hip Hop. As late rapper Dwight Myers, aka Heavy D, put it, "just because there are bad elements in Hip Hop don't mean that all of Hip Hop is bad." Indeed. However, it is the urban alpha male—by way of his belittling of women, explicit indulgence in criminality, and compulsion to emblazoning his licentious and lascivious loins in order to propagate his masculinity—that appears to mostly resonate with those who historically have been socially ostracized and stripped of representation.

Consider the troubles of the early '90s rap group, 2 Live Crew. Though not very talented yet extremely lewd and vulgar, the Miami-based crew incited not only unprecedented levels of controversy more so than any act or genre in the annals of pop culture, but also were the first to have their music censured via a circuit court ruling and pronounced as unfit to market and sell. Additionally, the ruling stipulated that any violations of this injunction could result in obscenity violations to vendors as well as sanctions for consumers. The US court of appeals would eventually overturn the obscenity ruling; indefensible, however, was the fact that in Hip Hop culture, decadence superseded contemplation and prudence in terms of notoriety and profitability, at least as far as public perception went. 2 Live Crew's third and most controversial album, *As Nasty as They Wannabe*, went on to sell over two million copies; a feat that Rakim and Big Daddy Kane—master lyricists and primogenitors of the genre's idiomatic and stylistic significance—had never accomplished in their entire careers. And although the genre maintained its cadre of artists who endeavored to preserve and, to some degrees, enhance the genre's sensibilities and social and cultural connectedness, the genre appeared to be tilted towards a trajectory bent on ensuring that it would be more extravagant than pedantic; more illogical than pedagogical; and more nefarious than conscientious.

Unfortunately, the path that Hip Hop dared to navigate would continue to take darker turns. And all that was good in Hip Hop, particularly from its grandiloquent and unexpected beginnings all the way to placing its first foot on the stage of infamy, seemed to be capsizing in an abyss of greed and exploitation. In other words, the ship that poor, disenfranchised, oft-maligned, and culturally-eschewed black and brown urban youngsters had built was being pirated and overrun—corporately and artistically. Because of the culture-changing accomplishments of gregarious and precocious youth—who had invented an art form in the parks and on the streets amid the squalor of urban decay and transformed it into the most influential and lucrative genre and musical art form in the world—were now crawling on arm and leg from dehydration in a barren desert; hence, the wings of institutional racism/white supremacy would swoop down on the soon-to-be carcasses like a ravenous vulture. This fact, alone, not only changed the culture and content of the music but also made it possible to where a seismic shift in power was so potent and pronounced that, despite the genre still being predominated by young males and females of color, a white rapper could come along and be christened as Hip Hop's version of Elvis, and boldly be proclaimed as being the genre's new King.

Hip Hop is dead. So who is now the Urban Alpha male?

"The endorsement of thugs is white people's fantasy of what they want us to be"
—CHUCK D OF PUBLIC ENEMY

In today's era of black passivity, despondence, and transparent affronting, it is easy for the white mainstream media to proclaim a white rapper as being the greatest asset to the genre. Troubling, however, is that these same representatives of white mainstream media are not at all in favor of the art form, nor are they supporters of the genre's commercial success and appeal. Instead, it is simply another sturdy display of the white supremacists mindset that predicates despite how baseless, frivolous, and whimsical they perceive the art form as being, a white person can came along and with little effort be the best at it (to note, just look at the out of the blue astronomical success of white female rapper Iggy Azalea). This statement might be perceived as disregarding the lifetime of pain, rejection, and perseverance that white rapper Eminem, who by his own admission has spent years and years trying to seek the approval and procure legitimacy from his black urban and Hip Hop peers. Well, actually it is not. In fact, the claim could not be any more relevant to the discrepancy that I will point out.

Eminem, born Marshall Mathers, who although is very talented and crafty with his wordplay, aligns his creativity with everything that is deemed profane and reprehensible to opponents and critics of the genre. And I would be remiss to not point out that he has done so unapologetically throughout his career. Similar to how wayward and criminal white youth are hypothesized by criminologists in their review of sentencing and incarceration reports as being driven towards criminal acts and compulsions because of external reasons (e.g., substance abuse, physical and sexual abuse), their black counterparts, on the other hand, are perceived as doing so because of internal (biological) character flaws. With that being said, it is interesting how Eminem is immortalized and revered for his clever rhyme schemes and craftsmanship with words, yet his lyrical predilections toward acts of interpersonal violence and depravity are cushioned as being remarkably human and inherently visceral. Oddly, these same lyrical cadences that certainly did not start with Eminem yet made him Hip Hop deity, were also the trademarks of the internal travails of artists such as Scarface, 2Pac, and Notorious B.I.G., but were largely dismissed as typical and conjectural ghetto rhetoric.

This should not at all be surprising in a racist society with such deep-rooted enmity for black males that it will even attempt to display its predominance and superiority, vicariously by way of one of its own whom, by all appearances, is as pro-urban and anti-establishment as the culture that he steadfastly embraces and aligns himself with. But is this not typical of the white, black dichotomy that America itself, unwaveringly, attempts to exploit? My answer would be that it is a linear and unimpeded track record that is indelibly etched in the fabric of cultural media by way of news coverage, films, and television portrayals, designed for the same purposes of inculcating to the public the realities of black and white encounters. For this reason, black males are perceived as either roving bands of miscreants, hell-bent on bedlam and impropriety; or, they are oversexed and lascivious predators and sexual deviants (e.g., Willie Horton, Lemuel Smith). Furthermore, when they are portrayed or depicted more positively than negatively, they are still several steps behind their white counterpart and not nearly as intrepid or sophisticated (e.g., *Miami Vice);* or, they are deemed and portrayed as corrupt and immoral (e.g., *Training*

Day), or have high-ranking law enforcement and political positions yet have very little to do with solving crimes or exuding judicious decision-making (e.g., take your pick...).

It is because of these factors that the black male in America may find that displays of masculinity are fruitless, career ending, and even life-threatening in a racist society. And the fact that Hip Hop music/culture is in the current state and predicament that it is in, is indicative of the claim that the aesthetic ambitions and cultural freedoms of the socioeconomically disenfranchised and culturally ostracized that was denied to their forebears was on a short life-cycle. Moreover, it was but a mere pipe dream for the young and precocious of an oppressed culture that sought liberation and cultural respectability with the same zeal as their older civil rights' contemporaries. Hence, the genre once appeared geared towards providing an outlet via art (graffiti), cultural expression (break-dance and deejaying), and voice (rhyme and free-style lyrics) for an oppressed urban culture long overdue for self-representation, particularly in a so-called new day in terms of race relations.

But, tragically, this coming to pass was not to be in a nation that is not only conscious of racial divisions but aims for one ethnic group (whites) to stay on top of the chain of command and dictate how the tides turn in terms of cultural influence. Consequently, the flamboyance of *B-Boys* died out as conditions in urban communities worsened (aftereffects of the war on drugs/poor blacks) and, as a result, warranted very little need or interest for self-professed unction and bravado that was based solely on rhyme skill levels. Additionally, the genre's socio-political acts were either bought out for their silence with the promise of Hollywood fame and glory (e.g., Ice Cube, Common, and Queen Latifah), or met the same fade from grace and prominence as did their *B-Boy* contemporaries. It was during this same period however that a new element of Hip Hop took form—the Iconic urban alpha male—a chimera of the genre that seemingly imbued all of the characteristics that previously had left the genre devoid of a single, solitary identity. No other artists exuded this new image more so than Tupac Shakur, or 2Pac. The son of former Black Nationalists was as intellectual as he was volatile, cerebral as he was unpredictable, and as insightful as he was haughty and superficial.

The birth of the Hip Hop Capitalist and reinvigoration of the urban alpha male

"Let me in now/ Let me in now/ Bill Gates, Donald Trump let me in now"[53]
—NELLY, COUNTRY GRAMMAR

The rise of Hip Hop Icons such as Tupac Shakur, contrary to popular opinion, did not raise the game in the genre nor did it raise the bar of artistic appeal; in fact, it only weakened it. More telling, the violent deaths of Shakur and east coast Hip Hop icon Notorious B.I.G., born Christopher Wallace—due to a fictionalized east coast and west coast war that became credible once exacerbated by an overzealous and derisive media machine—only succeeded in artists' confusing martyrdom and iconoclasm with pure unadulterated greed. As it is often said that "money is the root of all evil," never could such a forewarning have been more ominous than the rapid transformation of Hip Hop as an art form that was cultivated on pure artistic creativity and ingenuity to one that gradually ascended to bartering and renouncing those gifts and virtues for the assurances of excessive capital and wealth.

Take for instance artists such as New Orleans based Cash Money Millionaires, who in conceding their lack of pure lyrical prowess, attempted to transpose the art of rhyming to what they coined as "game-spitting, " which had very little to do with the craft of lyrical precision and clever wordplay and consisted more of convoluted and meaningless bantering over beats. Yet, commensurate to their namesake, this new approach to the craft represented the new era of the genre's multimillionaires. And as a result, the urban alpha male was no longer just a ghetto hooligan who, in tradition of the Black Nationalist power movement of the 60s and 70s, rebuffed and rebuked the social order for the purposes of establishing his own codes of conduct, mores, and standards; instead, the new urban alpha male capitulated to the same capitalistic appurtenances that created the separation between haves and have-nots, particularly among blacks as a whole. Because the game had changed, apparently so did the motivation of its young artists. For instance, research has purported that "rap can be a tool through which black youth negotiate their identity, 'cultural capital,' and develop authentic identities.[54] Therefore, it is this malleability among the young that renders them susceptible to the extemporaneous vacillations and trends that take place within the genre. Unfortunately, obstructions to the sudden trends that have become synonymous with the trajectory of Hip Hop music/culture have brought the genre to an impasse that renders it now mostly representative of the bejeweled, diamond-studded new urban alpha male.

This observation is in stark contrast to the gun-toting neighborhood menace or the bohemian Hip Hop intellectual or militant revolutionary. Also, this new urban alpha male is blinded by his own ambitions that dictate "MOB"—money over bitches—as well as money over tradition and artistic and creative conventions that were the hallmarks of the genre's rapid ascension. In the present state of the genre, for instance, an attack on another artist's lyrical proficiency and challenge to an artistic battle of wits is now deemed as an encroachment on one's innermost sensibilities. Furthermore, such an action can be perceived as a threat to another's marketability and money-earning potential; thus, a revamped and restructured infraction of the genre that consequently resulted in the deaths of two of the genre's iconic heavyweights. Hip Hop journalist Cheo Hodari Coker calls this era of the genre a "culture of excess."[55] More ominous, however, is that this obsession with an escape from the pecuniary conditions of urban life has precluded the sublime nuances that made both the music and culture as a whole, unique; instead, it has been reduced to one that is mockingly ordinary and predictable, despite being more profitable now than at any point in the genre's past.

Laugh now; cry later—all is fair in Love & War

Hip Hop is dead! As conceded by author, political activist, and social critic Kevin Powell in a 2007 article that was collaborated with professor, author, and social critic Michael Eric Dyson that asked the eponymous question. And I tend to agree. Sadly, Hip Hop music/culture has suffered the same fate as most of the profoundly-impactful and highly lucrative inventions of black innovators in a racist and oppressive society. Irrespective of how culturally relevant, entrepreneurial, socioeconomically feasible, and entertaining; in a capitalistic society such as this one, and one that is driven by white male-dominated patriarchy, nothing moves unless the all-powerful say so or give his (or sometimes her) stamp of approval.

Accordingly, Blues, Jazz, and Rhythm and Blues are musical art forms that whites simply wanted to come and prove that they could be equally as effective, if not better, than each art form's predominantly black base. What should be clear though is that these genres were never socially feasible or lucrative enough for an all-out takeover. Nevertheless, given the global impact and exponential profitability range of Hip Hop and, say, Black Entertainment Television, white people not only wanted in but also wanted complete control. For this reason, the black urban alpha male became the white capitalists and corporate executives' whipping boy; a puppet on the grand stage of the puppeteer because of his own capitalistic motivations and ambitions that left him weak-kneed and limp-wristed and internally filleted. In other words, the nobility of Hip

Hop was trumped by a burgeoning subculture of youth that seemed to confirm that what mattered most to their listening and viewing pleasures was the high-stakes corporate mantra that "glamour sells, violence sells, and graphic sex sells."[56]

Remarkably, this was confirmed by a panel of contemporary Hip Hop artists—some of whom are tremendously talented, some not so talented; some of whom are profoundly intelligent, and some not so intelligent—on a BET series called *Hip Hop vs. America*. Irrespective of the level of talent and insight, nearly all of the panelists confirmed that it is widely the content of today's rap lyrics that has enabled them to become self-made millionaires, despite the argument of many scholars and social critics on the same panel who asked the important question of "true, but at what cost?"

The question then of what is the proverbial price for glory is the overall point to what was and is still being discussed. Therefore, is the price of fame for a few worth the compromising of the virtues of an entire ethnic enclave and subculture that is invariably and inextricably linked to the worst of stereotypes and cultural debasement? It would appear that the obvious response would be an emphatic no, but American culture is also abreast to the fact that appearances can be deceiving. For starters, I think that few would argue that every artist in the genre engages in such depravity. In fact, and despite how financially appealing, some things are just not in certain people, and Hip Hop music is in fact a culture that is far from a monolith but rather is comprised of the most complex and ideological as well as the most mundane of individuals.

The second point is that it is not Hip Hop music/culture that is the problem overall. Instead, it is the constant rotation and airplay (via radio and video) of artists and music that by design is to make the genre appear to be an art form that his fraught with ghetto degenerates and overrun by those who are practitioners of confrontation over contemplation, degeneracy over stoicism, and decadence over artistic brilliance. And lastly, it is a culture that is rife with those who have hundreds of thousands of dollars of platinum dental work, as opposed to artists whose creative juices allow them to share their knowledge and sharpen their lyrical precision by constantly engrossing in PhD level books and readings, such as the previously mentioned Shakur; it is a culture that is now saturated with those who seek to sell out and race-trade via their indulgences in lyrical and artistic depravity and debauchery, which is in stark contrast to those who have repudiated the offer of traversing the path of a downward spiral for the money and fame and instead seek to preserve the roots of Hip Hop and their respective legacy in propelling the genre's initial ascent to prominence.

For these reasons, the claim that Hip Hop is dead is obviously a metaphor for an assertion that the genre no longer has character, heart, or even cultural respectabilities. Yet unlike some of the earlier musical art forms that preceded it, Hip Hop is far from defunct and is still vital enough to rejuvenate and reinvigorate itself. However, this can only be accomplished depending on the individuals involved and character of the young males and females who are inspired to reroute the trajectory of the collision course that the genre is widely perceived as headed towards. And even though the genre is still both commercially and financially viable, what is also obvious is that it is increasingly losing its appeal and credibility by way of public opinion. For instance, a Newsweek poll purported that while there is still a sizable proportion of the American public that either normally or occasionally listens to rap/Hip hop, almost two-thirds of those polled say the music is too violent; sixty-three percent of those polled say the lyrics are misogynistic, and the majority of those polled stated that the music contained too much sex.[57]

There is no doubt that the genre could benefit from a radical departure of its current standing, despite the fact that even the disproportionate numbers of those who cited rap lyrics as containing too many sexual references has a twinge of societal and cultural bias. Hip Hop is not the only musical art form that is overly-saturated with sexual references and coitus overtures; far from it. Nevertheless, if the genre is going to recapture some of its past sensibilities and measures of respect that crosses all age boundaries, particularly among black listeners, then the attitude of black males and black people in this society as a whole has to undergo a radical transformation. As mentioned earlier, Hip Hop music/culture alone is not the problem, but a mere microcosm of the same greed and avarice that has ensnared the vast majority in a country that reigns supreme in its capitalistic prose and standing. Even well into the new millennium, the black male's prowess in sports and entertainment has not nullified or mitigated negative views or improved public perceptions of him or black people as a whole, especially when compared to ethnic groups that are hardly visible in mainstream media. One would think that with the abundance of Hip Hop stars, pop culture celebs, and sports heroes, that the black male would be the pride of the American diversity pool; needless to say that this cannot be further from the truth.

In fact, statistics illustrated by authors Francis Dalisay and Alexis Tan purport that eighty percent of Americans hold favorable views and perceptions of Asians—deeming them as highly intelligent, inventive , and hardworking.[58] On the other hand, the abilities of black males to sing, rap, dance, jump high, and run fast has not shirked the label of ineptitude, sloth, and indolence. More tragic is that many Hip Hop artists, and black folk from various forms of entertainment, envelope themselves in racial stereotypes; thus, reinforcing these negative perceptions for the sake of individual recognition and celebrity status. Because of such outlooks and perspectives, the Japanese, for instance—whom, again, as American citizens, the country views more favorably than blacks— referring to the black male as a "sleeping giant" connotes the irrefutable fact of ignorance and unawareness with no excuses and without justification. Thus, institutional racism/white supremacy is one thing, but the discombobulating of priorities amid epidemic cultural crises is both unfathomable and unacceptable. Therefore, a plausible and proactive response to racism and cultural genocide does not entail spending a lifetime pretending that these things do not exist. Nor does it imply conditioning oneself to side with an enemy that will either never fully accept blackness and black people or never forget the obvious biological, genetic, and cultural differences that exist between black people and white people, blackness as opposed to whiteness; or, conditioning oneself to believe that the procuring of wealth—by any means—is the great equalizer of racial and caste divisions, as well as bartering one's virtuosity and integrity for the perceived guarantee of racial compromise.

In the 1993 Mario Van Peebles film *Panther*, a poignant scene depicted the late Black Nationalist and civil rights organizer Huey P. Newton uttering the phrase "I'd rather die on my feet than live on my knees." And despite the inner turmoil and vices that ultimately sealed his violent end, he is perhaps turning over in his grave, considering the masses of black males who have failed to heed the lessons that he imparted as well as those of other civil rights and social activists and organizers. Particularly more troubling is the fact that times have not at all changed since the days of the valiant works of Newton and others like him; if anything, the conditions of the black male and black people as a whole have only gotten worse. In fact, according to author and scholar Haki R. Madhubuti, black people's status in US cities is worse than those in many third world nations.[59] And that child poverty rates are higher today than they were in 1968, and unemployment in black communities rivals unemployment rates in third world countries, regardless of US policies such as affirmative action.[60]

For young urban black males these factors and conditions are even that much more ominous and disturbing. And because many of these young males are aware of this, gravitating towards Hip Hop culture is the ultimate form of self-expression and monetary viability; in spite of the various extractions that often accompany associations with this form of musical and artistic expression. As pointed out by Carl Taylor and Virgil Taylor, "throughout America, many of the young have lost hope; they live in the moment and believe that it is normal to die young."[61] And without question, such an outlook portends the evanescence of Hip Hop in the eyes of many of today's artists as a culture that glamorizes the prospect of living fast and dying young.

Ironically, to countermand this sub cultural collision of young urban people being buried before their parents, mothers such as Cheryl

KiloDavis—the author of *My Princess Boy*—have found solace and comfort in sacrificing and transmuting their young sons inherent genetic ascriptions to stave off the possibility of early mortality as a result of external demons and forces in a society that envies and fears black male masculinity. Despite the exercising of her maternal trappings, she, arguably, like so many in American society either fears the black male or understands the consequences of the threat of black manhood. This is perhaps the reason behind the semi-sensation and hoopla over her book that purports both her and her black male husband allowing their pre-adolescent-aged son to indulge in his desire to dress up in girl's clothing. Thus, it is not at all surprising that nowadays it seems that the absence of black masculinity is deemed as the salvation of black people and, of course, racist America!

Ten

THE DEATH OF THE BLACK POWER MOVEMENT AND BLACK NATIONALISM

Perhaps the greatest provocateur of racial animus and sordid race-relations in the annals of mankind is the black male. This has been the case, however, not because of his words or by his actions but rather his mere presence and very existence. Just check the history. Following the years of reconstruction, an era in which black people as a whole were constitutionally freed from chattel slavery, the most inflammatory of cross-racial enmity is the fuse that was lit when a white woman accused a black male of rape. More profound is that this fact has sustained itself even up to the present (there was recently an overly sensationalized case of the rape of a young white female in which an alleged black male perpetrator was involved; hence, emphasis on "overly sensationalized," considering that a rape is committed every 15 seconds in this country). Black scholars, historians, and intellectuals have attributed burnings, hangings, castrations, and other brutal murderous and heinous acts perpetrated against black males because of white racists' immense fear of black male genetic potency and sexuality, an assessment that is hard to dispute when considering the overly sexualized exploitation of black males that takes place even in today's times.

Amid racism and brutal acts of murder, mass incarceration, and repression, both the American mainstream media and, astonishingly, the black male himself have both equally exhorted the efforts of disseminating false and negative perceptions of the black male's very existence and psychopathology, by purveying the belief that the apex of black male self-worth lies in a contrived sense of sexual conquest, prowess, and predation. If the distorted images of black males as roving sexual predators are not unremittingly purported by news media, then blacks males themselves are on stage stripping to their skivvies and simulating coitus acts and gesticulations while singing love and romance ballads. Or, they are bombastically proclaiming their sexual mastery and subjugation of black females, who are just as much victims of the social order than their singing and rapping male counterparts. Nevertheless, this machismo modeling would not be so difficult to comprehend if it were not sullied by statistics that purport nearly seventy percent of black children are being reared in single-parent, fatherless homes;[62] underscoring the black male's failure to adequately support and raise his offspring in a racist society, despite his erroneously perceived libido and lascivious compulsions.

Television dramas and sitcoms and Hollywood films largely benefit financially from depicting black males as a subculture of weak and inept, milk-toast cogs. To counter these endeavors, black filmmakers, who are cognizant of the negative images and its potential residual effects, do so by depicting black males as hypersexual ghetto Romeos. Consequently, these efforts are trumped by overzealous and transparent ambitions, as well as underlining the fact that many of these filmmakers fall victim to their own need for truth serum as an emollient to make easier the concession that even in black circles, a "sexy black man" is a more common adage than one who is responsible, or one whose moral foundation is solidly intact. In fact, amid institutional racism/white supremacy and the panorama of cultural genocide, black male sexuality has managed to become such a mainstay that black males themselves have started an underground movement based on a voracious urge to have exclusive sexual relations with other black males (see chapter 7).

This observation is tantamount to the question of whether or not the virtues and objectives of the black male have changed. Or, perhaps more accurate, have those virtues and objectives been made more malleable to the conditions of institutional racism/white supremacy? Being race-conscious, culturally attuned, and anti-oppression, via the workings and trappings of the establishment can come with a price—a bartering of humanity over humility that the black male has learned from the past can result in the ultimate sacrifice. Yet, inexcusably, there was a time when many black males and black females unrelentingly and unapologetically put their lives on the line for a cultural identity and collective self-worth that had been denied to black people. This denial was largely because of a system driven to deprive them of the most basic and fundamental of God-given rights ascribed to human beings.

Dating back to the times of chattel slavery and forced subjugation of blacks, black activists such as Toussaint L. Overture, Nat Turner, and Harriet Tubman had a keen sense of the iniquity and inhumanity of enslaving, butchering, and mistreating human beings. And it was because of their virtuosity and intrepid nature, along with other likeminded individuals, that made the freedom of black slaves a reality. In contemporary society, a copious amount of untruths and distorting of history is the modus operandi of white racists in an attempt to absolve themselves of culpability of committing the greatest crime in the annals of humanity. For instance, based on Hollywood movies and books by authors that distort historical facts, Abraham Lincoln freed the slaves and redressed the evils of chattel slavery. This is analogous to the lies and untruths of history as pointed out by a Native American professor whom I had as an undergraduate, and who during a rousing speech brought to the audience's attention the specious nature of Hollywood's rendition of the torrent love affair between Pocahontas and English enslaver, John Smith.

It is this distortion as well as romanticism of facts that are designed to immortalize prominent European historical figures that the chasm between white people and their former slaves continues to perpetuate the grim black/white reality in America. Furthermore, it is white people's callous rebuking of the facts of black history and the real contributions of black people as a whole in American history, combined with black people's pernicious ignorance of their own past and contributions that the present conditions that exist, continue to exist. If this were not so, black folk would not subscribe to a celebration of black contributions offered on the shortest month of the calendar year. And while outright, unrepentant racist like Abe Lincoln are christened as cultural and moral icons, civil rights crusaders such as Marcus Garvey, Noble Drew Ali, Malcolm X, Martin Luther King, and Louis Farrakhan, each in their respective times and eras, have been vilified as racial rabble-rousers (yes, even King, which is why they killed him), and whose works and exploits are restricted to a minute sector of black history as just described.

The Movement

"A boycott is a passive act…In order for nonviolence to work your opponent must have a conscience. The US has none!"
—STOKELY CARMICHAEL

Since arriving on the shores of America, African slaves in some form or another tried to acquire rights that would open the doors to their freedom from chattel bondage and repression. Whether by brute force e.g., slave insurrections or passive resistance that was implicitly inoculated long before King's nonviolent campaign hundreds of years later, the purpose was to impress upon slave masters and slave owners a humanness that was widely regarded as being absent in African peoples. Thus, dubious were the challenges that would surface for a people who because of their enslaved status, certain rights or the power for the exercise of assembly were completely defunct throughout the hundreds of years of captivity.

For African slaves, all that remained after centuries of enslavement and servitude was an obligatory need for freedom that stemmed from an inborn certainty of humanness and a desire to make this fact known at any cost. However, the challenge that was as indefatigable as enslavement itself was the endeavor of vying for these needs amid the absence of governmental assistance, state or local legislation, or group or political representation. In his critique of Dexter Gordon's book, *Black Identity: rhetoric, ideology, and nineteenth-century Black Nationalism,* author Mark Lawrence Mcphail illustrates Gordon's claim that during the antebellum period, "blacks contending for citizenship grappled with inspirations of self-representation from their position of alienation."[63]

Eventually, and contrary to romanticized historical conjecture of Lincoln eradicating slavery based on sheer unadulterated benevolence and goodwill, slavery was abolished to amend the diametrically-opposed philosophical views of slavery being a natural condition for African peoples that was destroying the country internally. Yet even with the emancipation from chattel slavery, the mentality of white/euro supremacy remained unrelenting, and it is because of this that the advent of Jim Crow ensured death and suffering of unmeasured proportions for newly freed, former black slaves. Following the civil war, the reconstruction period between 1867 and 1877 allowed former slaves to enjoy unprecedented freedoms and sociopolitical and economic maneuverability. But it was the advent of Jim Crow laws that decimated any hopes of unabated freedoms, as subsidiary laws contrived by state and local governments trumped guarantees to unobstructed citizenship as guaranteed by repeals to the fourteenth and fifteenth amendments of the constitution. Moreover, white terrorist organizations such as the Ku Klux Klan were formed to extract both a mortal and psychological toll on blacks who dared to exercise their new-found freedoms.

Former slaves were forced with the realization that the wrong ethnic group had been classified as subhuman in the initial statute of the constitution. During the brief reconstruction period that followed the civil war, former slave owners as well as their sons and daughters demonstrated a complete disregard of acting within civil and moral parameters and boundaries in their dealings with their former slaves. Burnings, lynchings, castrations, and unfathomable acts of brutality against blacks were perpetrated at frequencies never before been seen in the annals of social functioning in the country's young history. Consequently, black leaders and prolocutors for black suffrage began lobbying for free land as a form of recompense and reparations for blacks when it became apparent that blacks were probably better off as slaves rather than beneficiaries of freedom in terms of their safety and physical well-being.

It was during this time that black leaders such as Sojourner Truth organized a petition seeking free land for former slaves[64]; hence, giving impetus to the notion that "forty acres and two mules" were owed to former slaves as recompense for their servitude and suffering as unpaid laborers and burden bearers. And because blacks were former slaves, the stigma attached to centuries of ownership and servility had rendered a unique and uncompromising position for blacks as opposed to other ethnic groups who had been on the receiving end of mistreatment based on racial animus. For example, the Civil Liberties Act of 1988 granted reparations to Japanese Americans for their internment in America's version of concentration camps for non-Aryans during World War II.[65] Hence, after the collapse of reconstruction, many former slaves found themselves susceptible to re-enslavement due to America s first construction of false imprisonment vis-à-vis mass incarceration, which was chattel bondage by way of peonage and restitution as the result of trumped up criminal infractions. Entering into the twentieth century, black provocateurs for social justice, by any means necessary, who would become known as black nationalists, paved and swathed a new landscape for black liberation—some more literally than figuratively. Self-made leaders such as Noble Drew Ali, born Timothy Drew, Marcus Garvey, and Wallace Farad Muhammad inculcated spiritual (some preached for physical) migrations back to their African homeland and *Asiatic* roots and renounced the values and customs of Europeans, including their names that were forced upon black slaves as a condition of slavery.

To become antiestablishment, of course, meant to become in essence anti-white; thus, pro-black. While some of these leaders lobbied for unity and peace among the races, all the while elevating the racial and cultural consciousness of former slaves, others such as Marcus Garvey and Wallace Farad Muhammad deemed Europeans as a race of "devils" that were inherently wicked by nature. It is because of such beliefs that these leaders stressed that the only means to escape the clutches of such ubiquitous iniquity was either a massive migration out of America and back to the land from which former slaves were indigenous, or a complete separation of the races and expropriation of territory and land of their own in America.

The advent of Black Nationalism signaled the outcry for massive reparations for the masses of blacks who not only had not been compensated for centuries of chattel slavery, but who were also under the most extreme of duress and mistreatment at the hands of their former slave masters. The belief among both black leaders and their millions of followers was that something was owed and should have been coming to blacks as long as they were still inhabitants of America. According to Bishop Henry McNeal Turner, blacks are owed an estimated forty billion dollars for centuries of unpaid labor.[66] To this day, however, black people have not seen a penny or a single acre or one mule. Instead, what remains of the legacy of slavery for blacks in America is a permanent underclass of unemployed or underemployed, masked by the visage of successful and wealthy blacks such as Barack Obama, Tyler Perry, and Oprah Winfrey, and the dearth and molasses-like growth of the so-called black middle class (again, it must be stated that in a system of institutional racism/white supremacy there are no class distinctions among blacks/victims).

It is as a direct result of the above claim that some black leaders took a different approach, particularly once it became abundantly clear that reparations were more of a pipedream than an eventuality. For this reason, leaders such as Malcolm X and civil rights groups such as the Black Panther Party, the latter being the successors of Malcolm's initial style, approach, passion, and vision, began making demands rather than trying to appeal to the sensibilities of whites by taking an innocuous, common sense approach as a means to procure concessions as to what was owed to blacks. It was this style and overtly assertive positioning that *Black Nationalism* became interchangeable with *black power*. This approach, however, was not centered on a decree for financial backing for blacks to vacate the country; nor was this approach an upping of the ante for a demand for the proverbial forty acres and two mules. Clearly, there were black individuals who understood that America was built on the backs of its African slaves, and if anything was owed as a result of such contributions it was the acknowledgement of unquestioned and unobstructed citizenship. And, as a result, what was definitely not taking place was the bargaining and quibbling for dubious rewards and petty privileges; especially not from the role of an auxiliary who represented the "other" of American classification, and whose role if it was not to serve white people had no place otherwise.

The Struggle: what is both wanted and owed

What black people wanted during those times, and still to a certain degree want, was equal representation of Americanism and the spoils of the drudgery of hundreds of years of chattel slavery. But unlike the circumstances of today which, by all appearances, is a push towards absolute assimilation or, better yet, absorption into the dominant culture, rendering blackness as a condition that is purely incidental, leaders of the Black Nationalist movement wanted full representation without resignations of sacrificing culturally aesthetic ties and sponsorship. Evidently, civil rights leaders such as Martin Luther King Jr. did not see blackness as a blessing or as a curse, but rather as a unique condition in a system through which all of its actions were driven by a doctrine of white supremacy. Unlike King, however, there were leaders such as Malcolm X, Elijah Muhammad, Stokely Carmichael, Fred Hampton, Huey Newton, and H. Rapp Brown who were emphatically propagating a model of an inextricable linkage of being both black and proud, and saw the posturing of black power as necessary for emphasizing black demands without concessions or compromises.

Essentially, what leaders such as King wanted was a movement; an advance that represented some semblances of change from the current social conditions. However, this was more of a tactical rather than a strategic approach to changing the sordid conditions of black people, as King, although brilliant and courageous, foresaw those changing conditions from a myopic lens; thus, failing to see that social justice that he was lobbying for had only so many miles left on the odometer and was only going to cover so much ground. Leaders on the other hand who opposed King's passive approach and nonviolent philosophy were considered as being true revolutionaries—fighting for radical changes and demanding complete reparations—and were willing to flirt with and engage in the most extreme of circumstances to achieve these goals. As stated by Haki R. Madhubuti in his book *Black Men: Obsolete, Single, Dangerous?*, "when a people does [sic] not have strong, resourceful, energetic, honest, serious, intelligent, committed, incorruptible, fearless, innovative, and fighting men in a world ruled by the force of men, then that people is in trouble."[67]

Perhaps even more so than land, what Black Nationalist leaders wanted in addition to complete reparations that was owed was the control of institutions, considering that the primary root of black power was group representation and distribution of control despite the lack of majority standing or backing.[68] Thus, it would be the exercise of the control of agency and self-governing that the lack of representation and equanimity of institutions and infrastructures that crippled blacks and rendered them null and void in the socioeconomic and political process, would then take the radical turn that would come to symbolize Black Nationalism and exactly what it entailed. In other words, whatever was owed, black nationalists wanted tenfold, in addition to whatever else could be negotiated as a means of full restoration. This was a far cry from the arm-chair negotiations for race-based acknowledgement and petty privileges that were far from commensurate to those of whites that many accused King and like-minded black leaders of settling for. Unsurprisingly, divisions manifested, as did the criticisms from both sides in terms of methods deployed.

Martin Luther King, although widely celebrated as a hero in black circles, and lauded for his penchant for passive and nonviolent resistance from white pundits, obviously had his detractors from more militant and less compromising blacks. And although there were also plenty who were swayed by Malcolm X's philosophy of the right to defend oneself, and the Panther's incorporating the methodology of the right to bear arms, black nationalism/power was not absolved of its critics either. Scholar and author Vernon Ford identified the flaws of Black Nationalism as a movement that "denies the essential 'Americanness' of blacks." He went on to concede, however, that this was the result of white America's failure to both identify and treat blacks as full citizens.[69] But criticism would turn out to be the least of the impending problems facing Black Nationalists and the black power movement of the 1960s and 70s.

The Downfall

History purports that some of the worst atrocities perpetrated towards human beings happened as a result of divisions among those who were sought out to be victimized or preyed upon. Ancient Greece and Rome ultimately were removed from their thrones as global powers because of rifts and dissensions among various contiguous nation-states and principalities that left them vulnerable. Accordingly, the *Maafa* or trans-Atlantic slave trade was made possible because of a failure of cohesion among African tribes, amid the incursion and seizure of slaves at the hands of marauding European slave traders. Also, Native Americans were practically wiped out because of the concentration of fending off opposing Indian tribes as well as repelling the genocidal ambitions of new world encroaching and conquest-minded Europeans. Even among Black Nationalists in America under the subjection of institutional racism/white supremacy, though there was a consensus for the need of immediate change and retaliation amid oppression, there also was disequilibrium as far as how to go about politicking and engineering whatever change(s) was needed. For starters, while there were black leaders such as Marcus Garvey and many of his followers that deemed it necessary to leave America and return to the land of their origin, other black leaders and citizens believed that America was indeed their homeland, thus place of origin. Furthermore, and even amid the most extreme of racism, oppression, and cultural ostracism, they were just as entitled to citizenship and rights guaranteed as citizens as were their former slave masters and the slave master's descendants.

These philosophical differences represented two types of Black Nationalism. For those who believed that America and western society and culture were not a reflection of black or its identity, and that consequently it would behoove people who were categorized as black to leave America were considered as *emigrationist* black nationalists. On the other hand, those who believed that America was just as much the land of the black "man" as it was any other contingent of men or race of people, yet could not possibly foresee a social and cultural compromise among black and white and lobbied for a separation among the two within the confines of America were considered as *secessionist* black nationalists.[70]

Unmistakable, however, were agreements for separation in some way, shape, or form from Black Nationalists and others involved in the struggle for black liberation. Of course, any method of opposition from former slaves in the most powerful nation on earth came at a heavy price. Despite the different philosophical views of various black leaders, then Federal Bureau of Investigation's Director J. Edgar Hoover saw any resistance to the status quo from former slaves as a threat. As a result, a *dissent list* was compiled of black dissidents operating in America. Additionally, COINTELPRO, an amalgam for counterintelligence program, and

America's version of the patriot act of the 50s, 60s, and 70s, was initially launched solely for the purposes of labeling civil rights activists as communists and antigovernment agents; hence, making it easy and legal for these so-called dissidents to be detained.[71] It would be amid the tumult of the racial crises during the era of civil rights that splinter factions of COINTELPRO were launched to infiltrate Ku Klux Klan organizations (1964), and neutralize the Black Panther Party because of their free breakfast program for kids in urban communities.

J. Edgar Hoover proclaimed the Black Panther Party's free breakfast program as the greatest threat to national security. And Hoover's campaign against the Klan was only the result of Klansman expanding their victimization pool from innocent blacks to whites as well. Thus, the truth being that J. Edgar Hoover and the grand wizard of any you-name-it chapter of the Klan were no different in their views and dislike for blacks, and the FBI and the Klan had the same ideations and agenda of either the subordination or extermination of blacks. However, Hoover's organization could not appear to be complicit in the random, cold-blooded killings of law-abiding white people, whose murders were strictly the result of their conflicted views with other whites as to how to address matters of race and race-relations. Nonetheless, the dismantling of civil rights organizations and elimination of black nationalists was underway. Throughout the 60s alone, the assassinations of Medgar Evers, Malcolm X, Martin Luther King Jr., and Fred Hampton was proof of white racists' murderous ambitions to preserve the status quo and maintain the repression of their former slaves.

Many other black leaders, activists, and civil rights crusaders were also either killed, imprisoned for egregious and trumped up criminal infractions of being political agitators; were forced into political exile; or descended into oblivion by way of drugs and poverty, conditions that many dedicated their lives to redress in order to improve the conditions of black people. Brilliant black minds and brave social activists such as Angela Davis, Joanne Chessimore aka Assata Shakur, Stokely

Carmichael, George Jackson, Huey P. Newton, H. Rapp Brown, Bunchie Carter, and Geronimo Pratt had fallen victim to the social order of an overzealous Government bent on maintaining white supremacy. Subsequently, many were imprisoned or exiled for being anti-American or were murdered not because they aspired to be troublemakers, agitators, or rabble-rousers, but because they aimed for the God-given rights of being classified as human beings and treated accordingly on the basis of those rights.

These black leaders, activists, and crusaders for social justice fought for the right to be treated as *men* and *women*. However, manhood and womanhood for Africans that were brought to America to be slaves had become obsolete once the ships departed the shores of West Africa and docked the shores of North America. And though it is true that human beings in flesh and blood survived slavery, the essential elements and essences of nature had been taken as a direct consequence. Hence, the American government capitalized on black males and black females fighting to reclaim their manhood by exploiting those unhealed wounds and reopening and chafing the scar tissue that concealed those wounds.

FBI infiltration tactics and subversive operations designed to transform the black on white war for liberation into a black on black war of cultural dissolution, succeeded in destroying black organizations by pitting them against one another; thus, making the essential and analogous causes of these organizations discombobulated and counterproductive. In other words, it was the failure of making the distinction of biological maleness to manhood that made possible factions such as the Black P-stone Nation and the Black Panther Party to lose sight of the ultimate, uniformed goal of liberation for the black male and black people as a whole, irrespective of organizational ties; as was the case with the Black Panther Party and the US Organization, and which is still the case when analyzing the current and seemingly unrelenting conflict between the Bloods and the Crips.

Death and reincarnation of...

"The problem with the world is white men" — MICHAEL BRADLEY

Black males and black females who fought, died, and sacrificed their very existence and well-being for what is right and what is in essence bestowed by nature were ultimately outnumbered as well as outgunned. Outgunned by those who represented the racist/white supremacist system and outnumbered by a fledgling breed of black interlocutors who saw Black Nationalism, vis-à-vis black power, counterproductive and problematic to what they deemed as the true goals of black people. This cadre of blacks espoused the claim that black power was just as derisive and erroneous as white power yet, paradoxically, did so from the position of victims and brutalized subordinates rather than from a position of morally credible and coherent equals. A position that is more of the equivalent of a hyena excoriating other hyenas for standing and fighting rather than fleeing from a pride of Lions when in the midst of the last carcass before the start of a sub-Saharan dry season. This hypothetical would ring of more truth if it was actually the Hyenas and not the Lions who had run down the carcass in a successful hunt, as is irrefutable the fact that America was built on the backs of blacks as former slaves.

During the civil rights era, black males wore posters that read "I am a man." And indeed, being a Man implies self-sufficiency, proprietary industriousness, and the ability to do for self. On the other hand, the approach taken by pacifists and conformists was a request to white people for a handout and pittance for the spoils that whites failed to acknowledge that blacks had anything to do with, particularly if what was to be bequeathed was left up to whites. Also, if what was deserved, as well as owed, was asked for rather than demanded, negotiated rather than appropriated—a course of action that was not only stamped and approved but also marked the death and silencing of the assertive black voice of the civil rights era—is perhaps the primary reason why black folk to this day remain in a state of total dependence of their former slave masters.

The precepts of the Willie Lynch "making of a slave" doctrine were conditions privy to keeping the black male in a state of utter dependency, and it is boys and not men who are by nature in a state of dependence— whether it be from parents or other designated care providers—thus assuring their subordinate and emasculated positioning because of that dependency state. And, certainly, as the aggressive Black Nationalist movement of the 60s and 70s waned, the embrace of Christianity not only intensified but persists to this day as the primary catharsis for black people as a whole, amid the scourge of racism/white supremacy. This is clearly where leaders such as Dr. King went wrong. His embracing and promulgating a religion that by its initial design was meant to pacify, debilitate, and occlude any fight or desire for freedom left him not only vulnerable but somewhat hypocritical; particularly when he decided to take a moral stance against those whom his actions seem to conclude were both influential and pedagogical in his own moral conditioning. And to this day, white people respect and celebrate the passive "I have a dream" King; however, they deemed it necessary to destroy the more outspoken and, perhaps even more militant, anti-war King.

In contrast, what militant black males seem to have known was that white racists and white supremacists were never going to align themselves to equal footing with the black male, nor were they then or do they even to this day have any desires at all to share anything with him (and no, Obama's ascent to the presidency was certainly not a passing of the torch of unimpeded power to him and especially not to black people as a whole). Clearly, King was blindsided because of his theological and neurotic delu- sions of grandeur, as is the case when considering the present-day mental- ity of many black people. However, those who supported the black power movement took the simplest of approaches and analyzed a man's deeds and what he is more likely or lease likely to do by way of his very nature. As a result, it should not at all be surprising that a renowned contemporary religious scholar and educator made a passionate plea to black parents, urging them to "take black children out of the churches immediately"; thus, going on the proclaim that "this is where 'miseducation' starts." On the other hand, learning to understand the true nature of one's enemy is where education starts and liberation will subsequently follow. It is therefore clear that the tribal, ethnocentric prose and nature of white people will simply not allow them to share power with a people who are unalike themselves; especially a people whom they have found it easy as well as economically feasible to oppress. This is the authenticity of nature, which should no way be confused with the spuriousness of organized religion.

Nature is science as science is nature. And, as even identified by Karl Marx, "man lives from nature i.e., nature is his body"; and that man must sustain a continuing suitable, healthy exchange with nature if he is to survive.[72] Religion, on the other hand, is a construct that was contrived by man to justify his actions and salvage his moral ineptitude when his actions are contrary to laws of nature. Understand that every species of man is tribal to a certain degree. It is what authenticates that particular species—their ways, their customs, their standards, their culture—from those of others. Therefore, nature dictates that even though what separates man from animals is the capacity to reason and the ability to rationalize certain actions; white people's actions towards blacks are indicative of those inherent distinctions. Yet the ability to reason and rationalize behaviors might also presuppose that despite those differences there is never any justification for mistreatment. This is why organized religion was contrived—to justify treatment based on those differences and to rationalize its obvious aberrations and conflicting viewpoint with the laws of nature.

Interestingly, we live in a society that advertises itself as a cultural melting pot. Yet the architects of organized religion illustrated a hierarchical stratification of human beings based on race, intelligence, and adroitness that happens as a direct result of the natural order of earthly existence. Thus, according to the same theological doctrine that was crafted by whites and held sacrosanct by their former slaves, a collage of race-mixing that in essence defies those tenets, obviously cannot and does not speak to true diversity at all. And it is because those tenets dictate that whites are naturally superior to blacks, diversity then to blacks entails kowtowing to whites. Also, such tenets encompass an existence that hinges on the precipice of white's social acceptance and tolerance of blacks. On the other hand, diversity to whites can be inherently troubling, as it goes against the grain of how they perceive nature and the natural order of the universe in terms of racial stratification. This is of course in addition to white peoples' unmitigated conviction to white supremacy and global domination that they have generation after generation immersed themselves in, as dictated by religious tenets and canonical precepts that of course white people themselves have manufactured.

Charles Darwin's theory of evolution by way of order of natural selection ensures that the better species slowly but surely displaces the less well adapted.[73] Furthermore, white people, world over, have supported and live by the creed of this theory. And as a direct consequence, the suffering and plight of black people across the globe has no bearing whatsoever on the consciousness of white people, as any semblances of conscientious morality is assuaged by the ubiquitous belief that this is the natural order of things; irrespective of the consistent analysis of the dubious distinctions of science and religion. Even with that being said, it is no less surprising that Roman Catholics, Episcopalians, and Methodists have given support to the theory of evolution and its teachings.[74]

As stated earlier, nature is science and science is nature, and man is as synonymous to nature as is every other living creature. It is because of this fact that nature dictates that Lions and Hyenas—two vastly different species of animals—fight, maim, and maul each other strictly by means of competition that is congruent to each species survival. For the reader who is scratching his or her head in attempting to make the correlation between the will and rationality of man and the pure instincts of animals, consider that for Darwinists this is not at all egregious or surprising. In fact, Darwin believed that there were no fundamental differences between man and other species of mammals in terms of their "mental facilities." Also, his theory went on to posit that if any differences do in fact exists, it was a difference of "degree and not of kind."[75] And among human beings in the United States, especially the dyad of black and white, there is clearly no greater method of competition than capitalism.

Fight the Capitalists with a raised fist

Capitalism in America is the "taking advantage of others misfortunes."[76] Also, it has been said that "you cannot be a black man in corporate America."[77] If there is any truth to these claims, and if corporations are driven by capitalism, then where does this leave the black male in America? How does he survive or what is it that he has to do in order to ensure his own survival? In a world of predator and prey—whether it be biped or quadruped—according to Jasper Doomen, in his review of contemporary Darwinian philosophy, "if a predator has evolved skills, they [prey] too must have evolved advantages to compensate this."[78] Certainly, in America, the wheels of institutional racism/white supremacy and the cultural oppression of the black male and black people as a whole, continue to turn as they did during the days of slavery. The only difference is that the wheels are now operating on an H3 Hummer SUV rather than on a wooden carriage. In other words, racism not only continues to be a harmful condition in this society but also is more deceptive and subliminal with the advent of time and technology. In America, there are still severe penalties and sanctions against blacks for speaking to whites in a certain manner; or for acting and carrying oneself in a manner that is outside of the comfort parameters of whites; or for daring to display any form of black male assertiveness or masculinity in a society that both fears and loathes such mannerisms, lest those actions are crafted and/or approved by white people in a controlled experimental setting i.e., on the set of a television or film production.

The claim that one cannot be a black "man" in corporate America has some profound relevance. Everywhere black males and black females go, and every day of their lives, encounters with whites who are either outright racist against blacks or have a heightened sense of alertness and awareness as to what type of blacks are in their midst is the inescapable reality for black people in America. And since black folk are overly cautious and aware of the fact that it is whites who determine their social standing in life—whether it pertains to a job, career, political affiliation, or cultural significance—blacks make whatever concessions or changes that are necessary, irrespective of the cost of one's virtue, morality, or cultural integrity. In her impactful book *Post Traumatic Slave Syndrome,* author Joy Degruy points out that for centuries black males have not been allowed to be and act as men, and it is because of this denial that black males' concept of manhood, as she stated, "has yet to mature."[79]

For this reason, *fight or flight* is both the clinical as well as natural reaction when confronted with a crisis. Unfortunately, black folk in American society are privy to the adverse outcome and consequences of black males and black females who chose to fight during slavery and the civil rights era. It is because of these outcomes that the option of *flight* over *fight* served as a more plausible alternative. Furthermore, black people have fallen prey to the allure of being a member of the upper echelons of the capitalistic, fraternal social order. In other words, there are unquestionably many blacks who are as quick to succumb to being bought out from taking a stance against social injustice as they are to waving the proverbial white flag of individual and group surrender. Take for example rapper turned actor Ice T, born Tracy Marrow. Long gone are the days when as a hardcore rapper and urban buffer, he offered insightful lyrics such as:

"Cops hate kids, kids hate cops/ cops kill kids with warning shots/ what is crime and what is not/ what is justice I think I forgot."[80]

Nowadays, however, Ice can be seen on television in partnership and in collusion with the intimidation and negation of the rights of people of color at the hands of the police (for a clear-cut example, see Law and Order: SVU episode "learning curve," 2012), both a somber and far cry from the systematized social and corporate evil that Ice so artistically and passionately spoke out against in his distant yet vainglorious past.

In retrospect, the controversial track "cop killer" which boosted Ice T's notoriety and at the time ascertained his infamy by placing him on the lists of Hip Hop's urban Robin Hoods, was arguably more of a ploy of seditious rhetoric and oratory displeasure with the status quo and bifurcated racial caste. At least that appeared to be the case until Ice, himself, was lavished with the best of amenities that Hollywood vis-à-vis corporate/capitalist America could bestow on a black male: steady work, a guarantee of prodigious wealth and, of course, a white woman (Ice T is currently married to a white woman, whereas he was involved with a black female during his Cop Killer days). However, Ice T is no exception to this omnipresent state of the mental conditioning and indoctrinating of the black male, be it the spoils of Hollywood fame or the barest elements and essentials for survival.

Another point of consideration is that Ice T was financially successful by way of his rap career long before his ascent to moviemaking and television. However, two additional factors must also be taken into account. First, the financial perks and benefits offered by whites is far more appealing and stable than the dubious rewards and benefits of rap record sales, particularly for an other than A-list lyricist such as Ice T (and in speaking honestly he was a far better rapper than he is an actor). Second, the "vanilla-wafer-caper" of racists' tactics is predicated on the strategy of eliminating and removing any threat to white supremacy—whether by way of outright death, mass incarceration, substance addiction, biological warfare, or the proverbial dangling of the carrot on the string to lure the hare which, in this case, is symbolic of true conquest of the American dream and not underground or sub cultural success—a strategy that Neely Fuller refers to as *racial showcasing*.

Racial showcasing is Mr. Fuller's claim of white supremacists' attempt to nullify my claim of racism/white supremacy, or anybody else's claim of racism in a so-called post-racist society that is based on the irrefutable proof of the success of certain blacks. This clearly speaks to the profound efficacy of the racist/white supremacists system that, tragically, many blacks believe that Barack Obama's ascent to a two-termed presidential bid is proof that racism, which was once considered the number one mental health condition/crisis in American society as well as the primary cause of mental health conditions, is no longer the case in Obama's America. Therefore, similar to anything in life that can be defined by logic, racism and racists practices work in layers and degrees. Thus, when white people have and continue to refer to Barack Obama as a socialist, it is merely the hullabaloo of those whites who cringe at the idea of Obama elevating the status of blacks to that of whites.

But for those whites who are not so myopic in their outlook and are much more insightful, know that Obama is anything but a socialist based on his politics thus far. Because of this awareness, they both elected him for his first term and reelected him for a second term based on his ostentatious zeal of demonstrating anything but a desire to change the current status quo. Black people, on the other hand, elected and reelected Obama solely based on the fact that he is black and arguably for few other reasons if any other reasons at all. This claim, once again, posits a glaring distinction between the strategic foresight of whites when compared to that of their wanton former slaves and continual black victims. Thus, it is white people's incomparable ability to be systematic, codified, industrious, and meticulous, as opposed to being confused, irrational, emotional, and indolent. These truisms are what separates white America from black America, superior from subordinate, master from slave, MEN from boys.

Eleven

HYENAS & LIONS/US VS. THEM

"The jungle creed/ says the strongest feed/
on any prey that it can/ and I was branded beast/
at every feast/ before I ever became a man"[81]
—JOHN HULL, *DEEP COVER*

The reason that the black male and black people in general have the shortest life span of any other racial or ethnic group in America is because of the failure to collectively recognize the war that is being waged against them. When Sun Tzu's historical and influential book *The Art of War* is referenced by Hip Hop artists and other urban youth, it is the war that is going on in the streets that is being spoken of rather than the war that is being waged for the purpose of cultural extermination by the hands of their enemies and oppressors. It is a collective failure to recognize that there is a competition for survival among the opposing ethnic groups that warrants an immediate proactive response, rather than mass confusion of what is actually taking place, or acts of cultural and ethnic self-destruction amid the confusion. Hence, it is due to collective, uniformed complacence and categorical self-destruction that racist whites can almost be certain that, as predicated by Darwinian Theory of natural selection, the competition will ultimately cancel out itself.

I can recall a conversation with a female coworker back in the mid-1990s, in which she made a comparison of the function of black males in the black family being metaphorically analogous to the function of male lions in a pride of lions. Be that as it may, it is because of my more broadened understanding of zoology and the fauna of certain animal groups and their respective ecosystems that it would be my claim that black people as a whole are more synonymous to hyenas as opposed to lions; particularly if I am going to entertain and incorporate such a metaphor. The jungle creed posits that the lion is the "king of the jungle," and sole master of its respective habitat. Well, the black male is far from king of any environment that he might reside or comprise here in the United States. This is true irrespective of the fact that many young Hip Hop artists might have monikers, titles, and even individual surnames that state otherwise. With that being said, one of the problems currently in American society is that there are far too many black folk who are entertained by the image of a black male impersonating the character of a female matriarch for the purposes of comedy, all the while claiming to acknowledge the serious message and connotations conveyed via the portrayal of this particular character. This is nothing new. In revisiting some of the theories of Dr. Francis Cress-Welsing in her groundbreaking work *The Isis Papers*, she illustrates a series of questions that she had for preadolescent youths pertaining to their approval or disapproval of Flip Wilson's famed character, Geraldine, in which nearly all of the children expressed their adoration and connection to the character. According to Dr. Welsing's assessment, these children stated that Geraldine was, if anything, "cute." The difference however is that these were children.

Tyler Perry's fan base is overwhelmingly adult females. Therefore, the fact that white people, particularly white woman, have never nor would they ever celebrate, glorify, or make an icon of a white male entertainer with a sordid compulsion to entertain dressed up as a female, clearly indicates that black people, particularly black females, do so for two reasons. First, this form of entertainment is supported by way of an unconscious neurological and psychological condition that foments black male passivity and cultural inferiority, especially in comparison to the status of the black male's white counterpart. Second, black people collectively, it seems, have conceded the emasculated condition of the black male, as well as their inferior, subordinate status in comparison to white people; hence, a great many black folk—both male and female—support images and representations that purport a matriarchal cultural milieu, suggesting that the black female is not only the life germ of black people as a whole, but also is the most visible and dominant figure in the challenges that black people here in America face on a day to day basis.

Racial stereotypes are conducive to reemphasizing the validity of cultural and ethnic hierarchical standings and the plausible advantages and disadvantages of the fortunate and less fortunate. Stereotypes derive from a theory that Walter Lipmann posited about the images or pictures that individuals hold in their heads in regards to other people.[82] Hence, stereotypes are so deeply absorbed and enveloped in the existence of black people in America that blacks themselves have embraced certain stereotypes and misconceptions as if they are somehow a pivotal part of the black social and cultural framework. Consequently, the success of Tyler Perry is actualized by symbolism and imagery that is nothing new to black folk and unfortunately seems to be perceived as unique, being that blacks seem to be the only ethnic group to either portray or support negative imagery and depictions of themselves.

Take for example in 1983, the cult film *Scarface* was so steadfastly rebuked and repudiated by Cuban Americans that the production of the film was practically driven out of Miami, where the film was to have initially been shot because of its large Cuban American contingent, and forced to resume production in Los Angeles. This happened for two obvious reasons: Cuban Americans were amid the torrent of unprecedented violence and drug wars in Miami during the era that the film was made and rejected any negative depictions of Cuban people as a whole. Additionally, and perhaps most telling, the film, even though it both depicted the exploits of a brutal Cuban refugee and had palpable political undertones of Cuban people's struggle to elude Castro's repressive Cuba, hardly had any Cuban actors. And while the film initially was eschewed and rejected by Cuban people and from its opening was a box office disaster, the film's vitality was revitalized by both a cult movie following and a fanatical underground constituency of socially, politically, and economically disenfranchised and ostracized urban youth.

In essence, black people's glorification of violence and societal malfeasance, that is a direct result of cultural destitution and despondence, is analogous to black folk's adoration and appreciation of a black male delivering comedy and supposed subliminal omniscience in drag and amid black male incapacity and cultural and social immobility. So, what the black male has failed in being able to accomplish, the black female must attempt to accomplish by default; particularly for failures of mutually setting their sights on achieving the same goal, a theme that is common is Perry's films. Perhaps even more profound is that since black females don't have the strength or the muscle to carry the weight and burden of black people as a whole on their shoulders, a chimera of the internal valor, adroitness, and virtue of the black female—infused with the physical stature of a black male—was both created and steadfastly embraced across the cultural stratum. Hence, the war between hyenas and lions was either reborn or revamped to reconstruct and ameliorate the moral turpitude of times, both past and present.

Is the Hyena actually laughing or crying?

The black male is living in a time where there is a push to illuminate black femininity at the expense of black masculinity being that both, although mutually exclusive, have either completely failed in the past or produced only snail-like progress in terms of any present and/or future assessment.

In addition to Tyler Perry's Madea, black folk's cultural iconoclasm of *big mama* is analogous to the hyena's role in the animal kingdom. Big mama in black culture is the robust and rotund all-powerful matriarch who, because of her omnipotence and omniscience, has no rivals in her respective habitat (in this case household or community). Similarly, the hyena is an animal that is comprised of a clan-based, social structure that is unequivocally dominated by the female. Tyler Perry as a six-foot five inch man, even when in drag, stature towers over everyone in his cinematic surroundings. Similarly, Big Mama in black folds and consciousness is not only big in status but usually is larger than all of the other females in her surroundings, and in some cases that includes the leaner, less rotund males as well.

Female hyena's exposure to testosterone during the early stages of development makes them more aggressive than any other female species of mammals on the planet.[83] Tyler Perry's Madea, in addition to her stature, is lauded in contemporary black consciousness as a highly aggressive, tough-talking, gun-toting matriarchal figure whose propensity for violence when provoked or deemed necessary, surpasses the subliminal Buddhist-like flare of enlightenment in which the character is also credited and, from all appearances, only Perry's targeted audience can gauge. Also, and as pointed out in an earlier chapter, Perry's predilections for donning a dress as his primary mechanism to entertain and deliver whatever message that he endeavors to convey takes on more symbolic significance than many would be lead to believe. This is particularly true as it relates to his primary base that seems to miss the overall point or fail to read the fine print. Nonetheless, in order for any of this to make sense, it must first be understood that every social activity in American society has an element of white superiority and white supremacists connotations. If this were not true then it would otherwise go against the racists and dominant culture's own codification.

It is therefore my claim that whenever Perry undergoes his transformation from whomever he actually is in real time and into his Madea character, he subjects himself into a metamorphosis that is symbolic of a more neutered and neutral amorphous construction that essentially contradicts the sex-role function and model from which his character is both admired and respected. Simply put, in black culture, the character of Madea has become something of a cultural icon, a claim that is hard to dispute when considering that on both New Year's Day and Easter of 2013, Tyler Perry movie marathons dominated the airwaves of Black Entertainment Television (BET). Presumably, the message that was sent loud and clear is that despite the dearth of black filmmakers, some of whom have made respectable to critically acclaimed films, it is Perry's work that is most accepted and admired. Or, of all the black filmmakers who continue to exists, albeit remain in obscurity, Perry's work is more representative of the black family—one that is historically exploited and misunderstood, loathed and objectified, marginalized and debased, and is hermaphroditic in its matriarchal symbolism.

Essentially, Flip Wilson (Geraldine), Tyler Perry (Madea), Eddie Murphy (*Norbit*), Martin Lawrence (*Big Mama's House*), represent and confirm the age-old racial stereotypes of the portly, quick-tongued, boorish, black female figure-head with the symbolic male phallus, which serves to amplify her omnipotent status in the black family. Similarly, because of testosterone in the utero, female hyenas have male reproductive organs that don't function in terms of reproduction.[84] Ironically, the gradual effeminizing of black males—with the exception of those black males who employ deception to mask their homosexuality and same-sex preferences—posits a stalemate in the reproductive processes of black people as a whole, adding credibility to the fact that these males function socially more as females; thus, negating their reproductive organs and abilities to reproduce. For that reason, the intrigue should considerably outweigh the irony of Perry being a man in his mid-forties and whom at this point is his life has abstained from the reproductive process, all the while becoming the highest paid entertainer in the industry on the strength of his highly successful and lucrative brand of impersonating a female matriarchal figure.

Similar to Perry's large stature, which probably accentuates the humor of his portrayal of a black female matriarch, dominant female hyenas are identified by way of being the largest and most robust of their respective clan-base. This fact, again, confirms additional credence to the metaphor of the big mama mythos, that likens the matriarchal system of hyenas to the movement of matrilineal domination in black families and communities—whether it is a natural adjustment or a permutation by default as a result of the conditioning process due to racism. Or, perhaps this conditioning is merely a manifestation of circumstances and hardships that black folk as a whole are overwhelmingly victimized, or a cultural conversion that is both accepted and celebrated as is often the case in Perry's films. This is not to imply that all black females speak, act, are similar in appearance, or conduct themselves similar to the Madea character or the big mama persona; however, what it does imply is that the most noble, deified, and celebrated figure in the black cultural landscape and family dwelling is the female elder vis-à-vis matriarch that more resembles Hattie McDaniels than, say, Halle Berry, and displays more of the uncouthness of Moms Mabley rather than the elegance of, say, Ruby Dee.

The struggle for survival in the plains

"A white dog does not bite another
white dog when black dogs are present"
—AFRICAN PROVERB

The jungle creed posits that the lion is the "king of the jungle." Unequivocally, in the jungles of North America, the white man is sole ruler of his respective habitat. And similar to Darwinian Theory of survival of the fittest based on competition for survival, lions and hyenas are sworn enemies driven by the pursuit of preservation of each respective species. Incredulously, what former slaves and contemporary victims of institutional racism/white supremacy seem to miss is the motive of the white supremacy mechanism to create a global and terrestrial mirage of white numerical domination and dominion when, in fact, white people make up less than one-tenth of the global population. It is because of such facts that the basis of the edifice of white supremacy is global control and maintenance by way of white supremacists codification.

It has been estimated that during the transatlantic slave trade, or the *maafa*, and throughout times since, hundreds of millions of black people have been slaughtered at the hands of white men and the system of institutional racism. Surprising, however, is that the black male and black people as a whole still resign their salvation, well-being, and fate to a precipice of uncertainty that hinges on white acceptance, sensibility, or humanitarianism. This failure to recognize the necessity of cultural preservation and survival based on obvious differences that are primarily the catalysts for racism and oppression is what leaves the black male on the cusp of impending extinction. Furthermore, failures to either recognize or fully understand that the premise or necessity for survival in human beings is no different than the same elements of competition and survival for animals in the animal kingdom. For this reason, survival of the fittest portends that only the strong survive, regardless of habitat or species; at least this is how it is by all appearances played out in the trials of life based on human as well as animal behavior, for those who reject such an assertion.

Similar to the hyena, the lion is also a member of a social system, called *prides*. Dissimilar however, and as a gift of nature, the lion is endowed with size, strength, and status that the hyena does not possess. Likewise, the system of institutional racism/white supremacy is constructed to where the global minority of white people work in tandem to maintain their monopoly of global power, with the white woman acting as coequal in the maintenance and preservation of this power base. What is interesting then, particularly if one has ever viewed programming that reports the social activity of certain animal species, such as programming on networks such as *Animal Kingdom* and *National Geographic*, is familiarity with the interactions of lions within a communal system such as a pride. The larger male lions dominate the feed of a successful hunt, often violently driving the females away during a feeding frenzy (the interesting factor being that female lions [lionesses] do most of the hunting).

When considering such an analysis, perhaps an even more interesting observation is how sexism and feminism as a direct response to patriarchal hegemony has compromised or, more accurately, brought attention to the discordance of the dyadic power dynamic between the white man and the white woman. This observation adds even more certainty to the fact that in the jungle habitat of both people and animals, nature dictates that there can be only one supreme ruler. This without question is not exclusively institutional racism/white supremacy in America, but is the terrestrial reality of people activity in terms of biological, ethnic, and cultural differences. It is a model of white supremacy that presupposes and practices the complete authority of and conservation of one ethnic and cultural order of rule. Hence, sexism and classism, although byproducts of the social order of unilateral ethnic and cultural preeminence, are essentially smoke screens to obfuscate the real endeavor of the subordination and/or extermination of nonwhites. Again, such an assessment foretells that the lack of solidarity among black folk—culturally, communally, and familiarly—has hastened the extermination process; has precipitated the emasculating and effeminizing of the black male; and has fomented the superimposed, arbitrary burden that has been placed on the shoulders of the black female. A factor that even amid metaphorical similarities makes black human beings, whom are victims of racism and oppression, unique from hyenas; considering that despite hyenas own environmental disadvantages, they are still considered in terms of zoological and geographical analysis at the top of the food chain in their respective habitat. Thus, the fact that hyenas social activity predicates that males play virtually no role in hyena cub's upbringing does not, however, weaken their environmental standing.[85] Yet on the other hand, the disproportionate number of black children being raised in single-parent, fatherless homes is a form of cultural genocide when analyzing people activity.

While the Madea character and the big mama representations of the black family are testaments of the enduring, unyielding, and unwavering strength, vitality, and dexterity of the black female, under the long-standing conditions of cultural and ethnic subordination and repression, it is still however foolish to believe and/or albeit create images and delineations to convey that an advance towards black liberation is weighted on the shoulders of the black female. A similar comparison would be just as zoology reveals that although hyenas can stave off attacks or drive off juvenile and female lions from their kills, they could never accomplish this when up against full-sized adult males.[86] In other words, physiological and biological factors eradicate the notion or idea of the black female positioning herself as a worthy or formidable adversary to the white man, even if she (or in this case he) symbolically creates a chimerical visage of herself as being endowed with both the courage and sensibilities of her own very nature, along with the size, strength, and physical dexterity of the black male.

What all this means

"Being a black man in America, it isn't easy.
The Hunt is on! And you're the prey"[87]
—MR. BUTLER, *MENACE 11 SOCIETY*

There are some who might find the concept of using an analogy between animals and human beings as a means to analyze the plight of blacks as erroneous and maybe even a bit frivolous and humorous; especially considering that what clearly distinguishes human beings from animals is intellectual capacities that engender both reasoning and rational thought, as well as actions. And though this may be true, there must at the same time also be an acknowledgment of the purposefully imposed distinctions among human beings in terms of procuring and having access to resources, commerce, and other necessities that are pivotal as they pertain to survival. Also, there must be tangible and plausible analysis as to the social dynamics that brings to realization those differences.

In the animal kingdom, the same struggle for survival between hyenas and lions is no different than the social dynamics that have taking place and continues to take place among human beings and, in the case of people of color in these United States, renders one destitute and on the brink of cultural and ethnic destruction.

Just as there is the dyad of masculinity and femininity, a dualism that presupposes the probability of cultural survival and perseverance or that hinges on the precipice of collective destruction, there also exist a concomitant that is comprised of predator and prey that serves as a barometer for the potentiality of survival or destruction. Hence, the only difference between animals and human beings that are based on obvious differences is that although irrefutably competition is just as much a factor, the method of the elimination of the opposition is meted out in a different way (although not in all cases). Similarly, the inequality and disequilibrium of the disbursement of survival necessities among human beings is rationalized and indulged by way of such contrivances as evolution of the dominant species that naturally ensures the destruction of those who are weaker. Or, survival, or an inability to sustain survival, is based on biblical or theological presuppositions that stratify a racial hierarchy; therefore, ascribing one group of people to divine preeminence and consigning the other group of people to outright destruction or psychological and physiological suffering throughout the course of their natural lives.

In the battle for survival and ecological control between hyenas and lions, both respective species kill the young of the other. This is done not for the purpose of eating and consuming the young of their enemies, which is extraordinary considering that both are predatory animals whose sole existence is based on eating and procreating. Instead, this is done for the purpose of eliminating the competition and ensuring that there are no potential rivals or competitors in the future for their offspring. As a result of the system of institutional racism/white supremacy, how many young black males slaughter each other on a day to day basis because of marginalized conditions that were crafted and superimposed for the assurance of the mutual destruction of black people as a whole? Furthermore, how many are ensnared in the clutches of confinement and institutions that are designed to ensure a lifetime of limited mobility and marginalization? More telling, how often do we hear of state and local officials shooting down young black males like wild game in an African safari?

As stated previously, the jungle creed posits the lion as being the king of the jungle. The lion is also the most feared predator in its natural environment and habitat. And, like most feared and efficient predators, lions roam and stick close to the open grasslands where there is an abundance of prey and enemies, such as hyenas to vanquish. When researching and analyzing police activities over the years, it is extremely difficult to miss (especially in a racist society) the prevalence of police officer's minimal reluctance of shooting down young black males in the streets for the most innocuous of reasons and the slightest of offenses. Take for instance in July 18, 2011; a nineteen year old black teenager was shot dead by San Francisco police officers for failing to pay a $2 bus fare. This incident, along with several other similar incidences in the years that have since followed, underscores the argument that clearly in terms of the reality of young inner-city blacks, urban ghettoes are the symbolic grasslands where young black males are the random prey and police officials are the predators. What should be clear as a result of this observation is that similar to the animal kingdom, the only way to ensure genetic and cultural survival for white people is the extermination of non-whites, just as the lion instinctively knows that the extermination of its arch rival—the officious, pesky, yet equally survival-minded hyena—guarantees its geographical preservation and perseverance and forebodes more entitlements and fewer headaches.

Hyenas and lions, because they lack rationality and the ability to analyze their own respective behavioral patterns, deal with each other in a manner none other than that which is purely driven by gut instincts—the most efficacious and cerebral weapon that each has been endowed by nature. On the other hand, factors such as the black male having the shortest lifespan of any other ethnic group; more black males being imprisoned presently than were enslaved during 1850 at the height of chattel slavery[88]; more black people both in America and across the globe being infected with non-curable diseases more so than any other racial group; and of the sixty to eighty million people across the globe who live in slave-like conditions, the majority being people of non-white caste clearly cast the shadow of impending doom and is a loud and indefensible proclamation of war being waged among human beings. And similar to hyenas vs. lions, this is a battle that consists of non-white vs. white, people of color vs. people absent of color, black folk vs. white people, US vs. THEM.

Trials of Life

"Children not taught by their parents will be taught by the world"
—AFRICAN PROVERB

Presently, there is a movement taking place in the southern region of the United States that is comprised of antigovernment and militia-minded whites (and maybe even some black folk with the slave mind as previously discussed), to buttress legislative power and authority on the state level in order to effectively countermand policies and legislation put forth by the federal government. One move in particular is the push for legislation to pass what is called the *Stand Your Ground Law*, which, essentially, is legislation for the right/power to defend oneself with the use of lethal force in any instance where one feels that his or her life is threatened or is at risk. On the surface, this sounds reasonable when considering the steady and, in some cases, gradually growing crime indexes of murders, rapes, violent assaults, burglaries, and robberies in a nation that already has undisputable claim of being the most violent the world over. However, the predatory stalking and killing of black teenager Trayvon Martin by a racist psychopath, who was subsequently acquitted of murder charges under the guise of stand your ground, calls into question not only its legitimacy but beckons the question of how to effectively draw a plausible distinction between victim and perpetrator.

When We Become Men

In a recent documentary on Current TV entitled *Right to Kill: Stand Your Ground USA,* the documentary eerily depicted the callous nature of gun-toting, right-wing, second amendment zealots and their desire and blood lust to use lethal force against other human beings ranging from the most extreme to innocuous of provocations. Driven by a theme of "dead men don't talk," the feature depicted the simulated training procedures and processes of how and when to shoot down would be assailants and wrongdoers, who, as simulated, when confronting their potential victims used such language and colloquialisms as "ay yo'," "what 'up homie," and "say bitch." When both clearly and thoroughly assessing the self-imposed and assigned vernacular of the-would-be enemy, it reverberates the perceived speech, thoughts, and actions of youths whose appearance is similar to Trayvon Martin's and certainly not Eminem's (even following Martin's murderer's acquittal, Martin was posthumously maligned and discredited for wearing gold caps on his teeth). Additionally, it prompted an outright upping of the ante of death and anathema against an ageless, common enemy of the good ole so-called red-blooded, law-abiding citizenry that did not start with Martin but was manifested once African slaves were seized and horded on slave ships. Also, racial animus and hostility were exacerbated when former slaves were emancipated, and was doubly aggravated with the procurement of civil rights enactment; and, lastly, was consigned and sealed in blood with the Reagan/Bush Administration's war on drugs (i.e., the urban poor).

One of the main points that I aspire to inculcate from the illustrations in this chapter is that racists/white supremacists have a code for everything that they do. And, as stated earlier, everything that involves any sort of people activity has a profound element of racist and white supremacist dictations. The problem for many black people is the failure to see, understand, and analyze this behavior. Thus, it is ironic that during the most tumultuous times of racism and global propagation of the most extreme forms of hatred and enmity against non-white people and their respective nations and societies, black people in America act as if they have either forgotten their own tragic historical dilemma or speak of freedom and justice for all and the pursuit of happiness for everyone. Fine. Nothing wrong with that! Paradoxically, however, black folk, former slaves and present-day victims of racism/white supremacy, seem to negate taking the time to analyze their own crisis, or ask the pivotal question of how is it that black folk have only gotten so far after over four hundred years of chattel slavery—adding a century, give or take, of second and third-class citizenship.

Another suitable question is whether it is wickedness or invariable racial animus perpetrated by white people that is responsible for the plight of the black male as opposed to the natural selection of the survival of the fittest species? If it is in fact the latter, then my efforts in writing this book are for naught and should be dismissed as frivolous literary nonsense. But if it is indeed the act of wickedness, then the question of reasonable doubt based on evidence and the historical track record of racist and white supremacists-minded whites is easily dismissible. And if white people are indeed truly wicked, then clearly I would suspect that they can live with that labeling being that they have done an extraordinary job of convincing the rest of the non-white world that not only is this claim untrue, but that nature endowed them with beauty, intelligence, and terrestrial divinity that the rest of the nonwhite world must bear witness to, greatly admire, and somehow aspire to be as such themselves; irrespective of the defect of having color.

Algorithms & Experimentation

In America, capitalism dictates that self-worth is predetermined by what one has or possesses. And the whiter one is, or the lighter one's pigmentation, the more apt one's probability to procure certain things. For this reason, institutional racism/white supremacy for the black male dictates that the more disinclined one is to race and issues involving race, not only is one more likely to have certain things but that individual is also more likely to hasten or prolong his or her survival amid the propaganda of racial extermination for people of color. With that said, effeminacy of the black male, self-hatred of one's own racial group, and preoccupation with wealth and material acquisition over cultural and ethnic persever-ance and preservation are all byproducts of disinclinations and abstract apathy of one's own survival and that of the racial caste that he (or she) is biologically, genetically, and culturally ascribed.

The mantra of "it is not what you know but what you can prove" couldn't be more telling and profound in terms of a thorough analysis of racial conditions and circumstances that portend imminent doom for those who just so happen to be on the receiving end of racial oppres-sion and victimization. In other words, either black victims as a whole will deny, are unaware of, or lack collective solidarity to homogeneously redress the social iniquities and forces that are gradually destroying them. In stark contrast, white people's codification could not be any more efficacious and indiscriminate in regards to their ability to hedge sordid racism and racists practices while systemically either eliminating, effeminizing, or devaluing the virtuosity and cultural worthiness of the competition.

The propensity for prima facie and pseudo displays of the financial and mainstream aggrandizement of certain blacks is as effectual a dis-play of trickery and deception as the devil's convincing the world of his nonexistence when, in fact, terrestrial existence as we know it is HIS pri-vate playground. Thus, the proof of the endeavor of genocide is presup-posed in actualities such as the global pandemic of HIV/AIDS infections among black people; reduced lifespan among blacks, disproportionate levels of incarceration of both black males and black females; as well as profoundly higher statistics of homicide victimization, infant mortality rates, substance abuse rates, and exorbitant levels of unemployment and underemployment. However, these factors become null and void when considering the success of black entertainers such as Will Smith, whose accomplishment of generating the highest number of box office rev-enues of any other cinematic actor or entertainer is extraordinary con-sidering his remarkably mediocre acting skills and abilities. Or Oprah

Winfrey, whose multibillion dollar status and corporate enterprise is equally as remarkable considering a life and career spent purposefully wallowing in self-obsessions, biases, dysfunctions, traumas, deceitfulness, and interpersonal failures.

In addition to the aforementioned, there is of course America's premiere, contemporary black infiltrator and aggravator of the moral angst and vulnerability of the black male. Unsurprisingly, one of Tyler Perry's most recent films, *Temptations*, has understandably generated criticism from those who are not as short sighted and myopic in their cultural perspective as are, apparently, the millions upon millions who support his works. Hence, *Temptations* is an endeavor that once again offers an inflammatory and incendiary depiction of the diabolical dualism of the black male and black female. And in staying commensurate to Perry's calling, it is the black male whom is depicted as the archenemy and primary deterrent to the progress of the black female, and not the institutional system of racism/white supremacy. Quite frankly, it is Perry's own imprisonment of his painful past and perhaps hatred of his own sexual identity that provides clear impetus and motivation to impugn and cinematically castrate the black male whenever he is allotted a budget by white studio executives to do so. Also, every sordid and nefarious black male that is purported in his films must be a symbolic image of his actual biological father. Because of this, Perry, providing his current financial status and mainstream appeal, endorses and pushes for an agenda that emphasizes that the onus of cultural correctness and countenances of the black experience in America is to be credited, understood, and appreciated by way of the suffering and travails of the black female.

When analyzing the fine print rather than being fooled by the heading, the agenda of the Tyler Perry's and Oprah Winfrey's of the world to encapsulate the soul and depth of black people as a whole by the virtue of the black female is nothing more than a concession of submissiveness that portends, if anything, the pliability of black people as going in whatever direction the wind blows. This is particularly the case depending on who it is that displays a greater mastery of the elements of the balance of nature or the natural order of things; or, at least, whomever is more meteorologically attuned. And so, either black male (Perry) or black female (Winfrey), who have a voice and who are driven by their own shortsightedness, base their program on sending a message to the world that the black female is ready to move past the black male and disassociate herself from the pithiness and ineptitude that the black male in general has come to be associated with. Demoralized by his invariable social impotency and immobility, websites that cater to black females seeking out white men for sexual relations and courtships, movies and films and television programming that juxtaposes black females in the same lane as white men, and a cultural horde of black females who champion the causes of a cinematically and artistically transgendered black male is a clear indication of both biological and psychosomatic reframing and reshaping of black male masculinity, as shown by way of the susceptibility of the black female and confirmed by the actions of the effeminate black male.

History purports that Cleopatra gave herself to Julius Caesar not because of her love or affection for him, but for the sole purpose of saving Egypt from assured destruction at the hands of the mighty Roman Empire. And, in E. Franklyn Frazier's *Black Bourgeoisie,* he points out how during times of slavery many black females gave themselves to white men (I.e., their masters) to gain certain advantages; particularly for their offspring whose mix-raced blood might assuage some of the suffering that was all too common for other black slaves.[89]

The bottom line is this: while nature dictates that animals are not endowed with the gifts of guile and cunning as bargaining chips for their survival and, consequently, are bound by outright brutality based on ascribed otherness; human beings, on the other hand, are only more sophisticated in the sense of utilizing such gifts for the purposes of prolonging the inevitable; although, tragically, many still lack the foresight of fully understanding what it is that the inevitable actually entails. And while these natural gifts are clearly what separates human beings form animals, it is however the failure of the black male to judiciously shake the shackles of racist oppression that continues to widen the gap and foment the rift between the black male and the black female. And it is this disjointedness and discord that makes both vulnerable and susceptible to impending cultural and ethnic annihilation.

Twelve

Unmasking the Face of Evil: Who is it that is responsible for the imminent death of the Black Nation?

*"There must be a way to escape this accursed land,
where the Devil and his children still walk with earthly feet!"*[90]
—Jonathan Harker, *Bram Stoker's Dracula*

In a racist society that is driven by a white supremacist mindset, the conditions and plight of the black male are of little concern to white people—regardless of whether they are outright racists or claim to be disavowed from racial prejudice or bias, yet continue to sleep on the bed sheets of social advantage and *white privilege*—the latter of which is now the politically correct term to replace racism. In fact, America, even in its present social condition and, conditioning, is nothing more than one large plantation that is still comprised of masters and slaves, bourgeoisie and proletariats, capitalists and subordinates, haves and have-nots. In addition, I will make the claim that the mere thirty percent of black households that earn between $30,000 to $75,000[91] per annual income are representative of house slaves on the plantation, and that the remaining seventy percent remain gridlocked in a dichotomy of those who are privileged and those who are consigned to abstract poverty and suffering in a nation with an abundance of resources and wealth.

These statistics are clearly not indicative of a society that can legitimately boast a claim of color-blindness and post-racial progress. The only way this can be done is by way of an honest admission and acknowledgment of the racial supremacy of whites and that the progress of blacks—regardless of how such advances are perceived in terms of expedience or stasis—hinges on the prudence or allowances of white people (i.e., acquiring employment, getting a homeowners or business loan, etc.). Consequently, because there is a black president, along with the specious claim of an existential black middle class—irrespective of how diminutive—these factors are what is widely perceived as black progress or is considered as America's determination of de facto social egalitarianism. Ironically, this is what is accepted and deduced as hard evidence of color-blindness and post-racialism, in spite of facts that encapsulate the true reality of the black male and black people as a whole in America; facts that purport that blacks are less likely to own homes than whites, don't earn as much yearly income as whites, and certainly do not live as long as a direct consequence of these disparities. Moreover, the earning power of blacks is about seventy-three percent to that of whites; blacks are twice as likely to die from disease, accidents, and homicides than whites;[92] and white people with masters degrees are more likely to live middle class or above middle class as opposed to blacks with doctorates.[93]

The strategic, much-placed emphasis and focus on the dearth of black entertainers and black millionaires is perhaps the most deceptive ploy and caper in gauging black advancement and progress and post-racialism and colorblindness; thus, illuming a symbolic love child of a pseudo dyadic romanticized union that inured such progress and advancements. In simpler terms, it is the "showcasing" of the success of blacks in an effort to hide true racism or the castigations directed towards the great majority of blacks, which can feasibly be surmised as percentages based on profits and losses. This is especially the case in terms of methodically and strategically enumerating and eliminating the longstanding dilemma of the black existence and representation in a society that from its inception, particularly following the eradication of chattel slavery, has loathed both.

Posttraumatic Slave Syndrome posits that black people as a whole in America still possess a slave mentality. A people who by way of their conscious and subconscious behaviors, subtle and obvious, demonstrate a collective inferiority complex that was indoctrinated with slavery as well as an unchanging status of subordination and inadequacy that has never waned. As a result, the venom and irascibility that was created due to conditions of slavery and oppression have not been directed against the palpable enemy and oppressor of black people, but instead has been inverted and, perniciously, continues to cause a deep chasm between the victims of institutional racism/white supremacy and cultural and ethnic subjugation that continues to be the sole catalyst for black confusion, weakness, passivity and, now, black male effeminacy.

It has always been common—past and present—for black people to slander, denigrate, and impugn other black people. And the vitriol that is verbally and physically expressed from certain blacks is more than likely directed towards other blacks. The gossip that is disseminated in reference to other blacks can almost certainly be traced back to a black source or black person or persons whom are the initial conveyors of the gossip. Also, the poison that is summoned by blacks that pertains to the actions and improprieties of other social groups is more than likely in reference to other blacks. I can recall years ago a conversation with an adult black female who fervently verbalized her distrust and disdain towards other blacks because of what she described as a lifetime of mistreatment and suffering primarily by the hands of these impudent and malfeasant individuals. This is shocking when considering a lifetime assigned to mental and physical bondage via conditions of institutional racism/white supremacy, a social reality that black folk not only have nothing at all to do with in terms of orchestrating and perpetrating but are also the most palpable victims of its practices.

So, say for instance a young black male who attends a prestigious University and notices that a cultural disconnect exist between himself and other blacks, particularly black females who fill these institutions in droves. Given the scenario, it is imperative that this individual understand that this is not at all personal, nor is it a reflection on him in terms of his character or personality traits. The fact of the matter is that black females and the dearth of black males who fill these institutions do not do so solely for acquiring a college education, but also for the purposes of Europeanization—procurement of such and/or certain mechanisms and social trappings as a means to assuage the condition of being black in a racist society—in order to make conditions that they cannot change more acceptable and tolerable for white people. Similarly, when a black person encounters white people in any setting whom are condescending, controlling, and haughtily expressive and purposeful in their explicit and implicit debasement of him or her, black folk in general, or other people of color, it should not be surmised as an encounter with one particular white person who happens to be rude or disrespectful. Instead, it should be concluded as the racists codification of white people in terms of how they interact with black people or any other person of color, in which the indoctrination of Americanism dictates that they are biologically, genetically, and culturally superior.

This is true regardless of time or place in western society that a black person might encounter white people, or anywhere you might encounter them in the world for that matter. The simple fact is that unlike their foolish and ignorant black victims of institutional racism/white supremacy, white people are not at all confused by race and practices of racial subordination. They understand what it means to be white in a society that from its inception has stratified whiteness far beyond any other caste of color or creed. And just as white people determine the growth or hindrance of the progress of a certain percentage of blacks—due to their unmitigated and unobstructed monopoly on corporate industry and the socioeconomic infrastructure—they also unabatedly dictate the terms of their relations and dealings with black people. It is because of these reasons that the white-washed, white-identified, and sub-Euro-minded black male or black female, who fail to understand the excessive consignment cost that is to be extracted for cashing in their individual and cultural respectability, strictly for the purposes of ingratiating themselves into the foray of those they deem as occupying the dominant and winning side of the chessboard, do so at their own peril and inexcusable unawareness that the institution of racism/white supremacy was patented and perfected strictly for the purposes of white genetic and cultural survival. Therefore, any beliefs or an idea of an amalgamation of the cultures that is based strictly on oneness under the penumbra of Americanism is an abstract fallacy that reeks of the squalor of massive neuropathology.

What is also confirmed is the complexity of collective inferiority that has long-since been indelibly implanted, particularly when considering that it is the inherent otherness and difference that whites are highly cognizant of and blacks have steadfastly attempted to downplay that are essentially the reasons why the institutional system of racism was crafted in the first place. In other words, white-identified blacks may only be prolonging their inevitable demise under the guise of colorblindness and enmeshing of contrived commonalities. Yet these same blacks remain grossly ignorant of the one true fact that there has never been nor could there ever be colorblindness in a society that was constructed on the premise of superiority vis-à-vis inferiority based on racial and color differences, and has since thrived under a system of racial supremacy for whites and collective subordination and oppression for blacks.

Heroes & Cowards

*"The revolution can't survive if the revolutionary
is killed. So the revolutionary has to be wise to
avoid the killing fields. Not for the sake that he wants
to live, but that the revolution may live
and thrive. So revolutionaries have to be wise,
not only courageous, but wise."*
—LOUIS FARRAKHAN

A hero is judged by his deeds amid danger and uncertainty. Therefore, what makes the revolutionary special and unique in regards to social conditions and constraints that affect the black male, and black people as a whole, is his or her unyielding pursuit of the abolishment and amelioration of those conditions. Also, this is despite the potential (and often inevitable) consequences. The revolutionary does not think and act on his or her own behalf, but on behalf of the masses of those who invariably face the most extreme and adverse of persecution and mistreatment. On the other hand, a coward is someone who clearly only thinks and acts on his or her own behalf; is terrified of the potential consequences of speaking and acting out against social injustices; and often will hedge or make null and void truths and the painfully obvious in order to appease and ingratiate himself or herself into the folds of the oppressor/s, rather than demonstrate sound discernment of morals and virtues. And even more destructive is that the coward carries his or her pusillanimous and self-centered proclivities like a virus, endeavoring to infect any and all by feigning to act and speak for the good of all—including the wrongdoers and enemies of the natural balance and order of humanity.

Given such a claim(s), a feasible question would be, what is it that taints or warps the senses of values more so than money and material acquisition? Furthermore, how could this ploy be done any more effectively against a people who have been historically jettisoned, ostracized, and deemed irrelevant to the socioeconomic and political infrastructure of the wealthiest nation on earth? It is not at all uncommon to hear hullabaloo from black artists and filmmakers such as Antwan Fuqua, a black male whose career could not be any more foretelling of cultural debasement and black exploitation, make an argument haranguing those who infer the racist tendencies of Hollywood and its exploitative zeal and campaign against blacks. Or rapper turned actor (racists' most effective method of silencing the voice of black, urban discontent) LL Cool J's indulgent blustering, along with country artists Brad Paisley, of none other than music being the most effective and plausible of platforms to open up the dialogue of race relations among whites and their hapless black victims. This spectacle, of course, is in addition to the prospect of Mr. Cool J further lining his pockets and/or earning more individual recognition, same as other persons involved.

Once again I make the distinction between biological maleness—a trait that one is ascribed by birth—and manhood that is confirmed by virtuosity and dexterity that is geared towards self and cultural preservation and the ability to sustain both, particularly amid external forces that are opted to quell such attributes and endeavors. While devoid of the true measures of manhood, the black male has indeed proven to at least be physically strong. Hence, LL Cool J, born James Todd Smith, possesses the ability to physically beat to a pulp a marauding intruder in his luxurious home, yet is devoid of the foresight to accurately as well as truthfully assess injustices that are still taking place in communities from whence he was himself socialized. Also, Mr. Cool J is someone who lacks the gall (and balls) to speak honestly about race, race relations, and the global hegemony exacted by the same people who pay his excessive salary. What is perplexing is that while defending the characteristics of urban youth who wear their pants sagging way below their beltline, he in the same voice points out the impropriety of North Korean nuclear weapons (and we have heard this lie before) being pointed at the United States, neither of which are the crux of the real problem in which his kumbaya, hand-holding soliloquy with his country-singing cohort was based. Not to mention the last claim being egregiously false. Nor do these things have anything to do with the social injustices that continue to be meted out by white supremacists America against blacks and other people of color.

Previously, I made the claim that America is still symbolically one big plantation that is comprised of a big house that is run by a master or an overseer. Accordingly, the small segment of the financially secure of black America are analogous to the dearth of house slaves who, during the times of slavery, worked in the master's house, slept in the master's house, formed close interpersonal relationships with the master's kinfolk, and admonished and excoriated the majority of field hands and slaves for taking issue with their position and status of being circumscribed to servitude and bondage. Subsequently, it should come as no surprise that the majority of the SO-CALLED middle-class of black folk in America either dismiss the question of race entirely or address racism as to how it affects black folk individually and not collectively. Moreover, these supposed well-to-do blacks seldom deduce racism as an institutional system that is designed to keep blacks and other people of color in a permanent state of arrested development. For what other reason would it appear that individuals such as Mr. Fuqua and Mr. Cool J come a dime-a-dozen in the entertainment industry, yet the Farrakhan's, Sharpton's, and other voices of discontent of the American social order seem to be comprised of an entirely different paradigm, despite the fact that all black people—regardless of class, rank, or privilege—are under the constraints and dictates of the racist, white supremacists system.

Black people who have access to wealth and who are the beneficiaries of fame and prestige seldom speak on matters pertaining to race/ism or still see issues of race as salient factors in American society; primarily, because they have been deluded in the belief that their personal or individual success is testament of the infallibility of the American creed that posits hard work, personal drive and ambition as determinants of American success and not color or color constraints. Accordingly, you have blacks who openly speak out against affirmative action policies, deeming them as Jim Crow props that are window-dressed under the guise of modern day liberalism. Hence, the politics of respectability is misleading and loses credibility by fallacious images and pseudo representations of the success of other blacks, as if these successes were made possible without the benevolent offerings of white people who understand the need to mask outright genocidal endeavors and exploits by bequeathing a certain segment of the black populous with certain resources, appurtenances, and financial opportunities, and do so meticulously and minus the expense of sacrificing their own powerbase.

Incidentally, the onus and emphasis of black celebrities is representative of individuals who are far and few between. However, the reality of the majority of black people, particularly young black males, is premature death, underemployment or unemployment, and mass incarceration. Yet, tragically, black pop stars, black athletes, and mainstream black celebrities are the folks who are revered and admired in this society. Urban gangs and gangsters, however, and who by the way are black folk's last line of defense—uncouth, uninformed, unorganized but ready to fight—are socially castigated, criminalized, and ostracized in both cultural circles. Consequently, it is my opinion that individuals such as "Monster" Kody Scott, aka Sanyika Shakur, are much more pertinent to the assessment of the balance between prosperity and destruction for black folk than are LL Cool J and Antwan Fuqua, Tyler Perry, Oprah Winfrey, Steve Harvey, etc.

Similar to the house slave that loved his or her master and spent a lifetime trying to curry the favor of his or her enslaver, while at the same time rebuking black identification and all of the conditions and ills that came with it, it is incumbent that contemporary black victims of institutional racism/white supremacy very thoroughly scrutinize and monitor the exploits and endeavors of black entertainers or those who have been erroneously designated to speak on behalf of either the black male or black folk as a whole. What should be clear is that they do not speak for black victims of racism/white supremacy, nor do they represent those of us who seek to escape both the house and the field. And, without question, in order to do this it takes the intelligence and judiciousness of a revolutionary, vis-à-vis a hero. The coward, on the other hand, can only affect the pursuit and motivations geared toward progress like a plague and, unequivocally, the disease that circumscribes the black male in America to sickness and vulnerability is the disease of racism/white supremacy.

Death of the Capitalists

> "Part of the mechanics of oppressing people is to pervert them to where they become institutions of their own oppression"
> —KUMASI

Haki R. Maduhuti has made the claim that persons in leadership positions in America are creations of "false and disguised images."[94] And how one is coerced to exude a false image and representation of oneself is by way of the offering of some sort of incentive that the victim of the decadent behavior believes that the means of the behavior are both justified and compensated for by the end result. Unsurprisingly, racism and capitalism go hand in hand in terms of controlling the progress or lack thereof of people by means of monetary and financial power, as well as controlling the thoughts, speech, and actions of people with the assurances of some means of compensation. During times of chattel slavery, slaves who by way of mouth thwarted slave rebellions and insurrections were rewarded for doing so with extra privileges, such as an extra piece of fatback at mealtime or a night's rest on a cot in the master's outhouse rather than the usual cramped conditions and discomfort of the slave quarters.

Capitalism is an evil that has not only kept people, irrespective of race and ethnicity, marginalized but also has sustained the institutional system of racism and has kept the black male in America socioeconomically wanton and perpetually ascribed to the status of "have not," in respect to the dichotomy of those who have and those who do not have. Perplexing, however, is that black people as a whole have stockpiled a two-hundred billion dollar "black economy" by way of working for white people,[95] yet the majority of black folk to this day remain both under and unemployed and remain at the very bottom of the economic totem pole of the world's strongest economy. It has been said that capitalism is a system that is designed to take advantage of the misfortunes of others. And in American society who is more misfortunate than the black male? Hence, in an era of black decadence and disillusionment, it is easy to be led to believe that poor Hispanic immigrants are not only at the bottom caste and lower rungs of the economic food chain, but that they are also the most vulnerable and susceptible to both institutional racism and group-targeted discrimination. However, the facts don't support such a belief. And although the previous assessment is true to some degrees, Hispanic groups as a whole are not as vulnerable to the uncertainties that blacks, as a whole, have been and continue to be. In fact, statistically, while white workers on average earn a medium wage income of $716, blacks earn $589 to $529 for Hispanics.[96] Nonetheless, and even though young Latino males make up a sizeable percentage of prison and correctional institutional detainees, the numbers are still not nearly commensurate to those of black males.

Furthermore, Hispanics do not boast nearly the same numbers of children being raised in single parent, fatherless households. And according to similar statistics, while only a third of blacks have entered the (SO-CALLED) middle class, more than half of Hispanic households have done so.[97] With the advent of *The Cosby Show*, which ran from 1984 to '92, and was a show that never touched base on issues of race, most black television dramas, sitcoms, and films attempt to depict a black middle class from a pseudo lens and myopic point of view that is robust and evanescent; moreover, attempt to do so from a perspective or point of view that is not much different from that of their white contemporaries. Perhaps it is this delusion that would compel Steve Harvey to make the assertion that "America is still the best thing going" in terms of the conditions of the black male and black folk in general. And maybe it is also this disillusionment that would prompt Antwan Fuqua, LL Cool J, and a large percentage of black America to have such a narrow and shortsighted purview of race relations in this society.

Even Bill Cosby, the ultimate black capitalist and newly crowned castigator and admonisher of the black, urban poor, as well as newly alleged sexual deviant, once made the claim that he did not think that black entertainers could win converts.[98] Well, I would make the claim that in regards to black liberation, they certainly cannot! Nor do they attempt to do so. And since it is hard to dispute that this is indeed the case in the entertainment industry, capitalism in terms of political maneuvering is packaged, stamped, and sold to appear much more palpable. Why not? After all, former slaves and victims of institutional racism/white supremacy can now boast for the first time in the history of western society and culture of having a black president. An important question however is whether or not Obama occupies the white house because of the fact that he is that good or is it more of a case that his opponents were that bad? So, for those who are paying particularly close attention, the smoke screen is the perceived outpour or outcry from the rightwing that Obama is a socialist, which he by all appearances and actions certainly is not.

Webster's definition of capitalism is as follows: an economic system that is characterized by private and corporate ownership of the capital acquisition of goods by private markets rather than state or federal control. Therefore, prices, production, and the distribution of goods and services are largely determined by competition of the free market.[99] Certainly, in a racist society that is controlled by whites, obviously the potential for economic prosperity of the free market is both restricted and limited to blacks and other people of nonwhite ethnic factions. Hence, capitalism, which its historical basis has been the conservation of class inequality,[100] ensures that the proverbial lion's share of wealth and the distribution of goods and services that cultivates wealth are determined by the species that tops the rank and order of natural selection, vis-à-vis survival of the fittest.

It was Karl Marx who stated that man lives from nature because nature is in him, and that in order for man to survive he must maintain a continuing dialogue with it.[101] However, natural selection also presupposes that competition in humans for sole control of land and all of its natural resources, although cruel, is natural and scientific.[102] Thus, capitalism is a social system that is comprised of haves and have-nots, in which whites mostly have and nonwhites have very little, if anything. So, as it stands, this can only be the case because the distribution of monetary assets and resources is at a gross disequilibrium, and it is the monopoly of such assets and resources that leaves one social group primed to preserve power and the other devoid and consequently on the verge of extinction.

Even Darwinism, and its connotations of natural selection, promotes what is termed as "biological-competitive capitalism."[103] What this means is that contrary to claims that state otherwise, there are indeed biological differences between the black male and the white man, black people, and white people. What this also entails is that there is, has, and always will be competition based on those differences; and that there are no resources that are more prized than monetary assets in western culture and society. In other words, he who has the gold indeed rules, and those who control the distribution of wealth not only rule but control the thoughts and actions of those who covet monetary procurement and financial stability. Consequently, not only will black males kill each other for paper with the face of a dead white man on it, but they will also sell their souls, virtues, and integrity to obtain it. Also, there are many who will sacrifice what is right and even attempt to justify bartering, selling, and sacrificing such attributes, all for the purposes of staying in accordance with the precepts and conditions of an unjust society that determines self-worth by what one has, or what one is willing to sacrifice in order to acquire certain things. And from the days when the first black faces stepped foot on these shores, the dictates of white supremacy and racism immediately minimized their self-worth and deemed them as a people not deserved of much, if deserved of anything at all.

According to Gary R. Johnson, in his article entitled "Social Darwinism in European and American thought, 1860-1945: Nature as a model and Nature as a threat," Darwinism, and his theory of natural selection, laid the groundwork for Nazism. Consequently, this act made it possible for Hitler to devise a specious Darwinist formula to legitimize his murderous and genocidal policies against Jews and other nonwhite ethnic groups.[104] One of Hitler's methods of carrying out his murderous campaign was to contrive negative images and false propaganda of Jews and other victimized groups in order to debase them and make their fate appear to be necessary for the purposes of national security and Aryan advancement, hence the natural order of things. Over a half century later, white racists, fascists, and Nazis still do not want to deal with blacks and cohabit with their former slaves, lest these dealings with blacks elicit individual and interpersonal gratification (e.g., sexual and other forms of coitus intimate relations). However, unlike Nazi Germany, who sacked their victims by blatant, brute force; neo-fascists America has with the advantages of time, technology, and resources, proven to be much more sophisticated in making the plight of its most hated victims appear to be the result of their own misdoings and uselessness. Therefore, when posing the question of who is responsible for the imminent death of the black nation, the answer lies in the actions of not only the victimizers but the responses of the victims and their erroneous and pernicious preoc-cupations. Certainly, nothing is more disarming and creates a more effi-cacious diversion than the preoccupation and obsession with acquiring capital and bequeathed monetary rewards for ones services or, in the case of many, disservices.

Mental health is based on self-love, and the post trauma of slav-ery and oppression that the black male has and continues to endure has greatly disrupted the balance of mental health and has instead fomented anguish, self-loathing, and a profound identification with the enemy of black people as a whole and those who seek to disturb the equilibrium and the collective well-being of blacks. Subsequently, for the sake of financial gain, rewards, and prestige, talented black males

and black females discard discretion in regards to what is morally, culturally, politically, artistically, and creatively correct for immersion in self-
destructiveness, exploitative prose, and the confirming of dissolution
and disregard of group representativeness. Consequently, black actors
such as, let's say, Samuel L. Jackson, who demonstrate very little prudence and discretion in choosing the roles that he plays and evidently
failing to fully understand (or perhaps he just doesn't care) that if art
indeed imitates life then perception can be as powerful as a nuclear
explosion.

And it doesn't end there. The list is endless. It was Van Goethe who
claimed that "none are more hopelessly enslaved than those who falsely
believe that they are free." Hence, it is the foolish and disillusioned black
person(s) in American society who believe that money is the great equalizer to institutional racism/white supremacy, or that success is the only
key to unlock the shackles of socioeconomic constraint and instead will
open up the floodgates to social and financial maneuverability and mobility. However, those folks who are susceptible to this caper fail to recognize
two very important facts: (1) Capitalism and racism go hand in hand,
particularly in terms of laying out the groundwork for the perfect divide
and conquer strategy. (2) This strategy is clearly designed by whites to
eliminate the seditious and the mere deadweight first, and then unabatedly eliminate the token blacks who were duped by the con that wealth
supersedes stealth, or financial gain eradicates oppressive pain.

Stone Killers

> "Alright! I'm coming out. Any man I see
> I'm going to kill him! Any son of a bitch
> takes a shot at me, not only am I going to kill him but
> I'm going to kill his wife, and all his friends,
> and burn his damn house down!"[105]
> —WILL MUNNY, *UNFORGIVEN*

Clint Eastwood's academy award winning film *Unforgiven* was highly acclaimed during the year following its release and continues to be one of the most celebrated of Hollywood's illustrations of white men being the world's most proficient and foremost killers and slaughterers of other human beings, as well as the world's premiere drunkards. The film is a character study of the white man's insight into his own imminent mortality as well as self-analysis of the fragility of life, almost as if subtly conveying that the apotheosis of murder and bloodlust among human beings will inevitably come at an extreme cost. Yet similar to all forms of illustrations and perusing of analyses as barometers for the forecast of white supremacy and global dominion, the black male is invariably a suitable culprit or, for all sense and purposes, the usual suspect.

For this reason, in the system of institutional racism/white supremacy, one of the film's characters, Ned Logan, played by acclaimed black actor Morgan Freeman, was the craven and cowardly representative of the yin and yang game of morality in regards to the social functioning of human beings. If Freeman's portrayal of this character seemed a little odd or, maybe even belittling, given his extensive pedigree and acclaim in film, this should not at all be surprising when considering that every degree of social functioning in regards to black and white is premised on a superior/inferior dyad. Subsequently, the character of Ned Logan did not actually spill any blood in the film; however, his own blood was spilled and violent death was implied for the retribution and sins of the murderous ambitions and exploits of his two white counterparts (another common racist mantra is that "it is always the nigger's fault").

And again, the list could go on. The point, however, of such films and cultural representations is to create a ubiquitous image of the black male as being a member of an inferior species that is psychologically inept, daunted, and incapable of ensuring his own survival, particularly if that survival hinges on his ability to compete with white men in terms of mental fortitude, virility, and dexterity (and in the case of the film *Unforgiven*, murderous predilections). This was the same campaign employed by Nazi Germany in its endeavor to exterminate the Jews and other nonwhite subgroups as a means to proclaim and legitimize Aryan supremacy. Hence, the real killers of the world, particularly in America, are ten thousand dollar suit-wearing politicians—both black and white—but mostly white obviously, as are real terrorists being men who occupy Wall Street. The architects and practitioners of institutional racism/white supremacy are aware of these facts; therefore, employ deceptive tactics and methods to make it appear as if senseless and wanton acts of violence are perpetrated by marauding urban black gangs and criminals, and surreptitious, politically-motivated brown-skinned foreign terrorists.

Human beings fight among each other in order to survive, and in a world that is driven by a "kill or be killed" mentality, the most sophisticated and skillful at killing is the one who is most primed to survive. Another common adage is that "might makes right"; hence, genocidal practices that are driven by racism and a white supremacist mindset is justified purely on the basis of the Darwinian model of survival of the fittest. Subsequently, greed, systemic oppression, exploitation, and the trickery of post-racialism amid a penumbra of covert racist tactics are obligatory and are utilized to ensure the extermination of the opposition or the perceived "other." One indisputable fact is that the black male is not at all free in a land that loudly proclaims the unmistakable benefits of freedom. Therefore, since the black male, and black people as a whole, are oppressed and certainly are not free, the proverbial land of the free for white people confirms the inferiority of blacks as well as those others who are weak; and unless those who are weak can radically change their weakened state they will surely perish!

Thomas J. Sugrue, author of *Sweet Land of Liberty*, made the assertion that it is now a plausible argument that in regards to human biology, race is an insignificant ideology being that other than variations in skin tone, it infers little else.[106] Additionally, a similar theory avows that the idea and/or concept of race is a social construct that is strictly attributable to white people. Hence, before the global encroachment of white supremacy and Euro-domination, the concept of race—particularly one based solely on differences in skin color—did not exist among the terrestrial human family. Even so, the fact that black males in America account for nearly half of the prison population speaks to both obvious and striking differences—whether biological or cultural—that are perceived as plausible and necessary enough to account for whatever incentive is warranted for their elimination and removal from society. And unlike blatant and outright murder in America's past (although this still happens), black males in the criminal justice system are not physically lynched but are lynched by America's racist and anti-black judiciary.

Meanwhile, the capitalist-minded black individual remains only interested in the procuring of capital, power, and social standing for the purposes of Euro-validation and fraternization; rather than pursuing these endeavors for the purposes of disentangling other black folk from the scourges of racism and imminent annihilation. Incidentally, the counterargument of having a black president means absolutely nothing, given that in more than six years of public service, Obama's budget is worse than George W. Bush's in terms of monies and resources allocated to drug treatment and prevention as opposed to increasing budgetary funding for tougher law enforcement policies. Proving once again that Obama is a black male who fraternizes and hodgepodges with wealthy white elites, and that his sole allegiance is to the preservation of power of this particular constituency, and the reinvigorating of the middle-class, vis-à-vis white socioeconomic base.

They aren't all bad

> "A hierarchal society is one that is
> based on poverty and ignorance!"
> —GEORGE ORWELL

In the history of culturally and ethnically-oppressed groups of people, black folk in America appear to be the only collective who attempt to both justify and minimize their oppression and mistreatment at the hands of their oppressors and sworn enemies. As stated throughout the entirety of this book, the post trauma of hundreds of years of chattel slavery has completely destroyed the zeal for egalitarianism and social autonomy and equanimity, instead producing the most profound effects of Stockholm syndrome. In fact, identification with former slave masters and their children is so profound and prominent that former slaves and victims of institutional racism/white supremacy fully embrace the names, religion, customs, and traditions of the people who to this day have demonstrated utter stubbornness in their acceptance, square-dealing, and treatment of blacks. Perhaps this is why black people in America as a whole are the last group of people on earth who remain in psychological and physical bondage, no doubt because they are the most accepting of ethnic discrimination and mistreatment, as well as most malleable to the abhorrent conditions that ensue and, consequently, are the least respected and most pitied (and perhaps most disliked) worldwide (and if there are any questions or objections to the physical bondage claim, check black and brown prison statistics and/or read Michelle Alexander's *The New Jim Crow*).

And if in case one so happens to disagree with the claim of black people being accepting of racial injustices and mistreatment, particularly if you are a black person, try striking up a conversation pertaining to racism with another black person and witness how a debate or outright argument gradually unfolds (coincidentally, I just recently had a dispute with an acquaintance in regards to race, class, and the socioeconomic status of black people as a whole in America). This fact is of course a sad and tragic climax being that the more natural response, based on the irrefutable reality of racism and discrimination directed towards all people of color, should be an automatic unification of this irrefutable fact, followed by whatever cooperation is needed or steps necessary to take proper action (To the author's knowledge and experience, I have never heard a Jewish person deny or question the certainty of the Jewish holocaust). This is where I would agree with the late Michael Jackson's prophetic soliloquy that nobody seems to like or respect black people.

In America, due to hundreds of years of the process of *inferiorization* and gradual effects of menticde, black people don't like or respect other black people!

A common truism is that it is hard to respect those who do not respect themselves. Therefore, a credible argument could be made that Malcolm X, during the time of his political and activist crusade, was more respected internationally than was Martin Luther King. Arguably, and during both of their respective heydays, Malcolm X was widely perceived as an unflinching, unyielding, and intrepid freedom fighter for a just cause for freedom and equality at any cost, and without any meager compromises. King, on the other hand, could have been perceived as another of what W.E.B. Dubois christened Booker T. Washington as being: a "great accommodator." Or, King could have easily been seen as a calculating flatterer, despite how stern and conscientious his commitment to the cause; thus, allowing himself to be reduced to a mere penny pincher for civil rights, if he believed that it would lead to a much bigger cause and open up more grounds for maneuverability for oppressed blacks in the future. This is why King's *Why We Can't Wait*, published in 1964, conflicted with his Job-like patience in terms of his political strategy, and could just as easily been interpreted as *why we can't wait to be heard in making an argument for the case of basic human and civil rights*, as opposed to *why we can no longer wait for rights that have long been delayed and are four hundred years past due.*

According to Sugrue, during the days of the struggle for civil rights, "equality required rash action, not polite discourse."[107] Yet the latter, which was more compatible to King's philosophy, and the armchair revolutionary tactics of those who both shared and embraced his vision obviously did not ameliorate or redress race relations in America. If anything, it only prolonged the inevitable suffering and subhuman standards and conditions that would be superimposed on black people by virtue of the sordid racist ideologies and practices that never waned but instead remained commonplace. Incidentally, "they are not all bad" is the pernicious and vacuous equivalent to King's description of "our sick white brothers" in response to the brutalizing, torturing, bombing, and maiming inflicted on blacks at the hands of racists whites. Indeed, the reference to whites as our sick brothers indicates that it is the kin folk and blood relatives of black people who also are the butchers, brutalizers, and present-day exploiters of black females and murderers of black children (As I write this, and as another prime example, the racist police officer who murdered Michael Brown in Ferguson Mo., was just cleared of any wrong-doing).

Presently, black people as a whole are fragmented primarily because of the dictates of institutional racism/white supremacy. Also, in today's times, the black female is nearly on par economically with educated whites—both man and woman—meanwhile, an educated black male makes three-fifths the salary of educated whites. Clearly, this is indicative of the attempt to disrupt the socioeconomic equilibrium and social functioning of the black family for the purposes of divide and conquer. Willie Lynch's "making of a slave" laid down the groundwork for this tactic centuries ago. And the reason this ploy is still effective (although to some degrees utilized differently) is that black people in America, although quasi-physically free, still possess a slave mentality. However, attempts to quash this claim are done solely by the success of black millionaires who found success by way of sports and other forms of entertainment. But the failure to understand that mainstream sports and entertainment are white racists' most indiscriminate and visible method of manipulating the REAL conditions of race-relations is also highly symptomatic of the massive neurosis and psychopathological conditioning of the black male, and black people as a whole, in terms of the susceptibility of being victimized by racism and ultimately total genocide.

Institutional racism and the belief in white supremacy is mostly perceived as either a relic of the past or a social ill that occasions rare instances of actions and words that can unsettle the sensitive black person or cause subtle distress. Furthermore, white people are not all bad; however, black people, particularly black males, are socially inept and malfeasant enough to bolster the worst conditions of social functioning since the years that immediately followed civil rights legislation, and wantonness and poverty in black communities rivals similar conditions in third world countries despite so-called, pseudo corrective policies such as affirmative action.[108] Certainly, seeing overweight white woman with biracial, mixed-race children in every state, city, and town hardly speaks to improvements in race relations; neither does seeing attractive, and is some cases professional black females, frolicking around with professional, yuppie white men. Instead, what it speaks to is America's proficiency and indiscriminate measures of window-dressing a social ill and crisis that started with the conceptualization of slavery and continues to exist to this day, because of the precepts and proscriptions that the legacy and visage of slavery dictated in terms of how to deal with its former slaves; hence, inferior blacks.

Institutional racism/white supremacy has inculcated that blackness is a curse and is a direct consequence of being on the shorter end of the genetic stick and, subsequently, has encouraged its former slaves to hate their own identity and, even more profound, their very own existence. Incidentally, survival for the black male and black folk in America is a resignation of being an enclave of flunkies and toadies to the superior caste of whites. In other words, blackness or, "being colored," as soberly verbalized in Tyler Perry's debauched melodrama *For Colored Girls*, "is a metaphysical dilemma" that black folk have yet to conquer. While on the other hand, white is not only normal but is culturally and biologically right vis-à-vis correct. Because of such ubiquitous (albeit absurd) beliefs, being black in American society is either completely deconstructed (arguably one of the most effective methods for whites to established any ties with blacks is an attempt to look past their blackness), used as an albatross to elicit sympathy, or is subverted by obvious transparencies and pseudo-self-exaggerations to maximize character and self-worth.

Thus, in today's times, if white people do not resort to the effusive and convenient criminalized portrayal of black males, then the penitence for such debauchery is the illumining of the Barack Obama-type, token black, whose Euro-elegance and detachment of typical blackness that has historically aroused deep-seated enmity is compensation for the stigma of his unchanging complexion.

On the same note, the neo-mainstream black female—with her hair weaves, warped sense of culture and values (e.g., reality television), and euro-eccentricities—and because she has never (nor will she ever) posed as a threat to the white establishment and social order, is showcased as equally prim and bitchy and as ambitious as the white female. Indeed, character traits that are contrived strictly on the basis of her birth defect of having black skin in a racist, white supremacist-minded society; compounded with, as previously mentioned, the aid of hair weave products, colored eye contacts, as well as carcinogenic skin bleaching creams. Similarly, just as victims of racism—male and female—have been taught to relish in self-hatred, the black female, on the other hand, is being systematically isolated as a means to cultivate her disdain and hatred of the black male and arouse pleasure-seeking and infatuation with white men, who generally speaking have never given a damn about the black female and whose ties to her on the surface have only been for the purpose of her mistreatment and exploitation. Just check both their history and present-day agenda.

This is far from coincidence or is in any way accidental. Institutional racism/white supremacy is a profoundly efficacious and indiscriminate system that is employed and operable based on a full understanding that the most efficient way to destroy a group of people is to stir dissension between the male and female of the targeted group. As a result, chattel slavery, unchanging deplorable social conditions, self-hate, and immeasurable infatuation and obsession with ingratiating into the dominant culture are precursors and main ingredients to collective self-destruction. Because of this claim, this is how I see this thing playing out. So, when asking the question of are THEY trying to kill Us? Or, better yet, who is it that is responsible for the imminent death of the black Nation? I would answer that it depends on one's interpretation or definition of "kill." Furthermore, who is the Us that is set to be eliminated? Either way, my overall assessment, as I will illustrate, infers a disastrous outcome.

Us & Them

"I'd rather be hated for what I am than loved for what I'm not!"
—CHUCK D, *PUBLIC ENEMY*

It is my claim that today's modus operandi of the institution of racism/ white supremacy is premised on the elimination of the base of black male constituency, or representativeness; in other words, complete annihilation. According to Michelle Alexander, mass incarceration is today's form of chattel slavery; and, as Todd Boyd, a USC film professor noted, the "penitentiary is the new cotton field." And certainly, prisons and prison growth is a booming, growing industry. Therefore, as long as institutional racism/white supremacy exist and the prison industry remains a booming and lucrative enterprise, more young urban males of color will continue to be the system's most ardent and relentless victims. And for those black males who somehow manage to avoid the scourges of mass incarceration, other social conditions that engender effeminacy, homosexuality, and transgendered and transsexual behavioral traits and characteristics will be left to the manifestations of collective and group self-destruction.

Presently, this is being done by way of an epidemic scourge of disease, massive neurological and pathological dysfunctions and deficits, and the inability to reproduce. Furthermore, the black female will be left to the whims of selective extermination practices depending on the need or, to be exact, will be determined on a need basis. What I mean is that the nearly seventy percent of professional black females who are currently unwed and, according to projections, will probably remain deprived of that privilege, will be left to concubinage and sexual gratification of the winner-take-all white male imperialists. Or, they will steadily gravitate towards same-sex unions—black females and white women—for those same comforts and needs. There was time in America's past that this indiscretion was brutally superimposed on the black female. What is taking place today however is proof of the gradual, patented proficiency of institutional racism and its psychological and, not necessarily physical, consequences imposed on its black victims. Today, a great many of black females, and provocateurs of black feminism (e.g., Oprah Winfrey, Tyler Perry, missjia.com, Oreo experience, etc.) have convinced themselves that the black male is the arch enemy of the upward mobility and salvation of the black female, and as a result of this belief perceive white men (or other black females or white women) as being better and more suitable mates for today's ambitious and goal oriented black female.

This would all make sense if the fact that the dearth of eligible and suitable black males, combined with a conspicuous zeal to redeem the social conditions and perceptions of black females and their children— irrespective of socioeconomic status—was being meted out as a means of recompense at the hands and doings of truly conscience and "wanna-do-right-by-them" white people. Unfortunately, this is not the case. A more accurate assessment is that the black female remains as objectified in American society as her black male counterpart, perhaps even more so. She just doesn't know it! Furthermore, and no less disturbing, is that spuriously designated cultural pundits such as Tyler Perry contrive images and delineations of today's black female priming herself for sexual availability and acceptance exclusively for white men. For instance, one of two of Tyler Perry's new dramas on his pal Oprah Winfrey's *OWN* network should be telling enough, precluding having to go into any details.

Frankly speaking, white-identified black males and black females are not at all interested in race or ethnic preservation, and because of the tireless and indefatigable efforts to intermix and deluge into white folds, both will perhaps delay their destruction more so than their black contemporaries who are not so fortunate to be products of some of the same social conditions and economic standings. The downside to this, however, is that even for these euro-minded blacks, under the auspice and aegis of racism/white supremacy, the inevitable will eventually come to fruition. Hence, white-identified blacks may succeed in procuring intermarriages with a miniscule number of whites; consequently, fostering a biracial caste that because of their being socialized and inundated with white mores and standards will in turn marry other whites or other mixed-race, white-identified non-whites. Ultimately, this course of action and/or trend will succeed in dissipating any semblances of blackness and African features completely—similar to theories of the grafting process that took place to produce a people who categorizes themselves as the white race—people who come from Europe and are devoid of melanin or skin pigmentation.

Can't beat'em, join'em

"There is no difference between a white
snake and a black snake. They'll both bite you!"
—THURGOOD MARSHALL

America is indeed a powerful country, but it might be as wicked as it is powerful depending on one's interpretation of wickedness or what can be categorized as wicked acts. Arguably, America's treatment of the black male is not solely the problem. While it is true that institutional racism/ white supremacy is the disease, the symptoms have been negated by a people who collectively have failed to decode and decipher the dynamics at play, in terms of why such futile and contentious race relations actually exist. Quite frankly, it is the black male's own failure to proactively respond to conditions that connote discrimination, exploitation, and outright oppression which is where either confusion or outright denial becomes a factor. White people are not all confused about issues of race and race relations. How could they be? They invented racism and all of the sordid conditions that presently exist as a result of such practices. Furthermore, the blueprint for maintaining racial superiority and meting out oppressive and harsh discriminatory policies, especially in order to do so effectively, have been passed down from generation to generation—similar to how a baton is passed in a relay race.

Again, whites have no disillusions about the practices of racism/white supremacy, regardless of whether these practices take place nationally or are conducted on a global scale. What they have done in the past and continue to do presently though is attempt to minimize the severity of race relations as a means to both assuage its overt practices as well as guilt and culpability for doing so. On the other hand, black victims seem to be endowed with a very minute concept of the practices of racism—its rationale, modus operandi, and overall purpose. For this reason, the black male and black people in general do not understand the art and concept of war. Failure of fully understanding this concept also entails that blacks as a whole do not understand the true nature and motives of their sworn enemies. If this is not true then black people would have never been brought to the shores of America as chattel slaves, nor would they be at the bottom of the socioeconomic latter and looking up from the bottom nearly five hundred years later.

If this is not the case, sixty to one-hundred million blacks would not have been slaughtered since the days of being considered as property to presently being considered as inferior, third-class citizens. If this is not true then scores of civil rights leaders and champions of black liberation would not have been murdered outright or forced to flee in exile for their lives for simply demanding the same human entitlements as their white counterparts. If I am wrong, then presently the black male would not be primed for mass incarceration in prisons and correctional institutions; he would not be susceptible to violent death at an early age; both the black male and the black female would not be the most vulnerable to an epidemic of incurable, life-threatening diseases; disproportionate numbers of black boys and girls would not be ravaged by the scourges of poverty; and black people—male, female, boy, and girl—would be amalgamated and culturally connected rather than disjointed and culturally exploited and taken advantage of.

As profoundly and provocatively harmful as racism and prejudicial discrimination is, incredulously, it is easy to write off or abate by those who practice it. A common theme of white people when confronted with a racial dilemma—whether legitimate or otherwise—is that it is not about race, or that the motives were not racially motivated. Even when racist whites go on racist tirades, an easy remedy that is nearly always concluded with impunity is the claim, "I am not a racist!" Hence, racism and practices of discrimination are a joke to white people; primarily, because they understand that as easy as they can provoke a racial crisis, they can just as easily quash it. Institutional racism/white supremacy dictates that the primogenitors and practitioners control all of the nuances and permutations of racism and racist practices and not their victims. Perhaps it is this impotence and vulnerability to racism/white supremacy that black people in general tend to suppress and dismiss its practices, or internalize the psychological duress and tumult that results from racist's ideology and systemic oppression.

Just as a common (sense) mantra dictates that there can be no law without justice; similarly, there can be no president—black or white— who boast of being a "man of the people" when those same people are morally, culturally, and socially fragmented and are over four hundred years removed from any semblances of ethical cohesion. For certain, what this entails is that Obama's presidency is the result of anything but a fruitful coalescing of two groups of people that remain torn from the visage and legacy of slavery and continual systematic racism and oppression. If this is not the truth then I would be more than happy to hear evidence that states otherwise; particularly evidence more plausible than the simple fact of America boasting its first black president. Is Obama the first black president who has demonstrated an expected and a necessary concern for the conditions of black people?

The answer is an emphatic no! To the contrary, he is a person who has demonstrated more of a commitment to the preservation of the capitalist's ethos of what his predecessor bombastically referred to as "the haves and the have mores." Black folk who do not know any better and those whites who do know yet, still, audaciously embellish the illusion of a post-racialized America would like to think or act like this is not the case. However, Obama's track record, his verbal diatribes towards black males that can be further researched, his continued occupation of poor Arab and Muslim nations, and his wanton drone attacks and air raids on so-called terrorists' cells and organizations speaks for itself, among a slew of other things.

Greek mythology posits that "a hundred good deeds cannot atone for one murder." The facts are that the Obama administration, similar to that of his predecessor, has murdered and taken thousands of innocent lives, confirming his own lawlessness based on these abstract and apparent injustices. So, when asking the question of what is the expected trajectory of black folk in America under the guidance of its first black president? My answer would be right back at square one. Moreover, and with absolute certainty, I would also make the claim that this is so because of Obama's own apparent bloodlust and propensity for injustice and genocidal tendencies and practices. From Roosevelt to Kennedy to Johnson to Clinton to Obama; it doesn't really matter. One thing for sure is that the perceived contributions to the terrestrial world from the days of Christ have not at all changed things or improved the conditions and circumstances of people, i.e., oppressed people of color. This is undoubtedly why black folk call on Jesus in their most critical time of need, and the "oh my God" outcry of white people can legitimately be perceived as nothing more than a cultural colloquialism, particularly being that the white man believes that he is the god of the universe (recently, there was another major motion picture depicting Christ as a white man).

These are some of the sordid realities that exist in America, as they are unfortunately the reality of the black male, regardless of the fact that many of these ideologies and practices do not work to his advantage. Hence, these realities have fomented and underscored that conditions and circumstances in America have gone from black males who once strived to be *men* and championed to be free, to black males who will don a dress if the end result is multimillionaire status. Or, black males who will frolic the streets in droves throughout major cities in women's garb, skinny jeans, and pants sagging to the knees, or black people in general who will passionately and fervently argue in favor of buffoonery and the revitalizing of adverse racial portrayals and characterizations for the sake of entertainment, during a time when entertainment should be as far from a priority of black people as measurably or conceivably possible.

Escape from Babylon: what needs to be done?

With a mighty voice he shouted: "Fallen! Fallen is
Babylon the Great!' She has become a dwelling for
demons and a haunt for every impure spirit, a haunt for every
unclean bird, a haunt for every unclean and detestable animal.
—REV. 18: 12

Institutional racism and the practices of white supremacy, as well as the national and global acceptance of racism/white supremacy have caused the black male in America, and black people as a whole, to be on the precipice of ethnic and cultural annihilation. Shockingly, the black male is either not aware of this fact or simply does not seem to care. Also, so-called projections of America as well as the rest of western society and culture gradually becoming an amalgamation of predominantly colored societies are completely misleading. What this implies is that a deluge of people of color from other nonwhite nations might continue their advances towards the shores of North America; however, that does not at all speak to the survival of the gradually shrinking minority of America's former slaves. And consequently, attempts at a physical and mental ingratiating with the sons and daughters of former slave masters will not hinder but only hasten ethnic and cultural erasure of the black male. In other words, interracial crossbreeding is not the answer, nor is attempting to live one's life under the auspices of a "white is right" mantra.

The word genocide, as coined in 1944 by human rights activist Raphael Lemkin, is not a mirage but is as real as the conditions of institutional racism and oppression as we know to exist. Because of this realization, it is foolish for a black male of any socioeconomic status to delude himself into believing that the feigning and imbuing of personal attributes and characteristics that appear to be suitable and disarming to white people is resultantly going to cause them to ultimately lose sight of the primary and obvious differences that has engendered antagonism and aversion in them for as long as both groups have been in existence on this planet. Nature has in the past dictated discord among people, and continues to dictate that human beings must fight with each other in order to continue to exist. And as long as there is black and white, the battle will indeed rage on until one group is left standing or reigns supreme in the demographic and geographical landscape of earthly existence.

In order to correct or redress a problem, it is of the utmost importance to know the source or crux of the particular problem in question. Even in 2015, the black male, who remains the most abject victim of racism—nationally and globally—does not seem to have a clue as to the workings and methods of institutional racism. This is what was meant when members of the black power struggle referred to many blacks as being in a state of deaf, dumb, and blindness. Clearly, the implications were the inability to hear the messages that were then as they are now geared towards true freedom and equality; the failure to thoroughly assess and collectively address the social conditions that are designed to incapacitate and assure that blacks remain in a perpetual state of physical and mental weakness; and the absence of the ability to see, understand, and decode the obvious.

Racism and white supremacy are not solely premised on white men being physically and intellectually superior to the black male. If this were true, the black body would not be the epitome of athleticism, virility, and the prototype of ideal physiological functioning. Furthermore, if this were true, black people as a whole would not have had sole rule and mastery of the world long before the ancient Greeks and Romans usurped the technology of math, science, and medicine in their own quest for global supremacy and domination. To the contrary, Institutional racism/white supremacy is a global system that is very meticulously utilized for the purposes of abating white genetic annihilation amid a world that predominantly consist of people of color and, in turn, ensures the survival of white people; hence, the monopoly and control of global resources and technology is obligatory in maintaining both their survival and preservation of power. Ironically, not only do many blacks seem to not understand the circumstances that keep them in both physical and mental bondage but, more telling, is that many seem to be either reluctant or completely obdurate in discussing such matters.

Recently, an acquaintance asked me whether the purpose of writing this book is strictly for offering solutions as opposed to just ranting and raving or using the "usual suspect" of social unrest as a means of garnering attention. In addressing the latter, I am certain that there are many other ways to get attention (after all, this is America). However, in mulling over the former inquiry, for some of the reasons just cited, my response would be that there really are no solutions. "You can't discuss solutions until people understand how problems are caused and how they operate. Ignorant people can't solve problems." These are the words of Dr. Umar Abdullah-Johnson, psychologist, author, educator, and lecturer. And it is because I agree with Dr. Abdullah-Johnson's sentiments that I will take a gamble and stand by my claim and not attempt to offer any. I will however point out the obvious and hypothesize how certain people, certain actions, as well as identify conditions that are contributing factors to these problems in the hopes that solutions will manifest themselves and perhaps foment a blueprint for those who truly seek liberation and long for an end of social injustices to follow. For starters, it cannot be emphasized enough that institutional racism/white supremacy is not some passé construct that is not relevant in today s social climate, and that white supremacy is not some product of the brooding psyche of disgruntled black folk. In fact, an important question to be answered truthfully is whether or not white people are superior to black people. And an equally important follow-up would be that if they are then wouldn't they have been here first.

Even their scientific studies indicate that that is not the case. And if they appear to be smarter, it must also be understood that they have had centuries and centuries of Europeanization that they crafted and to this day continues to work in their favor. Hence, IQ tests that assess intelligence in a society that both beautifies and smites intelligence is indeed as culturally biased as prevailingly opinioned and advertised. Counter to this, however, is that phrenology, which is the study and measurement of brain size, does not reveal any meaningful disparities as it pertains to brain measurement, which determines the storage of knowledge and the capacity for intelligence. In other words, white people do not rule over the darker people of the world because they are genetically superior both intellectually and physically. This is the case because they preeminently contrived an indiscriminate system that would counterbalance their tiny minority status on the planet. They also showcased murderous tendencies and employed divide and conquer methods and tactics that had never before been utilized in the annals of world history. Indeed, skirmishes have always existed among human beings, but nothing to the level of the enmity, anathema, and disdain towards other human beings to a point where the harmonious balance of nature was completely off-centered and corrupted. Thus, white people in America maintain their superior status over blacks because, unlike their hapless yet seem to be willing victims, they are not at all confused about racism or the politics of race that maintain the seeds of social disequilibrium and uniformed imbalance.

Perhaps a better way of describing the previous claim would be harmonious imbalance that is more so the basis for why the black male and black folk in general remain the perfect victims of racism/ white supremacy. Consequently, what is now taking place is generations and generations of social, individual, and group dysfunction that has compelled many blacks to gravitate towards sub groups and splinter factions that rest their laurels exclusively in causes and agendas that continue to obscure the overall goal of black socioeconomic liberation and empowerment. Therefore, it is beyond meaningless to point out that such an endeavor(s) can only subsequently muddle and compromise what should be one common and interchangeable cause. Incidentally, the commonality of having black skin is nothing more than window-dressing for the push for black feminism and for (black) gay rights, which for the most part has very little to do with uniting victims of racism solely on the basis of mistreatment due to distinctions of both color and class. Again, black skin is only incidental! Because of this unfortunate fact, black people in America are bombarded with images of rich blacks connecting with rich whites as some sort of indication of racial progress.

This is made possible strictly because of the fact that black people in America have been taught to hate their own black identity. Sadly, there are great many who do just that, although they won't admit to this fact. And there are many black people who need white people to validate their blackness, or they need the acclaim or prestige denoting success that can only be legitimized or confirmed by whites. As a result, no mark of success is more prominent than that of the mainstream black entertainer. So pronounced and admired in fact, all of the wrongs of black entertainers and celebrities are automatically righted by their mainstream popularity, cultural success, and appeal alone. And on the rare occasion that a successful black person puts character, integrity, and virtue before wealth, both black and white are quick to rush to the same harsh judgment and indictment.

Consider for instance when popular black comedian and actor Dave Chappelle, shelved an exorbitant amount of money because in his quest for manliness over acquiescence, profundity over the mundane, the internal fortitude of personal and cultural pride would not allow him to barter these attributes for wealth and prestige. Ironically, it was Chappelle, the critically acclaimed funnyman, who stated both his concerns and confoundedness of black actors and comedians being co-opted to wear women's clothing on the Oprah Winfrey show. The irony, also, was that these concerns were expressed to an individual who has developed both business and close personal ties with a black male whose claim to fame is mostly by way of his penchant for buffoonery while in drag. Nevertheless, my point is that although I concede being devoid of any tangible solutions as to how to nullify the system of institutional racism/white supremacy, I will first start by making a proposal that black people— both male and female—need to discern themselves and their circumstances due to racism from black entertainers and celebrities. Not only are these not real human beings, but they are folk who have absolutely nothing at all to do with the social conditions of blacks in a racist and white supremacist-minded society. If anything, they are black proxies for the preservation of white supremacy and superiority.

What entertainment entails in America is the distracting of people from thinking critically on REAL issues that have resounding effects on the day to day lives of REAL people. This could not be any more indicative of the black experience in America; it is as if blacks are pelted and inundated with various forms of entertainment to somehow mitigate and assuage the true circumstances enveloping black people, particularly the black male. Hence, BET, black entertainment television, is disgraceful because of its whimsical, nonsensical programming amid a crisis among blacks that has reached genocidal proportions. Programs that should be created and designed to be informative and culturally enlightening are instead curtailed by a maelstrom of buffoonery and programming geared towards invariable depictions of black cultural and social *genocide.*

Thus, if the ameliorating and preservation of black culture superseded corporate wealth, then BET would be renamed BIT—Black Information Television. Sadly, this is not the case.

The offering of solutions would imply that it is either black folk or white people who are either devoid of or are confused of the knowledge of institutions that both engender and ensure social injustices and the suffering of one group of people at the hands of another group. Surprisingly, there have been several thought-provoking and profound books over the years that have been written that provide thorough data and statistics fomenting substantial proof that adverse social conditions that affect blacks on a grand scale are in fact real. Moreover, there are great disparities that exist between black and white that are strictly caused by conditions of racism, discrimination, and oppression, although these terms and descriptions are seldom used. More telling is that the solutions that are often suggested are the opening of the lines of communication and continual dialogue under the presumption that these things and conditions are being ruminated and discussed. This is true only because there is an abject failure to understand the real conditions of institutional racism/white supremacy. Or, there is a failure to understand the white supremacist mindset of those who keep the wheels of institutional racism spinning and the ideology of white supremacy very much alive. In other words, dialogue and discussion are long overdrawn and outmoded; black folk need to stop talking and start doing!

Proverbs 29:18 states that "where there is no vision the people will perish." Hence, solutions are baseless if the black male in America, and black people as a whole, can't see the inherent error and perniciousness of the failure of grooming their children to be able to function properly and productively in a racist society that is driven towards both proving and stabilizing black inferiority, debasement, and passivity. Furthermore, solutions are senseless and egregiously preachy if black males can't see how culturally destructive is the failure of raising their black children in a society whose predation and frenzy is fueled by the spilling of blood of young black males and boys. And, lastly, they are fruitless, if black folk as a whole can't see the mental and psychological bondage maintained by fervently and proudly clamoring to the names and religion bestowed upon them by their former Christian slave masters. America is more than just a nation that is bifurcated by race, class, and ethnicity. America can also boast being a nation that is most proficient in unabatedly fashioning a white supremacist prose and methodology; hence, America is hands-down, bar-none the most effective brainwashing mechanism the world has ever seen and/or had to bear witness to its racist, sexist, xenophobic, hegemonic endeavors.

———

The black male and black people as a whole in America no longer are socialized to maximum efficiency as a means to coalesce among each other for the betterment of themselves, their offspring, and the improvement of socioeconomic conditions. On the contrary, blacks are either pre-groomed (i.e., pre-programmed) for status as a permanent underclass or find a way throughout the travails of their lives to groom themselves to hobnob and acquire white social acceptance. For this reason, successful (a relative term) black males who disdain black females seek to acquire unions with white women and other non-black females. Also, black females who harbor equal contempt for black males convince themselves that a partnership with white men is the key to corporate success, socioeconomic stratification, and a release from the shackles of loneliness and cultural ostracism in terms of social acceptance. Thus, it is obligatory the understanding that black females prime themselves for white men and white social acceptance via education and corporate success, same as they lobby for the end of racism and discrimination against their black identity for those same reasons.

America is a country undergoing a racially-hierarchal transitioning phase that is geared towards an amalgamation and mutually-exclusive respect among whites, Asians, and Latinos that will ultimately be to the detriment of blacks. For those who are paying attention, inclusion and exclusionary social practices among these distinct ethnic and racial groups are well underway. And what it amounts to are statistics that purport a consensus of white, Asians, and Hispanic groups having more tolerance and racial union among each other and mutually unfavorable views of blacks. In an article entitled "Black Americans and Interracial Marriage: A focus on Black Women," author Amadu Jacky Kaba points out how research has confirmed comparisons of the inclusion of immigrant European ethnic groups to that of other non-black ethnicities, stating that "the boundaries of whiteness are extended to include Latinos and Asians, but remain closed to blacks."[109]

If there are in fact any other solutions in regards to the plight of the black male to be elicited and offered then, lastly and most importantly, it would be the promulgating of the restoration of the black male to the black family structure. It is my hypothesis that the MOST crippling condition of black people amid the epidemic of institutional racism is the absence of the black male father figure. This point is actually where Mr. Obama and I are in complete agreement! As this is especially true in regards to both young black males and black females. The over seventy percent of black children being raised in single, fatherless homes is unconscionable and, outside of the conditions of institutional racism/white supremacy, is the most pressing factor in both the pathological dysfunction of both males and females, as well as arguably the exponential development of effeminized black males. Regardless of the ties that either bind or break between the male and female, the act of procreating dictates that both parents rear and socialize their offspring—period! Therefore, contrary to the feminists and matriarchal push for ethnic exclusion and autonomy that is being bolstered by the renegade, apostate, infiltrators of the dictates and machinations of black cultural advancement and preservation, true salvation and liberation and disentanglement from the clutches of institutional racism/white supremacy are determined by the acceptance of the responsibilities manifesting such a task by the black male with, of course, the aid and cooperation of the black female. And it is the black male's complete failure to assume such responsibility and secure her cooperation that has resulted in the continual weakening, pacifying, and effeminizing of the black male, and the devolution of black culture.

Epilogue

What a Nigger is: The search for De-niggerization

*"Niggers are like roaches, they're never gonna
go away. Learn from them what we should not
become, 'cause Niggers don't die."*
—The Last Poets

What group of people has a better sense of the meaning of words than white people? Are they not collectively the smartest people in the known universe? If this is not so, institutional racism/white supremacy would not be the most powerful and efficacious force of brainwashing and subjugating nonwhite people the world over. Furthermore, it would not be perhaps the second most powerful religion in western culture and society (money, arguably, being the first because both whites and blacks worship money). And it is their/white racists' use of the word Nigger in reference to black people as a whole that they verbally, as well as both systematically and indiscriminately, exercise and boast their dominance.

Khalil Baaqi

Foolish black folk, as a means to mitigate their condition of racial suffering and subjugation, as well as giving white people a pass for the practice of racism/white supremacy, have attempted to invoke the erroneous theoretical definition of the word Nigger as referencing any "ignorant" person or individual. This is actually beyond foolish. And for those who might disagree, I challenge them to prove to me a time when they either witnessed or overheard a white person angrily, and not in jest or play, refer to another white person as a Nigger. They cannot! Obviously, in a system of global racism/white supremacy, the only time that someone will hear white people either directly refer to someone as a Nigger, or act or treat someone in such a manner will be said or done in reference to or acted towards their inferior black and/or nonwhite subjects. Therefore, it is beyond foolish for black folk to believe that white people, based on the SUPPOSED definition, will refer to each other as Niggers; or, refer to other blacks as Niggers for the sole purpose of being trite and mean-spirited or for the purposes of making a distinction of certain blacks in comparison to blacks as a whole. Also, it is absolutely preposterous to believe that these mannerisms and actions are restricted to just a handful of white people.

In fact, because of white people's incomparable understanding of words, and an even more profound understanding of their global status in terms of racial, ethnic, and cultural stratification, they either verbally refer to black people as Niggers, think and act towards nonwhite people in general as functioning inferiors, and mistreat black people on the basis of ethnicity and culture because they fully understand and are aware of the substandard functioning and existence of black people. So, there is a reason why white people either directly refer to black people as Niggers, or perceive black people as Niggers even if it is not explicitly stated, same as there is a reason for institutional racism/white supremacy. With that said, I'll explain exactly what my definition(s) of a Nigger is and what being a Nigger entails.

(1). A Nigger is a (black) person/s who is not only cowardly but is ashamed of his or her own culture and ethnic origin. And, as a result,

314

ostentatiously demonstrates a desire to disavow his or her ethnic status and classification for a social positioning and ethnic categorization that they can never truly be a part of or belong to, and one that they are not biologically, genetically, and culturally linked. White people are aware of this!

(2). A Nigger is a (black) person/s who no matter what he or she accomplishes, could never be perceived as smart or as an intelligent person. True, some black folk may appear to be smart or intelligent, even smarter, more sophisticated, more articulate, and more white-identified than most other black people. However, in a socio-material order that is bifurcated and ranked by color and culture, these blacks merely exist same as the rest of nonwhite and black victims of the social order of western society/culture. As theorized by Neely Fuller Jr., in a system of racism and white supremacy there are the "smartest" people (racists/white supremacists), and there are the "smartless" people (nonwhite victims).[110] White People would not hesitate to agree!

(3). A Nigger is a (black) person/s who pretends to act in a certain manner (*racial showcasing*) in order to appease those who represent the dominant culture and past and present power-structure. These individuals wear a mask to save-face and vie for white people's (massa's) acceptance; although this is not at all who these people truly are in their normal existence. In fact, if you pay close attention to blacks that act in this manner, often they are the most weak, vulnerable, and dysfunctional in their personal and private lives. White people understand this wholeheartedly!

(4). A Nigger and/or *Negress* are (black) persons who willfully adhere to sexual play and engage in sexual activity with white racists or white people who directly and/or indirectly benefit from institutional racism/white supremacy, and who purposefully cooperate with ethnic and cultural exploitation. It is hard to imagine how a black person can believe that he or she is in love with a white person, or believe that he or she can either dominate sexual relations with whites or have equal say or power in these relations when, in actuality, black people as a whole are inescapable victims of institutional racism/white supremacy. In other words, since black people in a racist society are subjugated and oppressed by white people, sexual relations with whites is no different than an adult sexually violating and/or molesting a child. Hence, the bulk of black exploitation is based on the sexual exploitation of black people. And only when institutional racism/white supremacy ends can engaging in sexual activity with whites be legitimized in any way, shape, or fashion. White people know this as fact, regardless of whether they admit to it or not!

(5). A Nigger is a (black) person/s who because of his or her oppressed state and/or condition, channels and inverts this anger by participating in acts and behaviors that are to the detriment and disadvantage of other black people. As a result, crime, drugs, apathy, passivity, femininity, and communal degradation are rife in the lives and existences of black people, purely and simply because of institutional racism/white supremacy. Tragically, because of ubiquitous suffering yet a cohesive failure to gauge who or what it is that is the exact cause of the suffering has sown the seeds for the debasement, destruction, and exploitation of blacks at the hands of other blacks. Testament to the power, potency, and efficiency of the most powerful socio-material system the world has ever known. White people are both totally aware and benefit from this indisputable fact!

(6). A nigger, as perceived by white people, and especially in this instance, is a (black) person/s who dedicates his or her very life and existence to eradicating institutional racism/white supremacy, by fighting for the proverbial "truth, freedom, and justice" that not only are all human beings entitled to but is the natural order of the known and just universe. Consequently, this individual/s is most despised by those who practice racism/white supremacy, and unlike their more obsequious counterparts, are oft-most maligned, scorned, and derided.

Yet by the virtue of his or her deeds, actions, writings, and lectures, attempt to keep those of us whom are misinformed, informed. Furthermore, such an individual/s passes down to the next generation the proper knowledge, wisdom and, hopefully in due time, power to stand up to the system of global injustice and subjugation of nonwhites and black people everywhere. White people who practice racism/white supremacy are very much aware of these traits and characteristics in their black victims. It is because of this awareness that not only will they accept and/or reject blacks as such and for displaying such characteristics, but also refer to black people as niggers for the simple fact that: (1) they are black, (2) they are beneath white people because of their black identity, and (3) white people's unmistakable and unbreakable belief in white supremacy.

To all of the black males and black females who make money and procure subsistence on their own terms and without the aid of white people, who do not engage in sexual play or coitus activity with racist whites, who do not support or endorse black exploitation and stereotypical caricatures of any sort, and who look to plant the seeds of knowledge that will one day aid in the subsequent liberation of black people in America, and all over the globe— this book is just as much for you as it is for those of us who remain shackled and gridlocked by racist subjugation and oppression; particularly as a result of our ignorance and confusion. These are examples of exemplary black folk who can perhaps one day shine their light on all of those of us who seek liberation, the restoration of culture, and what Judge Joe Brown so boldly refers to as, the promoting of "Manhood."

Endnotes

1. *The Color of Fear*, directed by Lee Mun Wah (1994; Documentary, Ukiah, Ca).

2. Baldwin, James, *The Fire Next Time* (New York: Vintage, 1962, 1963)

3. Thomas Bartlett, "Black Colleges react to low point in Fashion" (Chronicle of higher learning 2009).

4. Ibid.

5. Learn in Race, College, and Teachers, "Only four percent of college students are black males", Feb. 7, 2012.

6. David W. Park, "Oprah Winfrey and the Glamour of Misery: An essay on popular culture by Eva Illouz" Columbia University Press, 2003.

7. Los Angeles Sentinel, "Oprah Winfrey makes second 5million donation to Morehouse College" Feb. 26, 2004.

8. Moe Bandy, Joe Stampley *Where's the Dress*, Live at Billy Bob's Texas, 1984

9. Cress-Welsing, Frances, *The Isis Papers: Keys to the Colors*, Third World Press, 1991.

10. Willie Lynch, *The Willie Lynch Letter and the making of a Slave*, African Tree Press, 2011.

11. Ibid

12. Potash, John *The FBI War Against Tupac Shakur and Black Leaders* Progressive Left Press 3rd Ed. 2008

13. Ibid

14. Madhubuti, Haki R. *Black Men: Obsolete, Single, Dangerous?:The African American Family in Transition.* Third World Press 1990.

15. *The Untouchables,* directed by Brian De Palma (1987; Chicago, Il, Montana; Paramount Pictures).

16. Diggs, Robert, F. Hunter, Jason. Jones, Nasir, Smith, Clifford, *Ya'll My Niggas,* Untitled Album, 2008.

17. *Deep Cover,* directed by Bill Duke (1992; Los Angeles, CA New Line Cinema).

18. Cress-Welsing, *Isis Papers.*

19. Ibid.

20. Hardiman, Tio. *African-American Males facing serious challenges* The Blog 2013.

21. The Black Star Project, *The Silent Genocide-Facts about the deepening plight of Black Men in America,* www.blackstarproject.org.

22. Hamm, Nia, *Black Folks suffer from Mental Health in silence,* The Root 2012.

23. Fanon, Franz *Black Skin, White Mask: The experiences of a Black Man in a White World* Grove Press, 1952, 1967.

24. Jackson, Jr. Oscar, *Bush Killa,* Sleeping with the Enemy, Scarface Records, 1992.

25. *Barbershop,* directed by Tim Story (2002; Chicago, Il, Metro Goldwyn Mayer, State Street Pictures).

26. Walker, M. Brittany, "On the trail of African American Roots in Christianity." Our Weekly (2011).

27. Fanon, Frantz. *The Wretched of the Earth* Grove Press, 1961.

28. Alexander, Michelle *The New Jim Crow: Mass Incarceration in the age of colorblindness.* The New Press/New York 2010.

29. *Malcolm X,* directed by Spike Lee (1992; New York, NY Forty Acres and A Mule Filmworks).

30. Streetlove, Cisco *Yesterday's Shame: The Atlanta Child Murders* Good Ship Publishing, 1st ed. 2012

31. *For Colored Girls,* directed by Tyler Perry (2010; Atlanta, Ga, Lionsgate, Tyler Perry Studios, 34th Street Films).

32. Moore, Robert III "Interracial dating as an indicator of Integration." The Last Word 1999.

33. Frazier, Franklyn, E. *Black Bourgeoisie* First Free Press 1997

34. Raymond, Kenneth "Do African Americans think like former slaves?" Black Quill & Ink 2011

35. Olomenji "Menticide, Genocide, and National Vision: the crossroads for Black America" *African psychology in historical perspective & related commentary.* Africa World Press 1996

36. Dyson, Michael Eric. *Is Bill Cosby right? Or has the Black Middle Class lost its mind?* Basic Civitas Books 1st Ed. 2005

37. Public Enemy, *Welcome to the Terror-dome*, Fear of a Black Planet, 1991, Def Jam Records.

38. Eller, David Jack *Cruel Creeds, Virtuous Violence: Religious violence across Culture and History* Prometheus Books 2010

39. Haley *Autobiography of Malcom x* 1965

40. Dyson, Michael Eric *Between God and Gangsta Rap: Bearing witness to Black Culture* Oxford University Press 1997

41. Alexander, Michelle *The New Jim Crow: Mass Incarceration in the age of colorblindness.* The New Press/New York 2010.

42. Kelly. R, Isley, Ronald, *Down Low (nobody has to know)*, 1995, Jive Records.

43. King, J. L., *On the Down Low: A journey into the lives of 'straight' black men who sleep with men* Urban Moon Publishing, 2005.

44. Eller, *Cruel Creeds* Prometheus 2010

45. Dyson, *Between God and Gangsta*, 1997

46. Dyson, *Is Bill Cosby* 2005

47. *Blood and Bone*, directed by Ben Ramsey (2009; Los Angeles, Remarkable Films, Sony Pictures Home Entertainment).

48. Degruy, Joy, Dr. *Posttraumatic Slave Syndrome: America's legacy of enduring injury and healing* Upton Press 2005

49. Dyson *Is Bill Cosby*, pg. 218 2005

50. Dewese, Mohandas, *God made me funke*, Funke Funke Wisdom, 1991 Jive Records.

51. Boogie Down Productions, *My Philosophy*, By Any Means Necessary, 1988 Jive/RCA Records.

52. Dyson, *Between God and Gangsta*, 1997

53. Haynes Jr. Cornell, *Country Grammar*, Country Grammar, 2000, Universal-Fo' Real Records.

54. Squires, Catherine R. "Evaluating Agency & Responsibility in Gendered violence: African American Youth talk about violence & Hip Hop 2006.

55. Samuels, Alison, Croal, N'Gai, et al. "Newsweek: Battle for the Soul of Hip Hop" (2000).

56. Squires, "Evaluating" 2006

57. Samuels, Croal. "Newsweek 2000

58. Dalisay, Francis. Tan, Alexis. "Assimilation and Contrast effects in the priming of Asian-American and African American stereotypes through television." Pg. 7

59. Madhubuti, Haki, R. *Black Men, obsolete, Single, Dangerous?* Third World Press 1st. Ed. 1990

60. Alexander, *New Jim Crow* 2010

61. Taylor, Carl. Taylor, Virgil. "Hip Hop is now: An evolving Youth Culture." Reclaiming Children & Youth 2007.

62. Webb, Kevin. "Seventy-two percent of African American Children are raised in single-parent homes." Atlanta Black Star 2012.

63. Mcphail, Mark Lawrence. *Black Identity: rhetoric, ideology, and nineteenth century Black Nationalism* 2004.

64. Allen, Robert. "Past due: The African American quest for reparations." 1998

65. Ibid.

66. Allen, *Black Identity* 1998

67. Madhubuti, *Black Men* 1991

68. Valls, Andrew. "A liberal defense of Black Nationalism." 2010

69. Ford, Vernon. "Black Nationalism in American politics and thought, a critique of Vernon Ford." 2001

70. Valls. "A liberal defense," 2010

71. Ewuare, Osayunde. "In the shadow of COINTELPRO: Intensifying the struggle to repeal the US Patriot Act." 2003

72. Foster, John Bellamy. "Ecology and the transition from Capitalism to Socialism." 2008

73. Orr, Allen H. "Darwin and Darwinism: the alleged social implications of the origin of species."

74. Ibid

75. Doomen, Jasper. "Comprehensive Darwinism." Review of Contemporary philosophy, 2012.

76. Joseph, Peter. *Zeitgeist: The Movie.* GMP LLC 2007.

77. *The Color of Fear* Documentary, 1994

78. Doomen "Comprehensive." 2012

79. Degruy, *Posttraumatic Slave Syndrome,* 2005

80. Marrow, Tracy, *Squeeze the Trigger,* Rhyme Pays, 1987, Sire/Warner Bros. Records.

81. *Deep Cover,* Directed by Bill Duke (1992; Los Angeles, Ca, New Line Cinema, 1999 DVD Release).

82. Dalisay, Francis. Tan, Alexis. "Assimilation and contrast effects in the priming of Asian American and African American stereotypes through television." 2009

83. Kneidel, Sally. "Female Hyenas, all hermaphrodites, bully males, steal from Lions." 2009

84. Ibid.

85. Kneidel. "Hyenas." 2009

86. Ibid.

87. *Menace 11 Society,* directed by Allen and Albert Hughes (1993; Los Angeles, Ca, New Line Cinema).

88. Alexander. *The New Jim Crow* 2010.

89. Frazier. *Bourgeoisie* 1997

90. *Bram Stoker's Dracula*, directed by Francis Ford Coppolla (1992; Osiris Films, Columbia Pictures).

91. Hardaway, Cecily. Mcloyd, Vonnie, C. "Escaping Poverty & securing middle class status: How race and socioeconomic status shape the mobililty prospects for African Americans during transition to adulthood."

92. *Jet* Magazine, "Urban league's black America's report still finds disparities in economics, home ownership, education," 2012.

93. Toldson, Ivory, A. Snitman, Aviella. "Editor's comments: Education parity and economic disparities: correcting education-attainment discrepancies among black people in the United States." Journal of Negro Education 2010

94. Madhubuti. *Black Men* Pg. 21.

95. Ibid. Pg. 22

96. Toldson, Ivory, A. Snitman, Aviela. "Editor's comments: Education parity and economic disparities, correcting education-attainment discrepancies among black people in the United States." Journal of Negro Ed. 2010

97. Ramirez, Rosa. "Why do blacks trail in benchmarks leading to middle class?" National Journal 2012

98. Dyson, *Is Bill Cosby* pg. 26

99. Farmer, Bryan. "Capitalism, Socialism, and Christianity." 2012.

100. Foster, John Bellamy. "Ecology and the tradition from Capitalism to Socialism." 2008.

101. Ibid.

102. Orr, *Darwin and Darwinsim.*

103. Ibid. Pg. 768

104. Johnson, Gary R. "Social Darwinism in European and American thought, 1860-1945: Nature as a model and nature as a threat."

105. *Unforgiven*, directed by Clint Eastwood (1992; Malpaso Productions; distributed by Warner Bros. Pictures).

106. Sugrue, Thomas J. *Sweet land of liberty: The forgotten struggle for civil rights in the North.* Random House trade paperback 2008.

107. Ibid. Pg. 83

108. Alexander. *New Jim Crow* 2010

109. Kaba, Amadu J. "Black Americans and interracial marriage: A focus on black women."

110. Fuller, Neely Jr. *United Independent Compensatory Code/System/Concept: a textbook/workbook for thought, speech, and/or action for victims of racism/ white supremacy* 1957-1980.

I am extremely passionate about social issues, particularly injustices that affect the lives of people. This book, which is my first, is one of the many contributions that I hope to offer in an effort to eradicate the myriad of social crises that continue to play a destructive role in the lives of people of color as a whole, but especially in the lives of males/men of color. I am a single father of two girls. I have spent several years working in social services, acquiring master's degrees in both criminal justice and social work along the way. Some of my other hobbies include reading, meditation, and personal boxing training.